Thinking and Writing in College

College Section Committee

Tilly Warnock, Chair, University of Northern Arizona
Lil Brannon, SUNY at Albany
Doris O. Ginn, Jackson State University
Brenda M. Greene, Medgar Evers College, CUNY
Linda H. Peterson, Yale University
James F. Slevin, Georgetown University
Joseph F. Trimmer, Ball State University
Art Young, Clemson University
James Raymond, ex officio, University of Alabama
H. Thomas McCracken, CEE Representative, Youngstown
    State University
Janet Emig, Executive Committee Liaison, Rutgers University

Thinking and Writing in College

A Naturalistic Study of Students
in Four Disciplines

Barbara E. Walvoord
Loyola College in Maryland

Lucille Parkinson McCarthy
University of Maryland Baltimore County

In collaboration with

Virginia Johnson Anderson
Towson State University
John R. Breihan
Loyola College in Maryland
Susan Miller Robison
College of Notre Dame of Maryland
A. Kimbrough Sherman
Loyola College in Maryland

National Council of Teachers of English
1111 Kenyon Road, Urbana, IL 61801

Staff Editor: Mary Daniels

Cover Design: Doug Burnett

Interior Book Design: Tom Kovacs for TGK Design

NCTE Stock Number 54247–3020

Library of Congress Cataloging-in-Publication Data

Thinking and writing in college : a naturalistic study of students in
    four disciplines / Barbara E. Walvoord . . . [et al.].
        p.   cm.
    Includes bibliographical references and index.
    ISBN 0-8141-5424-7
    1. Thought and thinking—Study and teaching (Higher)—United
States.   2. English language—Rhetoric—Study and teaching—United
States.   3. Reasoning—Study and teaching (Higher)—United States.
4. Learning.   I. Walvooord, Barbara E. Fassler, 1941-
LB2395.35.T47   1991
378.1′7—dc20
                                                            91-18272
                                                            CIP

To Mina P. Shaughnessy, who taught us to respect the "intelligence and will" that students bring to their academic writing, and who helped us see our world through students' eyes. She gave us a vision of teachers and researchers who "look at students' difficulties in a more fruitful way" and hence who learn "to teach anew."

Contents

Acknowledgments

At crucial points in the planning and drafting of this book, busy people who didn't owe us anything gave us the precious gift of their time and attention. Lee Odell of Rensselaer Polytechnic Institute listened to us and encouraged us at convention hotels over several years. He also reviewed the manuscript, helping us especially with consistency and organization. Carol Berkenkotter of Michigan Technological University, rooming with some of us at a convention, spent, literally, days and nights questioning, challenging, and supporting us. Later, she read the manuscript and helped us especially with our research theory and methods. Over dinner one night, and again in a review of the manuscript, Frank Sullivan of Temple University brought us his rare quality of mind, always reminding us that the story we constructed from our data was only one of the stories we might tell. Steve Fishman of the University of North Carolina at Charlotte, in his careful critique of the manuscript, let us see how a teacher in a discipline outside English would use our study. Hoke Smith of Towson State University read the emerging manuscript several times, bringing to it his powers of analysis, helping us construct our broad theoretical concepts. Barbara Mallonee of Loyola College in Maryland offered constant encouragement throughout the project, and her detailed critique of the manuscript helped us make it more readable.

Dixie Goswami of Clemson University gave us warm and generous support throughout the project, as well as the example of her own work and the work of teacher-researchers whom she has inspired. Bob Wall, of Towson State University, and David Abbott, of Bell Laboratories, helped us with statistical and research techniques. Anne Herrington, of the University of Massachusetts at Amherst, and Carol Berkenkotter responded to our research project as panel members at conventions. Many colleagues who attended the L. Ramon Veale Seminar of the National Council of Teachers of English listened to us describe our work and offered useful suggestions—among them were Linda Flower and John R. Hayes, of Carnegie Mellon University. Colleagues in a Baltimore area support group for writing researchers listened and responded; particularly helpful were Joyce Magnotto of

Prince George's Community College, Barbara Roswell of Goucher College, and Carolyn Hill and Dan Jones, both of Towson State University. Our thanks, also, to the anonymous reviewers of our manuscript for the National Council of Teachers of English and to the members of the Editorial Board.

The students in the four classes we studied, at Loyola College in Maryland, at Towson State University, and at The College of Notre Dame of Maryland, generously allowed us to eavesdrop as they worked. But more than that, they also worked hard to help us—they toted tape recorders, flipped tapes, dated drafts, marked revisions in different colored pencils, penned their logs at the ends of long days, saved and labeled their work, and submitted to interviews. This study was possible only through their generosity.

Michael Spooner has been a skillful editor, helping us to tighten the manuscript and showing patience when the team process or the complexity of the project caused delays. Project editor Mary Daniels's eye for detail and her tireless energy further helped us tighten the manuscript.

Each of us has had the generous support of spouse and children. We are grateful to our families for their patience and encouragement. And we welcome Billy Gazzam and Margaret Breihan, both of whom were born since we began work on this project.

We have had generous support, too, from our four institutions. Our research was supported by a Faculty Research Fellowship from the University of Maryland, Baltimore County. We also received grants from the Faculty Development Committee and the Dean of Arts and Sciences of Loyola College in Maryland, from the Faculty Research Committee of Towson State University, and from the Academic Dean of the College of Notre Dame of Maryland.

1 Preview of the Book

Barbara E. Walvoord
Loyola College in Maryland

Lucille Parkinson McCarthy
University of Maryland Baltimore County

What looked once to be a matter of finding out whether savages could distinguish fact from fancy now looks to be a matter of finding out how others, across the sea or down the corridor, organize their significative world.

—Clifford Geertz

The six of us who coauthored this book represent writing and four other disciplines—business, history, psychology, and biology. Although we come from four different institutions of higher education in the Baltimore area, we had worked together in writing-across-the-curriculum workshops before this study began. Virginia Johnson Anderson, John R. Breihan, Susan Miller Robison, and A. Kimbrough Sherman, the four teacher-collaborators who specialize in disciplines other than composition, collaborated in this research because they wanted to know more about how their students thought and wrote, and about how their teaching methods, influenced by the writing-across-the-curriculum workshops, were working. Thus, between 1982 and 1989, writing specialist Barbara E. Walvoord paired with each of the four, and, using similar methods to gather and analyze data, each pair conducted a naturalistic study of the thinking and writing of the students in that teacher's classroom. Lucille McCarthy, a writing specialist who joined the team in 1985, helped to shape and guide the data analysis, and critiqued the emerging chapter drafts written by the pairs. With Walvoord, she also coauthored the introductory and concluding chapters.

In our model, then, a writing specialist pairs with a teacher from another discipline to study the students in that teacher's classroom.

1

Elsewhere McCarthy and Walvoord have called this type of collaborative structure the "focused pair" (1988, 80).

PURPOSES OF THE BOOK

In this book, we, the six members of the team, have two purposes:

1. We present the results of our investigation of writing and thinking in each of the four classes taught by members of our team: classes in business, history, psychology, and biology.

2. We illustrate a model of collaborative, naturalistic classroom research in a college setting. This model proved, in our cases, to be not only a way to investigate how students thought and wrote, but also a powerful impetus to teacher growth and change.

Generalizations from our study to other classrooms must be cautious because, as James Britton reminds us, classrooms are places where "every variable is actively varying" (Britton et al., 1975). To help readers judge the applicability of our findings to other settings, we have provided detailed descriptions of the classrooms and the students we studied, and also of the methods we used to construct what Lincoln and Guba term "trustworthy" findings in naturalistic research (1985, 290–331).

Also applicable to other settings, we suggest, is our experience that systematic investigation of students' thinking and writing can result in discoveries that are likely to change teachers' understanding of their classrooms and, consequently, their teaching practices (Goswami and Stillman 1987). We suggest that even a limited investigation such as collecting students' logs or analyzing their drafts can be useful. Further, in our experience, interdisciplinary collaboration can lead each teacher to insights she or he might not achieve alone.

In addition to our collaboration with each other, a broader kind of collaboration must exist between us and those of you who are teachers. Dell Hymes (1972a) warns that an outside researcher's interpretation of a classroom

> does not suffice to change it. . . . If information and ideas from [classroom studies] are found useful and are implemented, it will be because the teachers in an actual situation, through their observations and insight, have made them their own. (xviii)

THE NEED FOR OUR STUDY

A number of researchers and theorists in composition have called for investigations about how students think and write in college. Langer (1985) calls for investigations that seek to explain the interaction of student writers and their social contexts (327), and Frederickson and Dominic (1981) call for research on the meaning of literacy to people in various situations (17). Herrington (1983) recommends research on a wide range of students' experiences with writing and speaking (76), and Collins and Gentner (1980) suggest research on novice writers' "difficulties" (53). Bartholomae (1985) proposes research on the conventions of the academic community and on students' writing to see the "points of discord" that arise when students try to write in the university (147). Odell (1986) outlines several reasons for studying student writers and suggests a list of questions about what constitutes good writing in academic contexts and whether students need different strategies for writing and thinking in various disciplines. Cooper (1983) suggests a similar list of research questions.

Our study thus responds not only to our own needs as teachers and researchers to know what is going on in our own and others' classrooms, but also to calls from a variety of quarters for research into college students' writing in academic settings outside the composition classroom. A few such studies have been conducted (Berkenkotter, Huckin, and Ackerman 1988; Faigley and Hansen 1985; Herrington 1985; McCarthy 1987; Meese 1987; Nelson and Hayes 1988; North 1986). However, these studies have covered smaller numbers of students and disciplines than our study, and they have emphasized the *differences* among classrooms, the differences among students in the same classroom, or both. Our study looks at more than 100 students in four disciplines at three institutions, and it concentrates upon the *similarities* among classrooms as well as the differences.

THE TEAM'S RESEARCH QUESTIONS

The immediate context for our research questions is the four classrooms. Like any community, the classroom encompasses complex interactions involving not only teaching and learning but dynamics of race, gender, culture, and power. Interaction within the classroom, as well as any study of the classroom, is historically and culturally bound, mediated by language, and infused with the ideologies of the classroom participants and the researcher. However, among the various ways of viewing the classroom, each of which would highlight different interactions, *we chose to view the classroom as a discourse community in which, under the guidance of their teacher, students learn the ways of thinking and writing that are deemed appropriate in that classroom by that teacher.* Our theoretical framework and our methods for data collection and data analysis are explained more fully in the next chapter.

As Walvoord and each teacher began the study of a classroom, they attempted to get as full a picture as possible of the context, but they focused on a single, salient event—students fulfilling their writing assignments. They collected a variety of data, including notes, drafts, finished papers, and logs from all or most students in each class; tapes of students thinking aloud as they worked on their assignments; tapes of student-peer response sessions; interviews of students; classroom observations by Walvoord and by paid student observers; teacher logs; textbooks and classroom handouts; and student characteristics such as SAT scores, gender, race, and age. The team then used various quantitative and qualitative methods to analyze the data.

As the study progressed, the team members came to focus on these research questions:

1. Within each classroom setting, what were *teachers' expectations* for "good" writing, thinking, and learning in the writing assignments?

2. Within each classroom setting, what *difficulties* arose as students tried to meet their teachers' expectations?

3. How did *teachers' methods* and *students' strategies* appear to affect, contribute to, or help overcome those difficulties? (Definitions of "strategy" and "difficulty" appear below.)

4. What were *differences*, and, especially, what were *similarities* among the four classes in each of the areas under 1–3 above?

5. When the biology teacher, in a subsequent section of the same course, changed her teaching methods to address the difficulties she and Walvoord had observed in her first section, *did the performance of the later students improve?* (The quantitative methods for answering this particular question are explained in Chapter 6.)

DEFINITIONS

We defined *strategy* as any action by a student (including a mental action we inferred from the data) that seemed intended by the student to help complete the written assignment. For example, considering a topic choice, using a model one has learned elsewhere, and making an outline are all strategies.

We defined *difficulty* as a point of tension between the teacher's expectations and the students' attempts to fulfill those expectations. A difficulty is present when the data show either or both of the following:

- *Struggle:* the student spent extraordinary time or effort or expressed "this is hard" or some other frustration.

- *Failure:* in the judgment of the teacher, the student failed to meet the teacher's expectations for learning, for thinking, or for the final written product.

The Concept of "Difficulty"

We don't think that a difficulty is necessarily counterproductive. Learning, in our view, often grows out of the difficulties of struggle and failure. Exploring these positive sorts of difficulties helped us understand how our students learned. But we also focused on those less positive points at which the struggle seemed harder or more time-consuming for students than was necessary, or where the struggle did not produce the learning or the texts the teacher had hoped for.

We do not view difficulties as solely the outcome of either teachers' or students' actions, but rather as the result of complex interactions across time among teacher and students in a particular setting, involving cognitive, cultural, academic, physical, and emotional factors. Some of these factors are outside the scope of our study. In constructing the factors that contributed to students' difficulties, we thus focused on those that teachers could most readily influence—teaching methods and students' strategies.

We recognize that our focus on difficulties reflects our own view of the classroom, and our own teacherly roles and interests. As teachers, the research team was accustomed to identifying and addressing what we think of as difficulties that our students are experiencing in learning. Another reason we focused on difficulties was that an important goal of our research was teacher growth and change. A teacher who understands the difficulties that arise in his or her classroom, we reasoned, would be able to shape teaching methods that challenged students, that helped students learn through their struggles, and that helped avoid unnecessary frustrations and failures.

We chose, in this study, to grant to individual teachers the validity of their expectations. For example, we do not ask whether the biology teacher's expectation that her students would learn to use the scientific method was a wise or justifiable one. Instead, we focus on the difficulties that arose as she tried to teach the scientific method.

Broadly, then, this book is our exploration and construction of students' thinking and writing in four of our classrooms, of our interactions with students, and of the difficulties that arose within those interactions. It also tells how we six teacher-researchers collaborated over a seven-year period in order to learn, in Geertz's terms, how the people "down the corridor organize their significative world" (1983, 151). And as we've learned about others' worlds, each of us has come to better understand our own.

SIMILARITIES AMONG THE FOUR CLASSROOMS

METHODOLOGY

We arrived at a number of similarities among the classrooms under study by comparing and contrasting our findings from them, using two operations:

1. Searching for common elements, even when teachers and students may have been using different language to describe those elements,

2. Stating similarities at a sufficiently high level of generality to cover all four classrooms.

We were aware of two possible problems resulting from these operations: first, a common language might too narrowly represent our findings, and, second, similarities might be stated too generally to be useful. We tried to guard against these dangers by bringing all our team members, with their different perspectives and detailed knowledge of their own classrooms and disciplines, into our discussion of similarities. In our discussions, we consciously tried to challenge each other's constructions of the similarities, and we also checked our constructions carefully against our data. So that the constructions would not overly influence our ongoing data analysis and interpretation, each pair completed most of its data analysis before we finally settled on the similarities.

Our construction of similarities among the classrooms does not deny the many differences that we also discuss. However, because other researchers (Faigley and Hansen, 1985; Herrington, 1985; McCarthy,

1987) have convincingly established that classrooms, even those within the same department, differ in many ways, we decided, rather, to try to construct similarities.

SIMILARITIES IN TEACHERS' ASSIGNMENTS

Good/Better/Best Questions

We realized, after data collection was completed, that *twelve of the fifteen major assignments in the four classes asked students for evaluation and/or problem-solving in the form of what we call good/better/best questions:*

Good:	Is X good or bad?
Better:	Which is better—X or Y?
Best:	Which is the best among available options?
	What is the best solution to a given problem?

According to the survey literature, good/better/best questions may be common in college classes.* Among our teacher-collaborators there had been no prior plan to ask good/better/best questions; they appeared as part of the teachers' normal course planning.

Our good/better/best questions include "evaluation" and "synthesis," the highest levels in Bloom's taxonomy of educational objectives (1956, vol. I). In other words, these good/better/best assignments required complex thinking. The major assignments in our four classes were never merely the "review" writing that Langer and Applebee (1987) found common in high schools, writing which valued "accuracy of students' recitations of newly learned material" (137). Rather, in our four classes, the students were asked to apply discipline-based categories, concepts, or methods *to new data and new situations.* For example, in Sherman's business class, students read a textbook chapter that described how to choose a location for a manufacturing business. In the writing assignment, Sherman asked them to apply those prin-

---

*Bridgeman and Carlson's (1984) study of faculty in 190 academic departments at 34 institutions showed that instructors favored two questions that resemble our good/better/best questions: "Compare/Contrast plus Take a Position," and "Argumentation with Audience Designation." In addition, Rose's (1983) survey of 445 essay and take-home examination questions and paper topics from 17 departments at UCLA found that most questions and topics required "exposition and academic argument," presumably tasks that would include our good/better/best questions.

ciples to choose a location for a different kind of enterprise—the
proposed new Baltimore baseball stadium, a hotly debated issue in
Baltimore's barrooms and boardrooms at the time.

Generally, the four teachers held, with Peter Elbow (1986), that
what constitutes "real learning" is the ability to apply discipline-based
concepts to a wide range of situations and to relate those concepts to
the students' own knowledge and experience (33). Our four teachers
shared the quality that Langer and Applebee (1987) found in the high
school classrooms they studied, where "writing was effectively used
to enhance student learning." In those classrooms, as in ours, "the
teachers' criteria for judging [students'] learning changed from the
accuracy of students' recitations to the adequacy of their thinking"
(137).

SIMILARITIES IN TEACHERS' EXPECTATIONS
FOR STUDENTS' ROLES

What did teachers expect students to do as they addressed good/
better/best questions? As our data analysis progressed, we came to
the notion of "role" to help us summarize the many expectations.
Basically, then, *all four teachers expected students to function competently
in the role of "professional-in-training."*

We define *role* as a set of behaviors associated with a given position
or status in society (Banton 1985; Corey 1984). To adopt a role implies
that one relates in certain ways to "role-others." For example, the role
of "doctor" implies also that there will be "patients." A person may
also assume multiple roles—a doctor may also be a parent. Then again,
people may fulfill a role only partially; they may also combine
characteristics of several roles, and role expectations or role behaviors
may differ among people.

Our concept of role provides throughout the book a conceptual
lever with which to view our classrooms—a lever that emphasizes the
social aspects of students' behavior and allows us to construct relationships among the wide variety of teachers' expectations and students'
strategies.

The Professional-in-Training versus
the Text Processor and the Layperson

All four teachers expected students to adopt the role that, as data
analysis progressed, we came to call "professional-in-training." The

two teachers of majors courses (Sherman in business and Anderson in biology) were educating their students as business decision makers and entry-level scientists in industrial research and development laboratories. The two teachers of CORE and elective courses (Breihan in history and Robison in psychology) saw their students more broadly as preparing for professions in a variety of fields and for participation in society as citizens.

Professional-in-training, then, means either a professional in the teacher's own field or a professional in some other field who would be able, as an informed citizen, to employ knowledge about the teacher's discipline. Although the specific characteristics of that role differed in each classroom, in all four classes the professional-in-training role always meant:

- focusing on the issues or problems outlined in the assignment

- using, not ignoring, the knowledge and methodology being taught in the course to address those issues/problems

All four teachers viewed the professional-in-training role as distinct from other student roles they often witnessed—roles to which, as our data analysis proceeded, we gave these names:

1. *text processor:* the student focuses centrally on processing texts in some way (summarizing, synthesizing, reviewing, commenting) rather than on addressing the issues and solving the problems outlined in the assignment.

2. *layperson:* the student addresses the issues and problems, but does not use the knowledge and methodology being taught in the course.

One example of a layperson role occurred in Sherman's stadium assignment. The students who addressed the problem as baseball fans, rather than as business managers-in-training, did not use the methods of business decision making being taught to them in the course.

The difference among the three roles is the student's *focus.* The professional-in-training must not only process text but must also make some use of what has been learned outside the course. Though teachers in some high school or college settings may sometimes ask merely for text processing, Anderson, Breihan, Robison, and Sherman were consciously trying to move students from text-processing or layperson roles to professional-in-training roles.

Role Categories in Other Frameworks

Categories similar to our three roles have emerged within other research frameworks. In a college freshman class called "Reading to Write," Flower (1990) asked students to write a "research paper" using source texts she provided. She deliberately kept the instructions ambiguous, to see what kind of overall "organizing plans" students would generate for composing their papers. Among students' plans were those we have linked to the text-processor role—plans to "summarize" or to "review and comment" or to "synthesize" the source texts. (The operations students performed on the texts might be more-or-less sophisticated but, in our configuration, they were all text processors because the focus of their attention was to process the texts in some way, not to address an issue.) Another group of students addressed an issue, but, like our layperson students, without much reference to the texts that were supposed to be the basis for the paper. A final group of Flower's students "interpreted" the information in the source texts for a "rhetorical purpose." Like our professionals-in-training, they focused on using information in the source texts to address an issue or problem.

Flower's study reveals the models her freshman students already knew and could use, or could construct, when instruction was deliberately vague and open-ended. Our study, however, is different in three important ways: First, it explores what roles were expected of students doing their usual classroom assignments in four different disciplines. The teachers did not change or construct the assignments with our study in mind. Second, the assignments were not deliberately ambiguous, as in Flower's study. Third, we did not operate within the cognitive process model that Flower used, but instead adopted the concept of role as our conceptual lever. Nonetheless, working from different perspectives, both we and Flower seem to be constructing similar categories of students' behavior in college classrooms.

Nelson and Hayes (1988) developed some categories that are both similar to and different from ours. They studied how sixteen paid college-student volunteers responded to the researchers' request to write a research paper for a hypothetical Latin American History course. Their assignment was to write on the topic of "some aspect of the relationship between the United States and Chile during the overthrow of President Allende in the early 1970s."

Although the study was conducted in a much more artificial situation than ours (the students were not actually enrolled in a political science class) and the instructions, again, were vague, Nelson and Hayes identified two "approaches" that in some ways may relate to our text-processor and professional-in-training roles. In what they call the "content-driven" approach, the students focused on finding any usable information on the broad topic of the relationship between the United States and Chile during the overthrow of Allende. In the "issue-driven" approach, the students focused on choosing "some aspect" of the topic, as the assignment had requested.

Nelson and Hayes's categories may be somewhat similar to our text-processor and professional-in-training roles if one interprets their findings to mean that their content-driven students focused on merely processing the text, while their issue-driven students, like our professionals-in-training, focused on addressing the specific task proposed by the assignment.

In that same 1988 technical report, Nelson and Hayes recounted a second study from which we want specifically to *distinguish* our findings. This time they did a naturalistic study of eight college students writing their assigned research papers in eight different courses at Carnegie Mellon University. In this study, Nelson and Hayes identified two groups "high investment" (of the students' time, energy, and caring) and "low investment." They do not equate, but seem to link, the content-driven approach from the first study with the low-investment group of the second study, or the issue-driven approach from the first with the high-investment group of the second.

On the basis of our data, however, a distinction should be sharply maintained between students' investment and students' adoption of the text-processor or professional-in-training roles. Some of our text-processor students invested a great deal of time and energy in taking copious notes from sources and summarizing them arduously in their papers. The text-processor role, then, is not always linked to low investment of time, energy, and caring.

Relevant Issues in Recent Literature

In addition to these studies, our notion of "role" is relevant to the current discussion in the literature on the "ethos of academic discourse," to borrow a phrase from Bizzell (1978). Aristotle focused on how the speaker creates ethos *in the text* by using rhetorical devices to portray the self as a person of good character. But contemporary discussions of the ethos of academic discourse have been linked with discussions of the self *outside of the text*—for example, Bizzell advises that students should ask "what kind of person the intellectual work of college seems to be asking them to be" (353). The notion of role allows us to sidestep the sticky question of whether or not there is a "real" self while also allowing us to go beyond the self as merely an artifact of text.

Our data show that students, aside from some tinkering with vocabulary to make themselves sound more academic, did not consciously manipulate textual features to construct a self in the text; rather, their construction of self in the text seemed to proceed from what we term their roles—their behaviors in a number of areas such as collecting information, relating to teacher and peers, planning the paper, and reading source texts. For these reasons, then, we propose that the discussion of the "ethos of academic discourse" and the "self" that a student must "be" could profitably employ the concept of roles that are expected and adopted in academic communities.

SIMILARITIES IN TEACHERS' EXPECTATIONS FOR GOOD/BETTER/BEST REASONING

The Five Tasks of Good/Better/Best Reasoning

What, then, did teachers consider "good" reasoning as students addressed good/better/best questions? *In all classrooms, students addressing good/better/best questions had to perform five tasks*:

Task 1. Define "good" so as to accommodate a number of variously weighted factors and address the issue of "good for whom?"

Task 2. Observe and analyze causes of the problem, aspects of the situation, and/or alternative solutions to the problem.

Task 3. Bring that information into disciplined relationship with the definition of "good" so a single judgment can be made.

Task 4. Integrate values/feelings with reasoning so as to reach a defensible position.

Task 5. During the process, conduct simultaneously the processes we term "solution-searching" and "rationale-building" (see explanation below).

Solution-Searching and Rationale-Building

To explain Task 5 a bit more fully: In all four classrooms, the good/better/best questions were what psychologists call "ill-structured" problems—that is, open-ended problems for which there is no "right" answer and for which all necessary information may not be available.

Because solutions to ill-structured problems cannot be tested in the scientific sense, they must be supported by a rationale (Voss, Tyler, and Yengo 1983). In studying how social scientists solve ill-structured problems such as how to increase Soviet agricultural productivity, Voss, Greene, Post, and Penner (1983) found that their subjects employed simultaneously two operations—looking for a solution to the problem and building a rationale for a particular solution they wanted to defend. Not only Voss and his colleagues in problem-solving research, but researchers in critical thinking have identified two intertwined elements in critical thinking: "the context of discovery," which is the inventive, creative part, and "the context of justification," which is the presentation of the argument (Kahane 1980; McPeck 1981). Similarly, all four of our team's teachers expected students, as they made good/better/best decisions, to integrate the two elements we call solution-searching and rationale-building.

An Example of the Five Tasks in a Classroom Setting

Another example from the stadium assignment illustrates how all five tasks apply in one situation. Sherman's business students had to choose and weigh factors they considered important in defining a "good" stadium—factors such as transportation, land costs, and tax revenues (Task 1). Then they had to analyze various possible stadium sites (Task 2). Next, the information about the sites had to be related to the definition of "good" so that they could decide which stadium site they would recommend (Task 3). Values and feelings, in Sherman's class, were integrated as the student chose and weighted the factors that they thought would constitute a "good" stadium (Task 4). There was no single "right" location that the student could determine merely by considering evidence in a "solution-searching" mode, but neither could the student merely seek a rationale for a favorite site without considering evidence; solution-searching and rationale-building had to be combined (Task 5).

Scardamalia (1981) has summarized research on children's cognitive development in terms that reflect the five tasks:

> Much of the story of cognitive development may be construed as taking progressively more variables into account during a single act of judgment. (82)

Our study shows how this ability to account for variables in making a single judgment translated into five identifiable tasks that were performed somewhat differently in each of the four classrooms we examined.

SIMILARITIES IN AREAS OF DIFFICULTY

Given teachers' expectations that students, in addressing the good/ better/best questions, would adopt and implement the role of professional-in-training, and, in doing so, would perform the five tasks of good/better/best reasoning—what difficulties, then, arose in the classrooms as students attempted to meet their teachers' expectations?

In each of the classrooms, difficulties arose in six areas of students' thinking and writing processes:

1. Gathering sufficient specific information
2. In the paper, constructing the audience and the self
3. Stating a position
4. Using appropriate discipline-based methods to arrive at the position and to support it with evidence
5. Managing complexity (i.e., avoiding what the teacher considered overgeneralization or oversimplification; considering various aspects of an issue; discussing alternative solutions to problems; acknowledging and answering counterarguments and counterevidence; in science, designing an experiment with appropriate operational definitions and control of variables)
6. Organizing the paper.

We use these six areas of students' thinking and writing processes under which to discuss the difficulties. We do not imply, however, that the difficulties belonged only to the students; rather, as we have said, difficulties resulted from complex interactions between the students and their teachers.

The survey literature suggests that many college teachers value students' performance in these six areas (Behrens 1978; Cooper et al. 1984; Gere 1977; Shih 1986). Our study seeks to help teachers and researchers better understand the difficulties that arose in our four classes as students attempted to meet their teachers' expectations. Particularly, we focus on how students' strategies and teachers' methods affected the difficulties.

ORGANIZATION OF THE FOUR CLASSROOM CHAPTERS

As Table 1.1 illustrates, the four classroom chapters are organized according to our research questions. The second and third classroom chapters cover only some, not all, of the six areas of difficulty. The first and fourth cover all.

A subhead such as "Students' and Teacher's Differing Approaches to the Textbook" appears under several areas of difficulty in each chapter. Each time the subhead occurs, we explain how the differing approaches to the textbook affected that particular area of difficulty in that classroom. The chapter organization thus allows us to explore differences among the four classrooms in students' and teachers' approaches to the textbook while also emphasizing that approaches to the textbook were a factor in many sorts of difficulty within all four classrooms.

Within the common plan as outlined above, each classroom chapter has a special focus, and its organizational pattern may vary accordingly (Table 1.2).

In the final chapter of the book, Chapter 7, we summarize similarities

Table 1.1   Basic Organizational Plan for Classroom Chapters

Topic	Research Question	Chapters Discussed
Teacher's expectations	1	3,4,5,6
Areas of difficulty		
Information gathering		3,6
Nature of the difficulties	2	
Teacher's methods and students' strategies	3	
Constructing the audience and self		3,5,6
[Subsections as above]	2,3	
Stating a position		3,4,5,6
[Subsections as above]	2,3	
Arriving at (and supporting) a position		3,4,5,6
[Subsections as above]		
Managing complexity		3,4,5,6
[Subsections as above]	2,3	
Organizing the paper		3,6
[Subsections as above]	2,3	
Similarities and differences among the classrooms are explored throughout each Chapter	4	3,4,5,6
Changes in teaching methods and improvement in student performance as a result of this research	5	6

Table 1.2   Special Focus of Each Classroom Chapter

Chapter	Class	Focus
3	Sherman's Business	How teacher's methods and students' strategies affected all six areas of difficulty
4	Breihan's History	How Breihan's teaching methods helped students overcome difficulties
5	Robison's Psychology	How the multiple roles Robison modeled affected the difficulties
6	Anderson's Biology	Changes in Anderson's teaching methods based on study of her 1983 class; improvement in performance of her 1986 class

and differences we found among the four classrooms, focusing on our research questions about teachers' expectations, students' difficulties, and the ways in which teachers' methods and students' strategies appeared to influence those difficulties. We conclude by reflecting on our team's seven-year research collaboration, its challenges and satisfactions.

2 Research Theory and Methods

Lucille Parkinson McCarthy
University of Maryland Baltimore County

Barbara E. Walvoord
Loyola College in Maryland

In this chapter we (the research team) present the theoretical framework and research methods of this naturalistic study of students' writing in four classrooms. We begin by describing ourselves and our student informants. We then discuss our inquiry paradigm and research assumptions, our assumptions about classrooms, and our methods of data collection and analysis. Finally, we explain our ways of working as a team and our ways of assuring the trustworthiness of our findings.

THE RESEARCHERS AND THE STUDENTS

All four teachers on our team whose classrooms we studied:

- had participated in at least one writing-across-the-curriculum workshop of at least 30 contact hours before the study of their classrooms began
- had subsequently presented or published on writing across the curriculum (Gazzam [Anderson] and Walvoord 1986; Breihan 1986; Mallonee and Breihan 1985; Robison 1983)
- were experienced teachers who received excellent evaluations from their students and colleagues
- held a doctorate and had published in their fields
- were in their 40s
- had been in their positions at least five years
- were tenured
- had been department heads (except Anderson)

Walvoord asked these four teachers to collaborate because she judged them to be interested in their students, open to new ideas, and sufficiently self-confident to feel comfortable with her visits to their classes.

The team and most of the students are white and from middle- or working-class backgrounds (Table 2.1). Most students were between the ages of 18 and 22 and were enrolled full-time in undergraduate day classes. Within that sector of American higher education, however,

Table 2.1   Characteristics of the Classes in the Study

	Sherman	Breihan	Robison	Anderson[a]
Institution	Loyola College		College of Notre Dame	Towson State U.
Type	Catholic liberal arts with strong business		Catholic liberal arts	Public comprehensive
Location	Baltimore City			Baltimore Suburb
Enrollment[b]	3876		691	11,086
Mean verbal/ Composite SAT, entering freshmen	516/1064		444/918	437/911
Course	Business 330 Production Management	History 101 Modern Civilization	Psych 165 Human Sexuality	Biology 381 Biological Literature
Year of data collection	1985	1985	1986	1983, 1986
Level	Jr./Sr.	Fr./Soph.	Fr./Soph.[d]	Jr./Sr.
Course enrollment[c]	44	27	30	13
Mean verbal SAT, course takers	460	542	448	n.a.
Female	52%	56%	100%	54%
Minority	7%	4%	23%	15%
ESL	2%	0	17%	8%
Age 24+	7%	0	10%	0

[a] Anderson's 1983 and 1986 classes are the same number of people; the same percentage of female, minority, and ESL students, and those students covered the same age range.

[b] Full time equivalent, total undergraduate and graduate school.

[c] Enrollment figures are for year of data collection.

[d] Course was planned for freshmen-sophomores, but due to unusual circumstances, primarily juniors and seniors enrolled.

our discipline-based teachers and our students represent a range: The teachers are two men and two women who teach in three different types of institutions: a large, comprehensive state university; a small, Catholic women's liberal arts college; and a middle-sized, Catholic coeducational college with a large business program. Both teachers and students represent the four major undergraduate discipline areas: business, humanities, social science, and natural science. The classes under study ranged from freshman to senior and included required CORE, elective, and majors courses.

OUR INQUIRY PARADIGM AND RESEARCH ASSUMPTIONS

Our questions, as we began the study, were broad ones about students' thinking and writing. They were the general questions that Geertz says are traditionally asked by ethnographers facing new research scenes: "What's going on here?" and "What the devil do these people think they're up to?" (1976, 224). We chose the naturalistic inquiry paradigm to ask those questions because it is based on the following assumptions regarding:

1. *The nature of reality*: Realities are multiple and are constructed by people as they interact within particular social settings.

2. *The relationship of knower to known*: The inquirer and the "object" of inquiry interact to influence each other. In fact, naturalistic researchers often negotiate research outcomes with the people whose realities they seek to reconstruct; that is, with the people from whom the data have been drawn. Research is thus never value-free.

3. *The possibilities of generalization*: The aim of a naturalistic inquiry is not to develop universal, context-free generalizations, but rather to develop "working hypotheses" that describe the complexities of particular cases or contexts.

4. *Research methods and design*: Naturalistic researchers use both qualitative and quantitative methods in order to help them deal with the multiple realities in a setting. Their research designs therefore emerge as they identify salient features in that setting—features identified for further study. Naturalistic researchers understand themselves as the instruments of inquiry, and acknowledge that tacit as well as explicit knowledge is part of the research process.[1]

We assume, then, that research questions, methods, and findings are socially constructed by particular researchers in particular settings for particular ends (Harste, Woodward and Burke 1984). We recognize that our own research practices were shaped by our discipline-based perspectives, by our perspectives as teachers, and by our desire to construct findings that would help the teachers of the four classrooms we studied improve their teaching. Our perspectives shaped, for example, our decision to focus on students' difficulties in meeting teachers' expectations and on those aspects of the classroom context—writing strategies and teaching methods—that were, we felt, most amenable to the teachers' influence.

Because we are aware that our research findings were shaped by our perspectives, we "reflexively" explain wherever possible our own as well as our informants' knowledge-construction processes, our research assumptions, our decisions about data collection and analysis, and the collaborative procedures through which we arrived at our findings (Latour and Woolgar 1979, 273–286).

Because knowledge in this collaborative study was constructed by multiple researchers with varying perspectives and varying relation-ships to the classrooms under study, we have been careful to define these perspectives and to have all team members tell at least parts of their stories in their own voices. (The relationship among the individual voices and the "we" voice in each coauthored chapter differs somewhat and was worked out separately by each pair.) This type of coauthored, multivoice, reflexive discourse has been called "polyphonic," and we believe it best reflects the intersubjective, "constructive negotiation" involved in producing our research findings (Clifford 1983, 133–140). Thus, we have worked to adequately represent the multiple and evolving realities of our students and ourselves as we constructed our various types of knowledge and texts.

OUR ASSUMPTIONS ABOUT CLASSROOMS

Recently, several scholars have attempted to describe the dominant schools of thought currently represented in composition studies. They have discussed those schools in terms of their theories of writing, their approaches to research and pedagogy, and their social and political implications (Berlin 1988; Faigley 1986; Nystrand 1990). Of the three major perspectives identified by Faigley—the expressive, the cognitive, and the social—our study clearly belongs in the latter category.

Our understanding of students learning to write in academic settings is underlain by theoretical assumptions concerning language use from sociolinguistics (Gumperz 1971; Heath 1982; Hymes 1972a, 1972b, 1974), literary studies (Fish 1980; Pratt 1977), and philosophy (Rorty 1982). A central assumption is that language processes must be understood in terms of the contexts in which they occur. In this view, writing, like speaking, is a social activity that takes place within speech communities and accomplishes meaningful social functions. In their characteristic "ways of speaking," community members share accepted intellectual, linguistic, and social conventions which have developed over time and govern spoken and written interaction. Moreover, "communicatively competent" speakers in every community recognize and successfully employ these ways of speaking largely without conscious attention (Hymes 1972a, xxiv–xxxvi; 1974, 51). Newcomers to a community learn the rules for appropriate speaking and writing gradually as they interact orally and in writing with competent members, and as they read and write texts deemed acceptable there. We chose to see the classroom within this theoretical framework.

In our view, when students enter a classroom, they are entering a discourse community in which they must master the ways of thinking and writing considered appropriate in that setting and by their teacher. We also understand their writing to be at the heart of their initiation into new academic communities: it is both the means of discipline-based socialization and the eventual mark of competence—the mark, that is, of membership in the community.

As students write, they must integrate the new ways of thinking and writing they are being asked to learn with the already-familiar discourses that they bring with them from other communities. As Bruffee puts it, students "belong to many overlapping, mutually inclusive knowledge communities" (1987, 715). We believe that students may experience conflict among these ways of knowing, as old and new discourses vie for their attention.

Further, we understand reading, as we do writing, to be an interactive language process that is at once individual and social. Readers, like writers, construct meanings as they interact with written texts and with other aspects of the social situation, such as their explicit purposes for reading and the implicit values of the community (Pratt 1977; Rosenblatt 1978).

Teachers, then, construct meanings as they read students' writing, and the success of a student's work reflects such aspects of the reading context as the teacher's current relationship with the class and that student, the meanings and values (tacit and explicit) that the teacher assigns to the text, and the expectations (tacit and explicit) that the teacher has for text content and structures. The success of students' work also depends on the teacher's expectations about the role the student writer should assume in the piece. Sullivan (1987), studying the "social interaction" between placement test evaluators and the student writers they infer from those essay tests, observes that "readers construct writers as well as texts" (11).

Similarly, we view the student's writing development as a social process best understood not only as occurring within an individual student, but also in response to particular situations. We are typical of naturalistic researchers in that often we are "less concerned with what people actually are capable of doing at some developmental stage than with how groups specify appropriate behavior for various developmental stages" (LeCompte and Goetz 1982).

These theoretical assumptions about the classroom have shaped our choices of research questions and methods, and thus, ultimately, they have shaped the construction of our findings and interpretations.

DATA COLLECTION METHODS

Because we understand writing to be a complex sociocognitive process, we worked to view it through multiple windows. We assumed that data collected from a variety of sources would give us such multiple windows and would help us construct as full a view as possible of students completing their assignments in each of the four classrooms. Our aim was to investigate the entire classroom community, but within that community to focus on a single "salient event"—the writing assignment—the outcome of which was crucial to the life of the community (Spindler 1982, 137). Because our initial research questions were broad, we collected a wide range of data about students' thinking and writing and about the classroom context. This, we reasoned, would be the basis for the subsequent narrowing of our research questions and foci at later stages of the project.

CHOOSING THE "FOCUS" ASSIGNMENTS

In the history and business classes, we tracked students' progress across the entire semester, and thus we asked them for process data on *all* their written assignments. In the biology and psychology classes, we asked students to collect data about their writing processes only for a single assignment that their teachers judged central to achieving their course goals. In all four classes we collected data about the classroom setting for the entire semester.

EXPLAINING DATA PRODUCTION TO STUDENTS

We wanted to separate students' data production from their concerns about their grades and to minimize the possibility that they might try to produce data that they thought would please the teacher. Thus, Walvoord, rather than the classroom teacher, initially explained the research project to students and collected all data from them, except drafts or final papers normally given to the teacher. Both Walvoord and the teacher assured students that the teacher would not see any student data until their final grades for the semester had been turned in.

Before the teacher explained to students the writing assignment that the research would focus on, Walvoord visited the class and did the following:

1. Described the research in very general terms and told students, "We are interested in everything you do and think about as you work on the assignment."

2. Distributed a list of all the kinds of data we wanted from them, explaining each type and answering their questions.

3. Conducted a training session for those students who would be making think-aloud tapes.

4. Walvoord then recruited two student volunteers who were enrolled in class. These students, for a stipend of $25.00, agreed to act as observers for each class session of the semester. After class she instructed these observers and gave them sheets to fill out about all subsequent class sessions during the semester. These students also submitted the same data as their peers.

5. Walvoord reemphasized to students that they should record in their data what they actually thought and did, and that they should work in their customary ways and places.

When Walvoord had finished her initial presentation to each class, the teacher explained that he or she supported the research and had slightly revised the course syllabus to allow for the extra time students would spend collecting data.

The revision varied from course to course. In the psychology and business classes, a short, end-of-semester paper had been omitted to compensate for time spent generating data. In the history class, no papers were omitted, but students received extra points for handing in data. In the biology class, no compensation was made or announced; students were simply asked for their help. (Because that biology class was identified as "writing intensive," the students expected to focus on their writing.)

After her initial visit, Walvoord attended each class several times to observe and to collect data. When she was not present, the teacher answered students' questions about data collection. At the next session after Walvoord's explanation, some students in each class expressed fears or reluctance about the data collection, especially about the think-aloud taping. In each case, the teacher reiterated his or her support for the project and urged students to give it a fair trial. In the business class three students came privately to the teacher or to Walvoord after they had tried think-aloud taping and asked to be excused because they found it too disruptive. We granted their requests.

In the description of our data sources which follows, we have divided the data into two categories: data generated by students and data generated by teachers.

DATA GENERATED BY STUDENTS

Data generated by students is summarized in Table 2.2. In the business, history, and psychology classes, 100 percent of students submitted some usable data. In the biology class 85 percent of the students did so.

Students' Logs

From all students, we requested a writing log in which they would record their activities and their thinking as they worked on the assignment. Activities included planning, gathering information, reading, note making, consulting with other people, drafting, and revising. Sherman's business students and Breihan's history students were asked to keep logs for the entire semester because we were tracking student development in their classes. Robison's psychology students and Anderson's biology students were asked to keep logs only during the weeks in which they worked on the focus assignments.

When Walvoord initially explained the logs, she asked students to date each entry and address the following questions:

Table 2.2   Data Generated by Students

Data	BUS	HIST	PSYCH	BIO
		Percent		
Logs	36	74	67	82
Plans/drafts	73	70	100	100
Final paper with teacher comment	100	100	100	100
Interviews by Walvoord	5	7	3	0
Peer response/peer interviews	68	89	97	100
Taped interaction with others outside of class	0	11	10	9
Paragraph describing self as writer	n.a.	n.a.	90	n.a.
Think-aloud tapes	46*	67*	77	91
Students' class evaluations	n.a.	4	100	n.a.

* Percentage of stratified sample asked to tape (about half the class: business: 24 students; history: 14 students)

N = Students who submitted usable data: 44 (business), 27 (history), 30 (psychology), 11 (biology)

- What did you do today on your project?
- What difficulties did you face?
- How did you try to overcome the difficulties?
- How do you feel about your work at this point?

The logs helped establish a chronological scaffolding within which other data, more detailed and specific about certain parts of the writing process, could be placed. We recognized, with Tomlinson (1984), that retrospective accounts in the logs are limited by students' memories, their interpretive strategies for telling the "story" of their writing, and their consciousness that these writing logs are for the researcher. Thus, as Tomlinson suggests, we included specific questions designed to keep students close to recall of the assignment they were reporting, and we urged them to write in their logs immediately after each work session. Changes in handwriting, pen color, and students' responses to those questions gave us some indication that many of them had complied with our request. Tomlinson notes that retrospective accounts provide valuable information about students' conceptions of writing. We found this to be true. The students' retrospective descriptions and reflections about each work session as recorded in their logs usually contained information about their processes at a higher level of abstraction than did their think-aloud tapes.[2]

Students' Pre-Draft Writing and Drafts
and Teachers' Comments

From each student, for each focus assignment, we requested all final papers (including any teacher comments) as well as all pre-draft writing (including freewriting, reading and lecture notes, charts, and outlines) and drafts. We asked students to number pages, to date each piece of writing, to label their drafts ("draft 1," "draft 2"), and, in their logs and think-aloud tapes, to identify the pieces of writing they were working on. If they revised a manuscript in more than one sitting, we asked them to use different colored pens or pencils for each separate session. Most students complied sufficiently to allow the researchers to agree on the chronology of their writing activities as they wrote a paper and to match think-aloud tapes to written drafts.

Walvoord's Interviews with Students

Between three months and four years after the course was finished, Walvoord conducted open-ended or discourse-based interviews with a few students in the history, psychology, and business classes (Doheny-Farina 1986; Odell, Goswami, and Herrington 1983; Spradley 1979). She interviewed students whose data had been, or promised to be, particularly useful. Information from these interviews added to, refined, and cross-checked information from our other data sources.

Peer Interviews and Peer Responses to Drafts

In each class, for each student, we arranged at least one tape-recorded, student-to-student interview or one peer response to a draft, either during the writing of the focus assignment or on the day it was handed in. Biologist Anderson followed her usual practice of having her students interview each other in class about the experimental and composing processes they were using as they worked on their papers. She gave students a question sheet she had designed to guide these interviews. Psychologist Robison followed her usual practice of using a checklist to structure in-class peer response to the drafts. For Sherman's business and Breihan's history classes, where neither peer interviews nor peer response to drafts were normally used, we arranged for each student to be interviewed about one of their assignments, on tape, by a student from one of Walvoord's freshman composition classes.

.

In training her freshmen to interview the business and history students, Walvoord explained that the purposes of the interviews were to help with this project and to get information about the kinds of writing they, the freshmen, might themselves someday be assigned. She gave her students a series of interview questions to which they were to add at least three questions of their own. Then she modeled an interview for them, had them interview each other about one of their freshman composition essays, and arranged times for them to meet with Sherman's and Breihan's students.

Although we were aware that the usefulness of interview data produced by unskilled interviewers would be limited, we did get frank responses from the history and the business students and a valuable sample of student-to-student language. Further, comparisons among students were possible because in three of the four classes, virtually every student was asked on the same day, "What part of the assignment was most difficult for you?" (These difficulties, as we have said, increasingly became our focus as the study progressed.) Information from this data source, then, served to augment and cross-check information from our other data sources.

Students' Taped, Outside-Class Interactions

In their logs or think-aloud tapes, many students described out-of-class interactions with classmates, parents, or others. A few of them actually recorded these interactions. In Breihan's history class, for example, five students made tapes of their student-organized study sessions in the dorm. In Robison's psychology class, three students gave us tapes of their conversations with peer helpers (in one case a roommate, in two cases a classmate). One of Anderson's biology students made a tape of his friend, a graduate student in biology, responding to his draft. These tapes provided particularly useful information about how students gave and sought help from others and how that help served them.

Students Describing Themselves as Writers

In Robison's class, where all students were asked to make think-aloud tapes, part of their training involved their thinking aloud as they wrote a paragraph in which we asked them to tell us "something about yourself as a writer." These paragraphs were then used as data.

Think-Aloud Tapes

We asked all the students in two classes (psychology and biology) and a stratified sample of about half the students in two of the larger classes (history and business) to record think-aloud tapes whenever they were "working on" the assignment. We wanted to get think-aloud information about their entire writing process, extending as it often did over days or even weeks.

At the beginning of the semester, in each of the four classrooms, Walvoord trained students who would be making think-aloud tapes. Her instructions to the students were modeled on those suggested by Swarts, Flower, and Hayes (1984, 54). She asked them to "say aloud whatever you are thinking, no matter how trivial it might seem to you, whenever you are working on" a focus assignment. That is, they were to think aloud during their entire writing process, from their earliest exploration and planning, during reading and note taking, through drafting, revising, and editing. Walvoord asked them to tape whenever and wherever they could, and gave those students who needed them tape recorders to take with them. She told them to work as they usually did and to forget the tape recorder as much as possible.

Next, Walvoord demonstrated thinking aloud as she composed a letter at the blackboard. Finally, she asked students to practice thinking aloud as they composed, at their desks, a short piece about an aspect of the course or a paragraph about "yourself as writer."

In order to minimize the disruptiveness of the thinking-aloud process, our instructions to the students about taping were purposely general, and did not specify particular aspects of their writing that we wanted them to talk about. We were aware of Ericsson and Simon's (1980, 1984) conclusion that though thinking aloud may slow the thought process, it does not change its nature or sequence unless subjects are asked to attend to aspects they would not usually attend to.

Although we were aware of questions regarding the extent to which writers' subjective testimony can be trusted (Cooper and Holzman 1983, 1985; Ericsson and Simon 1980; Flower and Hayes 1985; Hayes and Flower 1983; Nisbett and Wilson 1977), we reasoned that these tapes would afford us information about students' thinking and writing processes that we could get in no other way. Berkenkotter (1983), who also studied think-aloud tapes made by her writer-informant in naturalistic settings when she was not present, notes that "the value of thinking-aloud protocols is that they allow the researcher to eavesdrop at the workplace of the writer, catching the flow of thought that would remain otherwise unarticulated" (167). Throughout the project we understood that our request for tapes was, in essence, like asking our students to let us "eavesdrop" at their workplaces. More often than not, we were amazed at their generosity and hospitality.

Characteristics of the Think-Aloud Tapes

The information we got from the students' think-aloud tapes was rich and varied. Because students recorded them in various settings over extended periods of time with no researcher present, the tapes contained more types of information than do the composing-aloud protocols made in laboratory settings in a limited time period, often with a researcher present. These latter protocols generally record writers' concurrent thoughts—that is, thoughts verbalized while the writer is composing (Berkenkotter 1983; Flower and Hayes 1980, 1981a, 1981b; Perl 1979). Similarly, our think-aloud tapes contained students' concurrent thoughts as they composed their drafts, but in addition, the tapes provided us with several other sorts of information.

The first type of information was students' retrospective comments about what they had just done on the assignment and how they felt about it, what had been particularly hard for them and what they might have done differently. They also talked about their plans for further work on the assignment. At times students seemed to use this sort of monitoring of their writing processes to help them proceed.

At other times students appeared to be speaking directly to the researchers, informing us about their past or future processes, and how they felt about them. This latter situation often occurred when students had worked in settings where they could not think aloud— for example, in the library while gathering information, or in the college pool planning a paper while swimming laps. Such retrospective descriptions and analyses of their writing processes were also necessary when students found thinking aloud too distracting and had turned the recorder off.

Students were, however, able to turn on the tape recorders in many settings, giving us a third type of information: information about the physical conditions in which they worked. They turned on their tape recorders as they conducted scientific experiments, as they planned a paper while driving to school or when at work, and as they composed at home or in the dorm. Furthermore, these tapes reveal much about the affective conditions under which students work. They were, for example, distracted by personal problems, interrupted frequently by the phone or by roommates, worried about exams in other courses, or anxious about their writing ability. In addition they wrote when they were hungry, fascinated, tired, bored, or enthusiastic.

The tapes, although generally informative and useful, were not without their deficiencies. This is to be expected, since our students were trained only briefly and worked with no researcher present. From some students, we got only glimpses of their processes when we wished we could have had a steady gaze; for example, some were thinking aloud on tape when, just as things were getting interesting, they turned the recorder off. We then got from many of those students a summary of what we had missed, which they recorded later. Moreover, there were some students who never produced concurrent thoughts or useful introspection, but rather said aloud on tape only the words they were writing on the page. Nevertheless, these tapes still gave us some sense of the pace and tone of the composing session, and we used whatever they contained, along with our other data, as we worked to reconstruct our students' thinking and writing processes.

Classes differed in the number of students who complied with our request to submit think-aloud tapes. In Anderson's biology, Robison's psychology, and Breihan's history class, 67 percent to 91 percent of those who were asked submitted tapes of at least parts of their process. In Sherman's business class only 46 percent of those students we asked complied with our request. This was due, we think, to several factors:

- Sherman offered his class a short paper as an alternative to taping. By contrast, students in the other three classes had to make individual arrangements with the teacher or with Walvoord if they wanted to be excused from taping.
- Sherman's students were junior and senior business majors and thus perhaps more confident about not complying than were students in Breihan's freshman-level history class. That Anderson's junior and senior biology majors knew that their course was designated "writing intensive" may account for their high level of compliance with our request for think-aloud tapes.

In Robison's psychology class, which also enrolled juniors and seniors, the teacher habitually asked students to sign a contract stating their responsibilities within the class. In the semester of our study, she added to the contract their submission of data. We believe that the contract, together with the general ethos of the class, taught as it was within a small Catholic women's college with an honor code, contributed to the fact that 77 percent submitted tapes.

Awareness of the taping process appeared to vary widely among our students. Most students seemed, after the first few minutes, largely to forget the tape recorder's presence. One student so completely forgot it that when his roommate entered the room, he began a conversation on personal matters and had to be reminded by his roommate to turn off the recorder. Other students seemed more aware of the tape, at times saying "excuse me" after they sneezed, or explaining directly to us that "I'm going to turn the tape off now." In a study session in the dorm that a group of three students taped for us, one of them let out a few four-letter words, and a study mate shushed her because of the recorder. She replied with a laugh, "This is a high quality tape; it can take it," and the study session continued.

In two of the largest classes—business and history—we asked only a stratified sample of about half the students to tape. At the end of the semester we compared the course grades of those who made tapes and those who did not, in order to see if the taping procedures had been disruptive enough to change students' ability to write their papers at the expected grade level. We found that the final course grades of those who made recordings did not differ significantly from the final course grades of the others.

In sum, our students, as they thought aloud on tape, were self-conscious in varying degrees. But they also revealed much of what seems to be natural behavior, and they provided us with rich information about their thinking and writing processes. We concluded about our think-aloud data as Philips (1982) does about hers in her naturalistic study of law students: "Although some people assume recorders cause those recorded to alter their behavior, in fact those observed can't do what they are there for if they change much" (202). Our students did succeed in completing their assignments for their classes as they recorded their processes for us and—at least in the history and business classes—at the expected levels of competence.

DATA GENERATED BY THE RESEARCH TEAM

Teachers' Logs

After Walvoord and Anderson had teamed to study Anderson's biology class in 1983, Walvoord decided to ask each of the succeeding teachers with whom she paired to keep a log during the semester of data collection so that the researchers would have a more comprehensive record of each teacher's perspective. These logs, in which the teachers recorded their ongoing plans and reflections about class, were then compared with the student observers' records and with Walvoord's classroom observations.

Walvoord and McCarthy's Interviews with the Teachers

Walvoord conducted at least three hours of tape-recorded, open-ended interviews with each of the four teachers at various times before, during, and after the semester of data collection (Spradley 1979). The interviews focused on teachers' expectations for students' learning and writing, their teaching methods, the ways of knowing of their discipline, the history of the development of that particular course, and their own evaluations of the course. At times, during the many hours Walvoord spent with each teacher analyzing data and writing research reports, she tape-recorded or took notes on what they said about their students' thinking and writing, their teaching methods, or their teaching philosophy. McCarthy also observed and questioned the pairs during several of these interviews and work sessions, and at two points she independently interviewed the teachers. Her interview transcripts and notes record the teachers' continuing clarification and articulation of their expectations for their students' learning and writing, and they augment and cross-check our other sources of data about the classroom.

Teachers' Presentations to Faculty Workshops

All of the four teachers were involved at least once during the course of this project in a writing-across-the-curriculum workshop presentation to faculty members at their own or a neighboring institution. Walvoord's tapes or notes of these presentations augmented information from other data sources as we worked to establish the teachers' expectations and teaching methods.

Classroom Observations by Walvoord

In each classroom, Walvoord observed between two and five sessions spaced across the semester. From these observations she gained a sense of the classroom ambiance, the teacher's style, and the language the teacher used to talk about writing. Often these classroom observations suggested questions that Walvoord pursued in future interviews with the teachers.

Classroom Observations by Paid Student Volunteers

After our initial study of Anderson's class, we asked, in the other three classes, for two students enrolled in the class to record, on a sheet we provided, what was done in class each day, what was said about student papers, and what difficulties students were facing in working on their current assignment. The latter was to be based on any conversations the student-recorder might have had with classmates about their work. These student-recorders also submitted the same student data as their peers.

LIMITATIONS OF OUR DATA

We used a variety of data sources, aware that the strengths of one source or method could compensate for the limitations of another. Using this triangulated approach (Denzin 1978), we viewed through a variety of windows the salient event of students fulfilling their writing assignments in these classes.

A type of information that we did not collect is information about students' lives outside the classroom. Though we did learn a good deal about the physical and affective conditions under which our students wrote, we never questioned them directly about their family lives or their families' educational history, their socioeconomic situation, their ethnic background, or their prior reading/writing/schooling experiences. We were aware that these factors have been shown to be important influences on students' writing and thinking processes— and achievements—in school (Gilmore and Glatthorn 1982; Heath 1983; Whiteman 1981). We recognized, too, that students have different learning styles, but we chose not to collect data that would allow us to identify those for individual students. Rather, we chose to focus on the writing and thinking processes of all the students in a class, assuming that the class as a whole would represent the range of learning styles and the range of students' backgrounds that usually occurs within the primarily white, middle- and working-class population who attends the institutions in which we worked.

DATA ANALYSIS PROCEDURES

When the semester of data collection in each of the four classes was over, Walvoord and the teacher together analyzed the data from that teacher's class. Data analysis took place in three stages, each stage employing different methods; some qualitative, some quantitative. We viewed each stage as part of a cumulative process during which we further refined our questions and our research foci, each analytic method helping us understand in some further way the complex phenomena we were attempting to describe. The results of the analyses of the three stages worked together, augmenting, refining, and cross-checking one other. Our data analysis was guided generally by the work of Guba (1981), LeCompte and Goetz (1982), Lincoln and Guba (1985), Mathison (1988), Miles and Huberman (1984), and Spradley (1979, 1980).

ORGANIZING THE DATA

We placed all the data we had collected from the individual students in their own 11" × 15" envelopes, and we kept all the envelopes from a single class in a large box, along with other data about that classroom. We wanted our work with any part of a student's data to be rooted in our understanding of other aspects of that student's learning and writing and of the classroom setting.

In each student's envelope were between 10 and 549 pages of data of the types we have described above—logs, notes on lectures and readings, paper plans, drafts, tapes and transcripts of students thinking aloud and of student interviews, and students' papers with the teacher's responses—as well as any pages of notes that the researchers had made during earlier reviews and analyses of this material.

Stage 1: Interpreting Students' Writing-Process Stories

Recreating the Stories

We began our analysis by examining the data in each student's envelope in order to recreate the chronological story of how the student had produced his or her writing for the focus assignment(s) in that class. As we recreated each student's story, we drew upon all the data sources in his or her envelope, taking notes on these data and making charts or other visual representations (Kantor 1984).

The writing process stories of the students in each class on whom we had the most complete data were recreated by both members of the research pair—Walvoord and the teacher. At least half of each class was analyzed in this way. At times Walvoord and the teacher worked together; at other times they worked independently and then compared interpretations. Every student's story in all four classes, no matter how sketchy his or her data, was recreated at least once by

Walvoord, so that subsequent data analysis was always informed by our awareness of all students in that class—including the "negative cases" that called into question our analytic categories or our tentative findings about the sample (Lincoln and Guba 1985). Walvoord and her collaborators returned again and again to the envelopes of those students in which the quality of the data was particularly rich or the issues raised were particularly interesting.

Identifying Patterns and Themes

As we recreated the stories of students' writing processes, we read and reread all of the data in their envelopes as well as data about the classroom setting, looking for patterns and themes that would help us to organize the data and to focus subsequent inquiry. It was during this stage that the students' difficulties became a central focus for us. We also began to create categories of teachers' methods and students' strategies. We were guided in our theme and pattern analysis by the work of Gilmore and Glatthorn (1982), and Spradley (1979, 1980). These Stage 1 processes—reconstructing students' writing stories and identifying patterns and themes in the data—continued throughout the study.

Stage 2: Constructing Primary Trait Scales for Students' Papers

Although primary trait analysis was originally developed to score student papers for the National Assessment of Educational Progress (Lloyd-Jones 1977), we created primary trait scales not only to score students' papers, but also to help the teachers articulate their expectations for successful writing on various assignments. This process also helped us to understand students' difficulties from the teachers' perspectives.

To construct the primary trait scale, the teachers, after the courses were finished, examined a sample of their students' papers and identified the traits that a paper had to have in order for it to meet their expectations. They then constructed a scale for each trait, describing four or five levels of increasingly successful ways in which students' papers exhibited these traits. This process was powerful for all the teachers, helping them explicitly to articulate expectations that had been tacit.

After the four teachers had drafted primary trait scales, Walvoord checked the scales and independently rated a sample of student papers, looking especially for traits that had remained unarticulated. If necessary, the scale was then revised.

We found that the conversations between Walvoord and her collaborators regarding the primary trait analysis often led them to insights about the teachers' tacit expectations and about students' difficulties in meeting them. Those insights were a powerful impetus for change. In subsequent semesters, the four teachers used the primary trait scales as bases for more clearly explaining their expectations to students. A sample primary trait scale is included in Appendix A.

Defining "Successful" Writing

Our definition of successful writing relies on no absolute or standard criteria, but, rather, upon teachers' judgments. Reflecting our view of reading as a context-specific act in which the reader constructs the meaning of the text, our definition of *high success* and *low success* in each class is based upon the tacit and explicit values and assumptions of the teacher for whom the student wrote the paper. A high-success or low-success paper in this study is a paper that received a high or low grade during the course and *also* a corresponding score on the post-course primary trait analysis. We expected that the two judgments would reflect similar (but not identical) values since a reading act is never exactly the same on two different occasions.

Purposes of the Scale

We used the post-course primary trait scoring of papers for three purposes:

1. To construct a judgment about the paper that took into account the students' process data—information that had been unavailable to the teacher during the course. Process data were especially helpful in evaluating whether students' uses of sources and methods of inquiry had met the teacher's expectations.
2. To allow the teacher to give the paper a more leisurely consideration than had been possible during the course.
3. To help the teacher make explicit those expectations that might have been tacit during the course.

Stage 3: Conducting Detailed Analyses
of Specific Aspects of Students' Writing

During the first two stages of data analysis we worked, as we have said, to get an overview of students' writing production stories; to identify, refine, and shape themes and patterns in the data; and to begin to analyze, through primary trait analysis, teachers' expectations, students' success, and students' difficulties. The work during Stage 3 was designed to give us further information about these phenomena and their interrelations, and included the following:

- Constructing the sequences of students' writing strategies for particular assignments
- Analyzing students' revision practices
- Analyzing organizational structures in students' texts
- Other analytic procedures

Constructing the Sequences of
Students' Writing Strategies

To answer our questions about the writing strategies that were associated with students' difficulties, we further analyzed their writing-process stories by constructing chronologically ordered sequences that were, in essence, codified versions of the stories we had constructed in Stage 1. These coded sequences represented all of the student's strategies over the entire period during which he or she worked on the assignment. They also included codes for teachers' and peers' responses to drafts, which we entered into the sequence at the points in the process where they had occurred. Although the sequences of strategies are chronological, they do not indicate how many minutes or hours students actually spent on each strategy nor how much time elapsed between one strategy and the next.

We then divided the sequences of strategies into what might be called the "turns in the conversation" for that assignment. A typical set of turns might be: (1) student strategies up to the first time the paper was handed in to the teacher, (2) the teacher's draft comments and the student's textual revision, (3) further student strategies to the final submission, and (4) the teacher's final comments and grade.

The codified sequences of each student's thinking and writing processes were very valuable because they could be scanned quickly. Also they enabled us to count strategies, to compare sequences, and to relate strategies to other elements, such as a student's difficulties and levels of success. The findings from this analytic procedure often spurred further inquiry, sending us back to the data or to further interviews in order to find out more about particular strategies or relationships.

To capture each student's writing process for an assignment from beginning to end, we coded on the basis of *all* the data in his or her envelope—not just the think-aloud transcripts as has been done most commonly in previous studies. Twenty-eight percent of our strategy codes are based on more than one piece of data in a student's envelope. For example, a student might say in her log, "I revised my draft this afternoon," and the revised draft was in her envelope as well as a transcript of her thinking aloud as she revised. Based upon these three data sources, then, we would add an "R" (for "Revises") to her sequence code, and probably follow that by other letters and numbers indicating the nature and extent of her revisions.

Categories we used as we constructed students' sequences emerged from our data. In naming our strategy categories, we listened very carefully to the language our students used to refer to their activities; however, we did not completely follow their language because it varied so widely. For example, two students might say, as they produced very similar-looking pieces of writing, "I'm writing an outline," and "I'm making notes." In those situations we imposed a consistent term, often one from a previous study.[3]

A Student-Strategy Sequence

An example of part of a student's strategy sequence for an assignment appears below. In order to illustrate the various kinds of strategy codes, we have collapsed the sequence, omitting some codes that would normally appear. The numbers in brackets indicate the page numbers we assigned to the data on which the record of the strategy begins. Where there are two or more numbers, there were two or more data sources for that code.

> STRATEGIES TO FIRST HAND-IN: CT (6,19), TP (7), RLN2 (7,36), 01 (8,20), R-01-MA (20,36), 02-MA (44), DAO-MA (44), DAO-C-MI. INSTRUCTOR RESPONSE AND STUDENT'S RE-VISION: MEVI (61), RL-N, EPORG (61). STRATEGIES TO SEC-OND HAND-IN: R-DAO-MI (7,61), DAO-C-N (69). INSTRUC-TOR'S COMMENT: EEVI. STUDENT'S DIFFICULTIES: INF (245,249), OPI (19).

The codes indicate that this student considered the paper's topic (CT), and that the two sources of evidence for this begin on pages 6 and 19 in her data envelope. The evidence might have been, for example, a log entry and a portion of the think-aloud tape.

Next, the student talked with a peer (TP), then read a library source (RL) and made notes that had two levels of hierarchy (N2).

The student then wrote an outline of one level (01) and then revised that outline by writing revisions on those same page(s) (R-01). The revisions affected the outline at the macro-level (MA).

The student then produced another outline, of two levels, which differed from the earlier revised outline at the macro-level (02-MA).

Next, the student drafted all of the paper (DAO) making macro-changes from the two-level outline.

Finally, she made another draft, this time on the computer, with micro-changes from the previous handwritten draft (DAO-C- MI). Then the student handed in the paper.

In the margin (M) of her paper the teacher called for more evidence (EVI), and the student revised at a lower level than the teacher had intended, with no improvement to the paper (RL-N). For example, the student may merely have added an irrelevant quotation to the paper.

The teacher's comment at the end (E) of the student's paper praised her (P) for her organization (ORG). The student's strategies after she got the draft back included marking revisions on her draft at the micro-level (R-DAO-MI) and then making a new draft on the computer with no change from the previous marked draft (DAO-C-N). Her teacher's end comment again suggested that she should have included more evidence (EEVI). The difficulties this student talked about in her log for this assignment, her think-aloud tapes, interviews, or peer response session, were that she was not able to find enough information, evidence, or counterarguments (INF) and that she struggled to arrive at her own opinion or position in the paper (OPI).

A Collaborative Process

This inductive process of constructing strategy categories and sequences of students' strategies was collaborative. Walvoord first drafted the coding system and constructed sequences for two or three students from each class. With McCarthy observing, the teachers then checked Walvoord's coding of their students and suggested changes in the coding system. Using these suggestions, Walvoord revised the coding scheme, and then constructed sequences for certain groups of students in each class. The codings that became most essential to our findings in each class were further checked by members of the research team in various ways which we explain in subsequent chapters.

When we finished constructing the sequences of strategies, we counted the frequency of certain strategies, compared students' strat-egies with one another, and examined the relationships between strategies and other elements, such as difficulties and levels of success. The findings from this procedure gave us another window into what students' difficulties were, what may have contributed to them, and how students went about overcoming them.

Purposive Sampling

We did not construct a sequence of strategy codes for every student and every assignment. Instead, we coded the strategies of two groups of students in each class whom we chose through "purposive sampling"; that is, students who helped us "increase the range of data exposed . . . and the likelihood of uncovering the full array of realities" in each setting (Lincoln and Guba 1985, 40). The first sample, which we call the *focus group*, consisted of between 32 percent and 70 percent of the students in each class. We chose students who had given us particularly rich and/or extensive data and who represented a range within the class of age, race, gender, success level, class level, verbal SAT score, and first language (ESL students were included). Characteristics of the focus groups appear in Appendix B.

Sometimes, we used a sample of high-success and low-success students, especially to compare and contrast strategies of the two. The precise nature of each high-low sample is explained in the relevant chapters.

Analyzing Students' Revision Practices

Our second major data analysis procedure in Stage 3 was revision analysis. As we constructed a coding scheme to answer our questions about how, when, and with what outcomes students revised, we drew upon Faigley and Witte's system (1981, 1984), which classifies revisions on the basis of their impact on the text. We were particularly interested in what Faigley and Witte call *meaning-changing revisions*—revisions that alter the meaning of a text, rather than merely fixing the spelling or substituting one word for another of similar meaning. We distinguished, as Faigley and Witte do, between *macro-structure revisions*—revisions which "alter the summary of a text" and "affect the reading of other parts of the text" (1981, 404–405; 1984, 100) and *micro-structure revisions*—revisions which alter meaning, but to a lesser degree than macro-revisions. Our coding system differed somewhat from Faigley and Witte's, however, because of the ways in which revision was entangled with text production in our actual classroom settings, and because of our research goals.

We defined *revision* as a change that (1) is written on the current draft or (2) occurs either between one draft or outline and the next, or (3) between an outline and a draft. We did not count as revision any false starts, where the student wrote a word or passage and immediately scratched it out before continuing to compose. Because so much of this activity took place orally rather than on paper, we decided to eliminate all false starts, whether written or oral, in order to concentrate on those revisions where a student *returned* to the text to make changes. Unlike Faigley and Witte (1984), who counted each sentence of a macro-structure addition as separate revision (102), we counted each macro-structure addition only once, no matter how many sentences it contained. We also coded only the highest level of revision the student made on a particular outline or draft, rather than counting the total number of revisions in each paper as Faigley and Witte had done. This was because we were interested in *whether* the student was revising at the macro- or micro-level on a particular outline or draft, not in *how many* macro- or micro-revisions the student made or how many sentences those revisions contained.

The research team's coding of students' revisions was collaborative, using the same procedures as for coding the strategies. Following Faigley and Witte's observations that "the reliability of the taxonomy depends upon the shared expectations of those applying it" (102), we did not use outside raters to confirm our analyses, but rather relied upon research team members for inter-rater confirmation.

Were the Revisions Successful?

In addition to our interest in the highest level of revision the student employed at various times, we were also interested in whether, in the teacher's judgment, the text was improved as a result of the revisions that responded to teacher comments. For this analysis, we adapted a system used by Sperling and Freedman (1987), based on "response rounds" analogous to the oral turn-taking identified by Garvey (1977). (A *response round* consists of the student's text, the teacher's or peer's response, and the student's subsequent revision. This method allows us to study revision not as an isolated act but as part of the ongoing "conversation" of the classroom.)

We coded each teacher's and peer's response according to its topic (e.g., organization, evidence) and its purpose (praise or suggestion). Thus a comment might be coded "praises organization" or "suggests more evidence."

Next, we coded the student's revision by how it addressed the teacher's or the peer's response (revised as suggested, revised at a lower level than suggested, deleted the passage, deleted and substituted new material, made no revision, or the comment became irrelevant because of other, unrelated revisions).

Finally, we coded the student's revision by whether, in the teacher's judgment, it improved the paper or not. Again, as in defining "success," we relied on the judgment of the teacher in order to stay as close as possible to the context-specific set of tacit and explicit expectations for "good" writing that underlay the students' and teacher's interactions across the semester.

Analyzing Organizational Structures in Students' Texts

In Stage 3, in addition to analyzing students' writing-process strategies and revisions, we analyzed the organizational structures of selected students' drafts and final papers.

Meyer's Tree Diagram

The four classroom teachers were concerned primarily with content at high levels of generality in their students' papers and with the content relationships among large units of text. We thus drew upon a system for analyzing "top-level text structures" developed by Bonnie J. F. Meyer (1975, 1985). Top-level structures refer to the ideas at the three or four highest levels of abstraction in the paper. These are the levels of organization that a composition teacher might call "thesis and major subpoints," or that would be represented in an outline at the levels of Roman numerals, capital letters, Arabic numerals, and lowercase letters. Meyer's system of structural analysis, however, is not like an outline, linear and sequential; rather, it uses a tree diagram to display the relationships among the main ideas in the paper. Meyer's system contains more information than an outline because it not only displays the level of abstraction, it also names the types of relationship between ideas; that is, each new idea (or branch of the tree diagram) is categorized and labeled according to its relation to the one above it in the diagram. For example, an idea may be a *comparison* with a preceding idea, or it may be a *description* of the idea. From the diagram, the investigator can calculate the number of branches, the levels of the branches, and the types of relations among ideas.[4]

Figure 2.1 shows two levels of abstraction in the tree diagram of one of John Breihan's history student's papers. The student has been asked to use evidence from seventeenth and eighteenth century British and French history to recommend a government for a hypothetical country called "Loyoliana," which faces many of the same problems

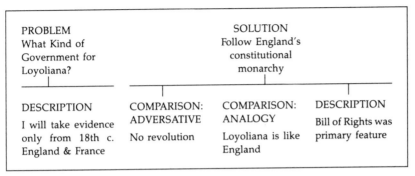

Figure 2.1. Using Meyer's tree diagram to display relationships between main ideas in a history paper.

that France and England did in that period. The entire paper is divided into two main sections, as the top level of the diagram shows: Loyoliana's problem, and the student's solution. The solution is developed by three main sections. A continuation of the diagram would show that each of those sections is further developed.

The tree diagram indicates the type of relationship between each idea and the one above it. The diagram also gives a short summary of each idea. This student's paper, one that Breihan deemed "successful," reflects Breihan's concern with high-level text-unit relationships of description (inserting specific evidence and explanation) and comparison (inserting historical analogies and addressing counterarguments).

In addition to the fact that the four classroom teachers focused on high-level text structures, we chose Meyer's analytic tool because, like primary trait analysis, it assumes that the textual structures deemed appropriate will vary from one setting to the next.

Our construction of these organizational diagrams was, like our other analytic procedures, collaborative. As Walvoord analyzed students' top-level text structures, she first constructed tree diagrams for a representative group of final drafts in each class. These were then checked by the classroom teacher, who suggested modifications in Walvoord's interpretations. Walvoord also at times diagrammed the structure of an earlier draft of a paper in order to help elucidate changes made during revision.

Other Analytic Procedures

In addition to analyzing students' writing strategies, revisions, and organizational structures, we also conducted several other types of analysis in Stage 3. These included counting the number of pages of students' pre-draft writing and calculating the percent of "specific historical material" in their history essays. We also counted such things as students' use of the word "thesis" and the frequency of certain errors and mechanical problems. We examined relationships among gender, grades, SAT scores, and certain features of students' texts. Finally, we analyzed differences in what Klemp (1982a, 1982b) calls "competencies" between high- and low-success students in these classes. Although we do not report findings from all of these procedures, they all contributed in various ways to our understanding of students' writing in these four classrooms.

OUR TEAM'S SHARED ASSUMPTIONS
AND WAYS OF WORKING

THE NEGOTIATED WE

Underlying our research team's seven-year-long research project was an assumption the team members all shared: to answer our questions, several heads were better than one. That is, we assumed our purpose was to arrive at a multiply constructed reality by working from a point of view that we called the *negotiated we*. From the beginning of our work together we valued knowledge and discourse that reflected the combined perspectives of researchers whose relations to the classrooms under study were very different. In making explicit, by collaborating and coauthoring, our assumption that several heads were better than one, we were perhaps only recognizing the unacknowledged co-researcher role that Clifford (1983) argues is actually played by all informants. (Informants, Clifford points out, ultimately control what researchers can know and thus the shape of their research findings.) By collaborating and coauthoring, we also challenge the discourse of educational research which often casts the classroom teacher as object. By contrast, in our study, teachers were in the subject position and were agents of research events.

Several ways of working made possible our team's collaborative construction of knowledge. These ways of working—establishing trust, using multiple coauthored drafts to mutually construct findings, and working to maintain a balance of authority among researchers—facilitated our team's research conversation and the achievement of a negotiated-we point of view.

Establishing Trust

We moved to create a climate of trust in which team members could—and did—say that their feelings had been hurt or that another team member's interpretation was inadequate or mistaken. For example, at one point in drafting their coauthored chapter, Breihan told Walvoord that her draft misrepresented a certain quality in his lectures. Walvoord, after hearing him out, agreed, and they reworked the passage. Because our purpose was to arrive at a multiply constructed reality by working from the negotiated-we point of view, we understood this sort of response to each other as a positive contribution to the process.

Using Multiple Coauthored Drafts

In addition to establishing a climate of trust, we used coauthored drafts to achieve the aims of our research conversation. We began drafting early in our data analysis because we believed drafting would facilitate the process through which mutually constructed findings and discourse structures would emerge. In the chapter on the biology classroom, for example, Walvoord and Anderson together conducted data analysis and agreed on the basic outline of their chapter. Anderson then wrote the first draft, with Walvoord questioning, changing, or rejecting parts of it, and then passing the revised draft back to Anderson. Walvoord and Anderson then worked together to complete the final draft.

Underlying our drafting process was the assumption that successive drafts would progressively refine our construction of findings and interpretations. Coauthoring helped us see our drafts not as personal interpretations to be defended but as vehicles for moving the team closer to what it wanted to say.

Sharing Authority

A third way of operating grew out of our concern about cooptation, or what anthropologists call "going native." In our project the danger existed that the outside investigator, Walvoord, might be so drawn into the worldviews of the discipline-based teachers that their interpretations would too much shape her own—or, on the other hand, that the classroom teachers would be overly influenced by Walvoord's expertise in writing. She was, after all, the writing specialist who had led the first writing-across-the-curriculum workshops that Anderson,

Breihan, and Robison had attended (later, Sherman and Walvoord both attended a workshop led by Breihan).

In order to prevent cooptation, we worked to maintain a balance of authority among team members by discussing and clarifying our roles and our viewpoints and by making our ways of interacting as explicit as possible. Sharing authority was facilitated because each of four classroom teachers, after the workshop with Walvoord, had become a leader or presenter for other writing-across-the-curriculum workshops—an expert in his or her own right. Also, to achieve trustworthy findings, we relied on techniques commonly used by naturalistic researchers, such as using multiple sources of data and methods of analysis, which we discuss later in this chapter.

Negotiating Discipline-Based Differences

In achieving the negotiated-we point of view, the team faced particular challenges in two areas: negotiating our discipline-based differences and negotiating classroom critiques. The six members of our team represented five disciplines. While we did share a common educational discourse, we differed among ourselves in our tacit notions about the nature of knowledge and appropriate forms of language, as well as in our working practices, our processes of inquiry, and our conceptions of the audience for whom we were writing our research reports. In his study of variations in discipline-based discourse, Becher (1987a; 1987b) suggests that even the terms that members of various disciplines use to praise or criticize research reports vary because these terms reflect tacit notions about knowledge in that field. And Bazerman (1983) warns that "communication between participants in separate disciplinary matrices is rife with misunderstanding and unresolvable conflict—unresolvable because there is no neutral terminology that will allow for making mutually acceptable judgments" (161).

Actually, however, some of our most interesting and productive moments occurred when our tacit, discipline-based notions about knowledge and texts and students' writing were called into question by other team members and, in the process, became more fully articulated. This happened, for example, when the four classroom teachers read and responded to a draft of this chapter. At times, McCarthy's and Walvoord's tacit ways of knowing in composition puzzled team members from history, biology, psychology, and business. For example, psychologist Robison asked, "Why all this theoretical self-justification?" and "Can't you cut this methods chapter in half?"

Questioning a sentence that used the word "speculate," Robison asked, "Do you use the word 'speculate' in composition studies?" This was the beginning of a productive team exchange about the role of "speculation" in each of our disciplines, the language used in each discipline to frame such speculations, and the ways we might handle speculation in this research report. This kind of clarification and articulation of tacit assumptions about discipline-based ways of knowing—and also about teaching, learning, and students' writing in each discipline—often accompanied our most interesting and productive work together.

Negotiating Classroom Critiques

In addition to the challenge of negotiating discipline-based differences, the team's second challenge was to negotiate our critique of classroom activities. Particularly since the classroom teachers were members of the research team publishing under their own names, readers might wonder whether Walvoord and McCarthy conspired to make them look good and to gloss over their weaknesses and mistakes.

The classroom chapters will quickly make clear, however, that the teachers do not always look good in this study and that we often explore how their methods appeared to contribute to students' difficulties. This kind of critique was possible in our study for two reasons: First, each teacher's original purpose in entering the collaboration was to see how his or her teaching methods were working and how those could be improved. Walvoord invited them onto the team precisely because she judged them to be secure, student-oriented teachers who were open to change.

The second reason why we could honestly examine how teaching methods sometimes contributed to students' difficulties is that in a collaborative, coauthored study, teachers do not need to look good as people who never make mistakes; rather, they can look good as researchers participating in a useful investigation. Because the classroom teachers were not afraid to critique their own teaching methods, their insights are part of our study. For example, biologist Anderson pointed out that her methods of guiding student peer groups had been useful in helping students with "specific operational definitions" but not with "comprehensive operational definitions." Walvoord and McCarthy did not have the training in science to make the distinction or, hence, the critique. Because our findings incorporate their responses, the teachers are shown to be thoughtful professionals working hard

.

to understand their students and to learn how to help them more effectively.

Our study and this report, then, are the products of our negotiated-we point of view. Though we on the team did represent differing perspectives and different relationships to the classrooms under study, we also shared common concerns as teachers and a common educational discourse. It is this discourse that has provided our common language as we have constructed knowledge and texts. Though our book's chapters vary somewhat according to the discipline of the teacher-coauthor, in all chapters we focus on the teacher's expectations for students' writing, on students' difficulties in meeting those expectations, and on students' strategies and teachers' methods that were associated with these difficulties. Our shared educational discourse shaped our inquiry, and it also inevitably shaped our research report.

ENSURING THE TRUSTWORTHINESS OF OUR TEAM'S FINDINGS AND INTERPRETATIONS

Our aim as naturalistic researchers has been to adequately construct and present the multiple realities of the students and teachers we have studied. We used a number of techniques to ensure that the findings and interpretations we produced would be trustworthy and could thus be used by our readers with confidence.[5] The techniques we used to ensure trustworthy findings included:

1. Triangulation by investigator, data source, and analytic method.
2. A search for "negative cases"; that is, cases that lie outside our tentative categories and findings.
3. Extended periods of engagement with our informants during which salient factors were identified for more detailed inquiry.
4. Credibility checks ("member checks") in which we checked our findings with informants.
5. Internal checks of various analyses by other team members.
6. External checks on the inquiry process, our methods and our biases, by established researchers who knew nothing about the classrooms under investigation.

Throughout this report we have described in detail the classroom contexts we studied so that readers may judge the transferability of our findings to their own settings. Further, we have, wherever possible, compared our findings about students' writing to findings reported by other studies.

In conclusion, our study of students' writing is a local one because we believe, with Brodkey (1987), that "writing is best understood as a set of observable human practices . . . and any attempt to study writing, even writing as literature, must entail situating writers and writing practices within a social, psychological, historical, and political context" (80). Thus, our study is, as Geertz says, "another country heard from . . . nothing more or less." Yet, "small facts may speak to large issues" (1973, 23). Studies like the present one of actual student writers at work in local settings can help inform theories and generalizations about writing in academia and about how students learn to think and write there.

Notes

1. See Guba, 1981, and Lincoln and Guba, 1985, for further discussion of the naturalistic inquiry paradigm and how it contrasts to the scientific or rationalistic paradigm.

2. See Sternglass and Pugh 1986, for another study using students' writing logs.

3. Studies from which we drew in various ways as we constructed categories and sequences of students' thinking and writing strategies for particular assignments include Berkenkotter 1983; Flower and Hayes 1980; Perl 1978; Selfe 1981; Swarts, Flower and Hayes 1984.

4. For a discussion of how a system like Meyer's, which displays high-level organizational structures and names the relationships among them, differs from the prose analysis schemes which focus on paragraph or sentence level structures and roles, see Colomb and Williams 1985, and Cooper 1983.

5. See LeCompte and Goetz 1982, and Lincoln and Guba 1985, for a discussion of trustworthiness, validity, reliability, and objectivity in naturalistic research.

3 Managerial Decision Making: Sherman's Business Course

Barbara E. Walvoord
Loyola College in Maryland

A. Kimbrough Sherman
Loyola College in Maryland

This chapter begins the discussion of the four classes the research team studied. A. Kimbrough Sherman's production management course is a required course which deals with the operational aspects of a business, such as what goods and services it provides, where it locates, and how it organizes resources, people, and processes. The course has two major thrusts: (1) strategic and tactical decision making and (2) standard (mostly quantitative) decision techniques. Writing in Sherman's course was directed at the strategic and tactical areas. We (Walvoord and Sherman) collaborated in gathering the data and writing the chapter with generous help from McCarthy and other team members, who helped to shape the study, check data, and critique chapter drafts.

Like the other classroom chapters that follow, this chapter addresses our research questions (p. 4) through an examination of Sherman's expectations and each of the six areas of difficulty we constructed for all the classrooms, focusing on how Sherman's methods and the students' strategies appeared to have affected the difficulties. (We follow the basic organizational pattern we outlined on p. 15. Our definitions of difficulties and strategies appear on pp. 4–5.) At the end of this chapter, we address two other topics that transcend any single area of difficulty:

1. Students' pre-draft writing (any writing that precedes the first draft that contains two-thirds of what the student intended to be the full paper)

2. Sherman's responses to drafts and students' revisions on the final paper of the course.

The characteristics of Loyola College, of Sherman's class, and of the focus group of students we used for some of our analyses are on p. 18 and in Appendix B. Note particularly the overrepresentation of women among students who submitted data in Sherman's class. Other classes were more balanced.

SHERMAN'S EXPECTATIONS

Our analysis of Sherman's expectations relies on Sherman's in-class instruction as recorded by Walvoord during her classroom observation and by Sherman in his log, his responses on students' papers, his interviews and working sessions with Walvoord as they analyzed data and discussed student papers, and his post-course primary trait analysis (p. 35).

THE BUSINESS DECISION-MAKER ROLE

"In management, people don't merely 'write papers,' they solve problems," said Sherman in an interview conducted by Walvoord during the production management course he taught during fall semester, 1985. His class was composed of 44 junior and senior business majors at Baltimore's Loyola College in Maryland. Sherman's expectations for his students' learning and writing grew from his goal of "teaching students to make decisions, not just teaching them *about* decision making."

The "business decision maker," then, was Sherman's version of the professional-in-training role that all four classroom teachers expected of their students (pp. 8–9). He tried to move his students from the roles of text-processor or layperson into that of decision maker.

A key word Sherman used often was *complexity*. In an interview with Walvoord he explained that he wanted to construct situations where students would have to "wallow in complexity" and work their way out, as managers must. His course was therefore centered not on covering topics but on teaching a process, a methodology. Sherman also believed that writing was his most effective tool for getting students involved in the complexity of decision making. "Writing," he said, "helps students put their thoughts together [and thus] helps me teach and them learn."

Like most assignments made by the other three teachers we studied,

Sherman's three assignments all posed good/better/best questions and asked students to apply textbook knowledge to new situations (p. 7). The salient features of the three assignments appear in Table 3.1. Three differences among them—the names Sherman gave to the papers ("analytical assignment" and "term paper"), the length, and the source of information—all appeared to influence how students responded to the assignments, as the rest of this chapter will show.

DEFINE/ANALYZE/PRESCRIBE: SHERMAN'S EXPECTATIONS FOR GOOD/BETTER/BEST REASONING

One of Sherman's ways of describing good/better/best reasoning to his students was his oft-repeated rubric, "define/analyze/prescribe." In this process the decision maker (1) *defines* the problem, defines relevant terms, and defines what a "good" solution would be; (2) *analyzes* the parameters of the problem and the qualities of various possible solutions; and (3) *prescribes* the best solution.

A Class Discussion: Lessons About Reasoning and Roles

Sherman's expectations for good/better/best reasoning, as well as the roles he and his students played, were embodied in a classroom

Table 3.1   Salient Features of Sherman's Three Assignments

Sherman's Name for the Paper	Topic	Learning Objective	Source of Information	Source of Methodology
Analytical Assignment 1 (1 page)	What is the best location for the new Baltimore baseball stadium?	Learn how to make decisions about locating a business.	Memory Media	Textbook Lecture/Discussion
Analytical Assignment 2 (1 page)	Evaluate layout and work design of McDonald's and Popeye's.	Learn how to analyze and evaluate production processes.	Observation	Textbook Lecture/Discussion
Term Paper (8 pp. draft; 5 pp. final)	What are the best ways to raise productivity in the United States?	Learn broad problem-solving processes for a national issue	Library	Textbook Lecture/Discussion

discussion Walvoord observed. In this discussion Sherman modeled and structured define/analyze/prescribe, showed students how to manage complexity, and communicated the nature of business problem solving. Throughout, he treated his students as professionals-in-training.

As the class began, the students were gathered in what one of them described as "the typical lecture classroom"—lectern and blackboard facing raked rows of tablet armchairs in a room with the high ceilings and tall windows typical of older classroom buildings. They had just submitted drafts of their productivity term papers to Sherman, who would return them for revision after he commented on them, and now they began to discuss how the United States could enhance its productivity.

Modeling and Structuring "Define/Analyze/Prescribe"

From students' contributions Sherman constructed three blackboard lists: a list of possible definitions of *productivity*, a list of possible causes for lagging U.S. productivity ("analyze"), and finally a list of possible solutions to the problem of lagging U.S. productivity ("prescribe").

Showing Students How to Manage Complexity

In the discussion Sherman insisted on recognizing and managing complexity. He suggested that students use new categories to produce solutions to the problems of lagging productivity: "Try to think of more institutional things, like laws and customs." This category helped students get away from overly simplistic prescriptions that the United States should simply do what Japan does, and helped students to realize the extent of differences in laws and customs between the two countries.

Sherman also warned students against oversimplification: "Don't take the simplistic view that unions that are resisting automation are doing something wrong." He often suggested complexity by adding information students might not possess, such as information about automation in mining, or pushed students to think more deeply: "Do you think you could do that with . . . ?" or "What about . . . ?"

Sherman modeled the use of counterargument, thus adding further complexity to the discussion. For example, in response to students' suggestions that industry should automate, he insistently voiced the objections and needs of the workers who would be replaced. Yet he was careful not to attack the students' positions as "wrong," and he made his devil's advocate role clear to them. At one point, soliciting a critique from the class to counter a student's contribution, he said in a smiling aside to the student, "I'm trying to make your example look bad." The student grinned back, obviously understanding that he and Sherman were involved in a cooperative endeavor, and that Sherman was modeling the ways of thinking that the class was trying to learn.

Communicating the Nature of Business Problem Solving

Sherman demonstrated that there were no absolute, right answers for the problems. Students were expected to keep an open mind and consider all the evidence, but their values and preferences might also be part of the decision. At one point he said, "We've addressed quality. Is that what everybody decided to do—go for quality? Didn't anybody decide to automate?" The lesson was that there was no one solution he expected. When he offered his own position, he took care to distinguish it as just one of several possible positions. At another point, he said to a student, "I believe more strongly than you do that . . ." and then gave his reasons for that belief: He was emphasizing Task 5 of good/better/best reasoning[1]—combining solution-searching with rationale-building.

Treating Students as Professionals-in-Training

Sherman consistently resisted setting himself up as the only authority. Rather, he treated his students as potential businesspersons who already had completed part of their training, who had valuable contributions to make to the discussion, and who could choose and defend their own positions. When a student asked him a question at one point, he turned back to the class with, "Is there an answer to that?" At another point, as he tried to remember a series of events in the mining industry, two students readily supplied the information without first raising their hands, and he, without embarrassment, integrated their expertise into the ongoing discussion. At a third point, when a student raised a logistical problem about the assignment, Sherman listened, then changed a due date. (Walvoord observed one student turning to a neighbor with a smile and whispering, "I *like* this class.")

Sherman transcribed students' contributions on the blackboard, but he did not appropriate them. In making his blackboard list, whenever he shortened or changed the student's wording, he asked the student's permission: "Will I ruin it if I say 'creativity'? I'm just looking for a single word."

In discussion, Sherman did not repeat students' contributions, but expected the class to listen to one another. When one student spoke softly, he asked her to repeat so that everyone could hear.

SUMMARY OF SHERMAN'S EXPECTATIONS

In a post-course interview with Walvoord, Sherman made a statement about the third paper, the productivity paper, that can serve as a summary of the writing, thinking, and learning he expected from his students and the role he expected them to play:

> I want them to reach a perception of the complexity of the problem, and an attempt at a solution, and then see how that solution is good and bad, and communicate the bad parts and brag about the good parts of whatever solution they have.

Sherman admitted that to "see the complexity and yet come out with reasonable solutions—that's tough. But that's what management is all about, and that's what business is all about."

In this chapter, a number of difficulties arose as Sherman tried to use his three writing assignments as vehicles for helping students move into the role of business decision maker. Those difficulties, we emphasize, are not the "fault" of either students or teachers, but result from complex interactions among them.

DIFFICULTIES WITH GATHERING SUFFICIENT SPECIFIC INFORMATION

THE NATURE OF THE DIFFICULTIES

One difficulty students experienced was with gathering sufficient specific information for their papers. By *sufficient* we mean enough information to meet the teacher's expectations for each assignment.

In Sherman's first assignment students were to propose and defend a site for the new Baltimore baseball stadium then being hotly debated in the public forum. To get more specific information about the controversy and about proposed stadium sites, many students, in Sherman's judgment, should have gone to the library to find back issues of either the local newspaper or *Baltimore Magazine*. Yet in our focus group of 14 students, only one student did. Not only Sherman, but also the students—especially after they had handed in their stadium papers—identified locating sufficient specific information as a difficulty. One student said to her freshman interviewer with a wry laugh, "I didn't even know the stadium was moving." Another remarked, "I would have done better if I'd researched it more."

In the second assignment, students had to visit the local McDonald's and Popeye's to gather information about each restaurant's layout (physical arrangement of work space) and work design (distribution of tasks among workers). Again Sherman thought many of the papers did not contain enough specific information about those aspects. Some students expressed frustration at not being able to identify differences between the restaurants, though there *were* differences that some students found.

Clearly, many complex issues were at stake in these difficulties with gathering sufficient specific information. We focus, however, on the teacher's methods and students' strategies that appear to have contributed to them. Throughout, we read the data in terms of students' success in adopting the business decision-maker role that was Sherman's central expectation.

TEACHER'S METHODS AND STUDENTS' STRATEGIES

Sherman's Language on the Assignment Sheet

For the stadium paper, one factor contributing to difficulties with information gathering seemed to be Sherman's language on the assignment sheet. To understand the sheet, we need to know something of Sherman's goals for this first assignment as he articulated them in class and in interviews with Walvoord:

- To introduce students to business decision-making processes—particularly decisions about where to locate one's business.
- To capture students' interest.
- To show students how business decision-making processes can be applied in "real world" situations.
- To present students with a business decision that forced them to apply the textbook discussion to a new setting.
- To allow students to draw in part upon their current knowledge so that they would not have to spend large amounts of time reading about an unfamiliar business before they could make decisions about it.

- To give students practice in the conciseness required in business writing.

To meet these goals, Sherman constructed and gave to his students the stadium assignment, which he called "Analytical Assignment 1" (see Figure 3.1).

We will return to this assignment sheet to discuss various difficulties. For now, we only want to point out that though Sherman mentioned the media as a relevant source of information, he restricted the word *read* only to the textbook, and he told students to consider the information they had *heard* mentioned. Sherman assumed, but did not specifically state, his expectation that students would go to the library if memory was not sufficient for their needs and gather information as professionals-in-training.

Students' Strategies for Using the Assignment Sheet

The Assignment Sheet as "Recipe"

We have said that difficulties arise as part of a complex interaction between teacher and students. In this case, Sherman's miscues on the assignment sheet were exacerbated by the way students actually used it. Students in all four classes typically used the assignment sheet as a kind of recipe for completing the assignment. The sheet seemed often to supersede other models or instructions given in class or remembered from other situations. Students usually kept the assign-

---

Analytical Assignment 1

The newspapers and television bring up the need for a new stadium to replace Memorial Stadium almost every week. Several reasons are given each time the subject is brought up, and each time the story is discussed, a different location is proposed.

   Consider the factors you have heard mentioned in the past year or so, read the text chapter on location of facilities, and present, in 250 to 300 words, your choice of location, either as a real site or an ideal imaginary place.

   The justification of the site you choose may involve some choice as to the type of stadium you foresee, and it is fair to mention this, but center your presentation on the locational choice.

   Your paper is to be typed and double spaced, and is directed to the members of your class, rather than to the decision makers.

Figure 3.1. The stadium paper assignment.

ment sheet beside them as they composed, consulting it frequently, especially when they felt confused. They tended to see themselves as following step-by-step the explicit instructions contained in it, and they often interpreted it very literally. We have no records of students asking themselves what were the teacher's broad intentions or larger goals, or asking, "I wonder whether the teacher really intended this to be read as I'm reading it?"

An example of the way in which the assignment sheet circumscribed the task is provided by a student we call Kurt Larson, who wrote in his log,

> [I] experienced frustration [because] my paper is very vague. I don't know enough about possible sites for the stadium to interject that into the paper. At least I'm making a full effort.

A "full effort" seemed to him not to include going to the library to get needed information—that wasn't part of the assignment as Larson saw it. For the final term paper, however, Larson, like every other student in the class, went to the library.

We located within the situation a number of cues that *could* have led students to act like business managers-in-training, going to the library for specific information they needed for an informed decision about the stadium. These other cues were found in:

- The textbook chapter, which, our data indicate, every student read at least in part. It describes a method in which the business manager gathers extensive quantitative and qualitative information about possible sites before making a choice.

- The assignment sheet's reference to "newspapers and TV" as a source of information about the stadium controversy.

- Students' own oft-expressed sense of frustration that they lacked sufficient remembered knowledge about the stadium.

Most students did not use these three cues. They put the assignment sheet's explicit instructions, as they interpreted them, ahead of everything else.

A plausible explanation, we believe, for their reliance on the teacher's explicit instructions rather than on their own felt need for information or on other cues, is that students in a new classroom setting are unsure about which cues to follow and which prior experiences to draw upon. Moreover, in all four classes, teachers warned students not to use certain models they had learned in other settings. Students writing science reports, for example, were told not to use the "transitions" their composition teacher might have emphasized as necessary to "good" writing. In the business class Sherman emphasized that he wanted tight, condensed, but straightforward writing for a business setting, rather than the more elaborated writing students might have learned elsewhere. We wondered whether teachers' words helped students to distrust experiences that were not directly related to the assignment at hand.

Differing Approaches to the Textbook

Declarative Knowledge versus Procedural Knowledge

Cognitive psychologists have distinguished between declarative knowledge (knowledge of *what*) and procedural knowledge (knowledge of *how*).[2] In Sherman's stadium paper, the relevant declarative knowledge was knowledge about the stadium problem and about various sites. The textbook contained procedural knowledge of how to make a decision about a location problem. The students who adopted a text-processor role, however, treated the textbook's description of the decision-making process as declarative knowledge simply to be summarized, rather than as procedural knowledge to be used as a guide in making the decisions they should have defended in their papers.

Berkenkotter, Huckin, and Ackerman (1988) have emphasized that both declarative and procedural knowledge were important to the learning process of a doctoral student in rhetoric. Our study of Sherman's business class indicates, in addition, that undergraduate students may confuse procedural with declarative knowledge. Sherman's assignment sheet might have helped by instructing students not just to "read" the textbook chapter "and" write the paper, but actually to use the textbook's methods in making the stadium decision.

Oral or written exercises, too, might have helped students through the decision-making process. One of the successful teaching methods we will see in both Breihan's history course and Anderson's biology course is to present procedural knowledge procedurally—that is, by actually leading students through the process and methods they should use, rather than merely relying on written or oral descriptions of that process.

Use of Models from Other Settings

"Term Paper" versus "Reflective Paper"

The genre labels Sherman gave to the papers, and the models for genre that students brought into the class, also appear to have influenced the students' difficulties with gathering information. The productivity paper was called the *term paper* by students and teacher alike, and all students went to the library—an action consistent with common notions of researching the term paper. For the first two assignments, however, Sherman's syllabus and assignment sheets used the label *Analytical Assignment*. Students did not pick up this term: No student referred to these papers as "analytical assignments." Ron Eton, who was interviewed by one of Walvoord's freshman writing students (pp. 26–27) just a few minutes after he handed in his stadium paper, described the stadium assignment as a "reflection paper" that needed no research:

> *Interviewer*: Tell the story of how you wrote the paper.
>
> *Ron Eton*: I sat down two days before it was due and wrote a rough copy. I just wrote all kinds of baloney, just everything that popped into my head. And then I came back the next day and rewrote it, um, and just—it wasn't difficult . . . It was a reflection paper. You didn't have to research anything. That's not very hard. You just sit down and write it and the thoughts come easily.

In Sherman's judgment, Eton's final paper had too much "baloney" and not enough specific information.

Sherman had never used the term "reflection paper." Eton therefore appeared to be using a model familiar to him from other settings. Richard Larson (1982) criticizes the practice in composition courses of confining library use only to the so-called "research" or "term" paper, because it gives students little idea of the importance of research to many other types of writing. Certainly Sherman's students associated library research only with the term paper and did not use it on their analytical papers in ways that would have benefitted them.

Streetcorner Debate

Some students who adopted a layperson role for the stadium paper used the streetcorner debate model, in which one draws on memory to argue a current "hot" topic. In the following think-aloud tape selection, Marsha Harrington is planning her stadium paper, and she is picturing herself as a baseball fan engaged in a debate with someone who is "standing there" arguing an opposing position. She muses:

> Hardest part is to decide whether to argue as if you're arguing for your point . . . as if someone were standing there arguing for it in the city, or whether to just argue for it in Catonsville and

totally disregard the fact that a lot of the people in Baltimore would be wanting it in the city.

The streetcorner debate model appears to have been evoked for students by Sherman's phrase on the assignment sheet, *you have heard mentioned;* by his designation of peers as audience; and by his use of a hot topic that actually was being debated in dorms and bars and on streetcorners. Sherman wanted students to use the information they had gathered in the public forum but not the roles or the styles of reasoning. Some students, however, adopted the whole package. Our conclusion is that for an assignment using a familiar setting, topic, or genre label, teachers need to clarify the models they expect.

Differing Ways of Assigning Value to the Assignments

Ron Eton, who had called the stadium assignment a "reflection" paper, also commented, "that's not very hard"—a sentiment echoed in several other interviews. He also said he thought the assignment was "not a good one" because it was "too easy." Yet Sherman had intended the analytical paper to be the result of careful information gathering and reasoning, condensed into a tight, one-page argument. But the one-page length, Sherman's advice to students to recall what they had "heard mentioned," and the familiar subject all seem to have conveyed to students that the assignment was not very important.

A related notion also implied in Eton's interview is that there is "research" and then there is "baloney." Students seemed to devalue papers that were not labeled research or term papers.

Students' Strategies for Using Peers' Information

Some students relied on peers to help them gather information for their stadium papers. Usually, their conversations with peers as revealed in the students' logs, tapes, and interviews tended to generate more heat than light, and to follow the model of dorm room or streetcorner debate. However, Kelly Rice acted more like the model of professional-in-training when she sought specific information from a friend she phoned because, as she wrote in her log, the friend "knows more than I do about Memorial Stadium and its planned location." Then she took notes during their phone conversation.

Seeing how students used peers to gather information made us realize that, while in some cases peer interaction may be useful for students, in other cases it can be a weak strategy unless they choose peers who truly do have the specific information they need, and unless they assume the role of formal interviewer—part of the larger role of professional-in-training.

Sherman's and the Students' Specialized Categories for Observation

Assuming a professional-in-training role involves observing with a professional's specialized categories. That was the task set by Sherman's McDonald's/Popeye's assignment (see Figure 3.2). Table 3.2 reveals that less successful students visited the restaurants *before* reading the textbook chapter and relied on their memories of visiting McDonald's rather than revisiting it for the purposes of analysis. They thus acted as though all types of observation were similar. They failed to realize differences between the customer's and the business professional's categories for observation. The less successful students typically observed details in such customer-oriented categories as service, menu, and food quality, but as they did not yet have the textbook's categories, they did not gather detailed information about layout and work design.

The assignment sheet (Figure 3.2) does not clearly specify a sequence of reading *then* observing at both restaurants. Particularly, it

- waits until the last sentence to mention the textbook readings,

- uses "and," not "then" to link reading and site visits in the last sentence,

- says a visit to both restaurants "may be unavoidable," thus introducing the possibility of not visiting McDonald's.

Analytical Assignment 2

In 250 to 300 words, compare and contrast the layout and work design of Popeye's and McDonald's restaurants on York Road. Evaluate the two on the effectiveness with which each serves its customers. A careful evaluation of what each restaurant is trying to provide should precede or begin your analysis, and such concepts as line balancing, type of processing, and specialization should be included. This is a short paper, so your writing must be efficient. Chapters 7 and 8 in the Stevenson text can provide guidance, and a visit to each site may be unavoidable.

Figure 3.2. The McDonald's-Popeye's assignment.

A revision of the assignment sheet might include making clear to students the importance of reading the chapter first, of visiting both restaurants, and of using the textbook's categories of observation.

Students' Pre-Draft Writing Strategies

We give the term *pre-draft writing* to any writing (e.g. notes, freewrites, outlines) that takes place prior to the student's first draft of at least two-thirds of what the student considered to be the paper.[3] The functions of pre-draft writing and its role in students' success are important themes in our study. Table 3.2 shows that high-success students took notes at the restaurant; low-success students took notes after the visit or not at all. The notes of high-success students served several functions which were common for the pre-draft writing of successful students in other classes:

- to help the student act the role of professional-in-training rather than layperson
- to store specific information for later use in the paper

Table 3.2 Grades and Information-Gathering Strategies (McDonald's-Popeye's Paper)

Student (by verbal SAT)	Read Text, Visit Both	Both	Notes at Rest.	Visit, then Read Text	Visit Pop. Only	Notes After/No Notes
			Paper Grade "A"			
570				X	X	X
510	X	X	X			
430	X	X	X			
410	X		X		X	
400	X		X		X	
n.i.*	X	X			X	
			Grade "B" or Lower			
520				X	X	X
490				X	X	X
440				X	X	X
410				X	X	X
310				X	X	X

N = 11 students (focus group of 14 students, omitting 3 students about whom we were not sure we had complete data).

* No information.

- to access that information efficiently in writing the paper
- to organize and/or structure the information (many students took notes under categories or in columns)
- to identify different kinds of information or different functions for information in the paper
- to reorganize information easily

The Importance of Topic-Specific Knowledge

Recent research in cognitive psychology has emphasized the importance of domain-specific knowledge in the problem-solving process (Larkin, Heller, and Greeno 1980; Simon 1979), and the role of topic-specific knowledge on the writing of high school students (Langer 1984). In Langer's study, students in two classes were asked to generate information about a topic by free association in response to key words. The knowledge thus generated was compared to the quality of the students' school papers on the same topics. Her study suggests "a strong and consistent relationship between topic-specific background knowledge and the quality of student writing" (146). Further, she found that when students had to present a thesis, analyze it, and defend it, the degree of organization of knowledge (as opposed to simple fluency) influenced the quality of their writing (146). She suggests that when students have only fragmentary knowledge, they may fall back upon simpler writing (summary) that demands less structured knowledge, rather than more complex writing (analysis) (147). Her chapter is aptly entitled "Where Problems Start."

Our naturalistic study in a college setting supports Langer's findings with high school students. Difficulties in information gathering led to many other difficulties throughout the entire writing process, as illustrated by a log entry written by Kelly Rice. Rice was a junior with a 520 verbal SAT score who wrote a low-success McDonald's-Popeye's paper. Her weak information-gathering strategies included:

1. visiting Popeye's but not McDonald's
2. visiting before she read the textbook
3. eating but not taking notes at the restaurant

In shaping her final paper, one of Rice's contributing problems was that she had observed no differences and not very many specifics about the layout and work design of the two restaurants. Yet Sherman had emphasized in class that students should not merely compare and contrast the two restaurants, but should formulate a "theme" and should "evaluate" which restaurant's procedures were better in meeting that restaurant's goals. Rice's lack of specific information meant that she had no basis for evaluation and therefore no theme.

Kelly Rice's Log for McDonald's-Popeye's Paper

10/15:   I visited Popeye's & ate lunch there. I took mental notes about the service & the layout of the restaurant. Tonite, I read part of each of the chapters in the textbook about the areas our paper is supposed to cover.

10/18:   I wrote my first draft today. I hadn't really thought about the theme until I started to write the paper. I knew basically what the body of my paper was going to be, though. We were supposed to include certain points in the paper so that is what I based my paragraphs on. I really couldn't think of a good way to end my paper. I don't want to have too much of a conclusion really, because the paper can't be any more than 1 page long. My paper just sort of stops, but I really don't know what to say exactly to make it end smoothly and keep within the 1 page limit.

The Textbook-Items-as-Points Strategy

Kelly Rice's weak information-gathering strategies yielded little specific information about layout and work design in the restaurants. So, in her paper, she strung together a pageful of paraphrases of the textbook's definitions of the various technical terms Sherman's assignment sheet had asked students to cover. Rice called these terms her "points": Rice's textbook-items-as-points strategy was linked to her lack of specific information.

We mentioned that students in all four classes often adopted "text-processor" and "layperson" roles rather than the "professional-in-training" role their teachers wanted. Here Rice's lay role as customer in the restaurants resulted in a lack of appropriate topic-specific knowledge leaving her little choice in the paper except merely to summarize textbook points in a text-processor role.

In sum, then, we have identified a number of teaching methods and student strategies that appeared to affect the difficulties with information gathering, and we have shown how information gathering was linked to difficulties in other areas and to the students' roles as they planned and wrote their papers. Sherman, after our analysis of the data, wrote a piece called "What It All Meant to Me," in which he concluded,

Our research, as it progressed, made me aware of several aspects of my assignments and grading and of my students' perceptions and writing that had not been apparent to me before. Principal among these are that the length of the assignment and the way I present that assignment to students has a strong influence on the importance that they attach to it, the care they take with it, and the depth of their research.

DIFFICULTIES WITH CONSTRUCTING THE AUDIENCE AND THE SELF

THE NATURE OF THE DIFFICULTIES

Aristotle used the term *ethos* to refer to the writer's creation of self, and others have noted that both the self and the audience are created by the writer through features of the written text.[4] In our view, the writer's creation of self (or ethos) and of audience are linked to the roles students adopt for their work in class and the roles students envision for their teachers and classmates. Students in all four classes experienced difficulties with constructing the audience and the self in their papers, but we limit our discussion to those assignments where students were asked to address a peer audience in addition to their teacher. The largest number of the teachers' assignments were of this type, and students' difficulties with peer audiences reveal some complex and interesting aspects of how they created the audience and the self.

Sherman's stadium paper assignment directed the students to address an audience of classmates. In constructing the audience and the self, students adopted two approaches that did not meet Sherman's expectations: Some wrote as baseball fan to other fans; others wrote as student text processor to teacher checking textbook knowledge.

Baseball Fan to Other Fans

Marsha Harrington, who used the model of streetcorner debate to plan her stadium paper, failed to meet Sherman's expectations because she created her self and her classmates as baseball fans rather than professionals-in-training, as Sherman had wanted. Here is part of her final paper:

> Catonsville is the best location because it is a midway point between Baltimore and Washington. Neither the Baltimore or Washington fans would have to drive to another city to watch

the Orioles play ball and neither would be using an outrageous amount of gasoline to get to the game.

Land purchased in Catonsville would come at a cheaper price than land bought in the city. Ticket prices, therefore, would not soar to an absurd amount, and all the fans could see their fair share of games.

Fans would not have to pay a premium to park their cars either. . . .

Notice Harrington's constant references to fans and her use of the language fans might use in conversation. But more than that, her three points are based on the assumption that her audience has only the very narrow interests of fans—gas money, ticket prices, and parking. Sherman wanted her to consider other factors, such as labor supply and wider implications such as economic impact, factors that were covered in the textbook and that were important to a balanced, managerial consideration of stadium location.

Student Text Processor to Teacher
Checking Textbook Knowledge

An example of the text processor is the second paragraph of Dawn Shale's stadium paper—virtually a straight paraphrase of the textbook:

There are many factors that are involved when a business is looking at possible locations for facilities. For the typical company, there are three main factors that should be considered. The regional factors, which include location of raw materials and markets and the availability of labor. The community factors, which include development support, attitudes (pro/con), facilities and services, and regulations. Finally, site-related factors which include such issues as the land, transportation, and zoning restrictions. These factors are many of the factors that are involved in finding a location for the new stadium in Baltimore.

Shale has merely paraphrased the list of factors in the textbook, keyed to a manufacturing firm. She has not selected or created the factors that should enter a decision about a stadium. She has also ignored any audience other than the teacher checking textbook knowledge. Shale's many uses of "there are" reflect her presentational stance; her long lists enumerate textbook categories; her sentence fragments probably stem from the fact that the factors were listed in the text as individual items in a chart.

Contrast the baseball-fan and the text-processor-to-teacher papers with the paper by Kelly Rice, a student who successfully creates her classmates as businesspersons-in-training and herself as a thoughtful decision maker. In the second paragraph of her paper, Rice sets out on the same task as Shale—to indicate which factors should be considered in choosing a stadium site:

> An ideal new location should be close enough to the public so as to be accessible but far enough away from the center of the city so that there's not as much congestion in parking and traffic as there is now [at the old stadium site]. A location farther away from residential housing would surely make those homeowners happy as they won't have people parking on their lawns or making a lot of noise late at night. A new site should not take away all of the stadium's revenue from Baltimore City as that has been a loving home for the stadium for many years. [She goes on to cite other factors that are important.]

Absent are the "there are's" and the long, enumerated lists of items. Instead, Rice has chosen the factors she thinks are most relevant for the stadium.

Explicit assumption of the business-manager-in-training role is illustrated by Fritz Earhardt, who recommends a site far from the center of the city, where his emotional allegiance lies. He concludes his paper:

> After looking at the proposals and matching factors, I have come to a conclusion I really dislike. . . . Do we give up profit to keep a tradition going? As a businessman I would have to say NO.

Rice and Earhardt avoid merely a lay or a text-processor role, but they do not sound like professional business consultants writing formal recommendations either. The ethos Sherman looked for was a complex amalgam. Sherman's assignment required a complex business-manager-in-training role which skillfully combined elements of other roles to create a self and an audience unique to this school's setting and this classroom's audience. In other classes, too, the assignment of a "peer" audience was a more complex requirement than the teacher had envisioned, as we will see.

Earhardt's reference to himself as a "businessman" highlights gender as a factor in students' adoption of roles and their construction of self and audience. Undoubtedly many other factors were also at work; however, this study focuses on how students' strategies and teachers' methods affected the difficulties that arose in the class as a whole, including both male and female students of various backgrounds.

TEACHER'S METHODS AND STUDENTS' STRATEGIES

The Role of Information in Creating the Self

The surprise is that Kelly Rice, whose stadium paper so clearly communicates a decision-maker ethos, is the same student who adopted weak information-gathering strategies and a text-processor role for the McDonald's-Popeye's paper. Rice's lack of information about McDonald's and Popeye's contrasts with the rich information about the stadium she gathered from memory and from a formal telephone interview with a knowledgeable peer (p. 62). Perhaps guiding students' information-gathering strategies is one way to help them assume the role and create the ethos of a professional-in-training.

The Assignment Sheet: Sherman's Language and Students' Strategies

We mentioned that the assignment sheet affected students' information gathering; it also affected their constructions of audience and self. By designating as audience for the stadium assignment "the members of your class, rather than the decision makers," Sherman wanted students to avoid the one-sided advocacy by which various neighborhoods and economic interests were attempting to influence the mayor and the city council, the actual decision makers in this case. Instead, he wanted students to use the language and decision-making methods that were being taught in the class and that would be respected by classmates who were business decision-makers-in-training. However, an inappropriate baseball fan ethos is directly traceable to the assignment sheet. We have already quoted the section of Harrington's think-aloud planning where she imagines herself "standing there arguing" with her audience in what we have called the "streetcorner debate" model (p. 60). Following that portion of the tape, Harrington's thoughts turn to the arguments she could use to support her position that the stadium should be located in Catonsville.

She opens her textbook. Temporarily, she switches to the classroom model of reasoning: her diction is more academic and she mentions a number of relevant factors from the textbook. Most of those factors should have made it into the final paper, but none of them did, because, in the next section of the think-aloud tape, she looks again at the assignment sheet and shapes her plans by its statement that the audience is to be "the members of your class rather than . . . the decision makers."

> Now, Dr. Sherman made a note on the paper the assignment's on that we're directing this analysis to the class, not to the decision makers themselves, so I've got to keep this in mind, that I'm not trying to win over the people who are locating the stadium. I'm trying to win over the class to the stadium's location. Now the best way to go about this is to think about the thing that affects the class themselves when thinking about the stadium and that would be their pocketbooks. They're the ones that are paying the ticket prices and all. So I've got to try and convince them that moving the stadium to Catonsville won't drive up the ticket sales—ticket prices, rather—as much as if the stadium were located in the city.

Next, Harrington plans her three fan-centered points—gas, ticket prices, and parking—for the paper reproduced earlier (pp. 66–67).

Considering only ball fans' needs is one of the most common shortcomings of the stadium papers as a whole, in Sherman's judgment. This shortcoming is partly due to difficulties with information gathering we discussed earlier: students simply didn't have enough specific information to address a variety of factors, especially those that business managers would consider. Nonetheless, the narrowness of their considerations seems at least partially attributable to the ways in which students, triggered by the assignment sheet, constructed their readers and themselves.

So should teachers give up assignments that ask students to address peers? Bartholomae (1985) has maintained that assigning a "peer" audience to students is an "act of hostility" because it does not help students learn to assume the "expert" persona needed in academic writing (140). But Sherman's intention was precisely to give students this kind of practice in writing as an expert. He wanted to construct the class as a business community and to help students practice writing to others within that community. He knew that addressing multiple audiences, each with different levels of expertise, is a common situation writers must face in business.

We believe that what caused difficulties on the assignment sheet was not that Sherman assigned a peer audience but that: (1) Some of his students did not easily see themselves and their peers as professionals-in-training, and (2) Sherman did not communicate effectively to all his students his expectation that they would do so. Our advice would be that teachers specify their expectations and help students adopt the appropriate roles.

Our chosen view of the classroom—as a place where students, under the guidance of their teachers, are learning to be competent communicators—lets us construct Harrington's story as the story of a student trying to learn an appropriate role and ethos acceptable to her teacher, and, in this case, missing the mark in certain ways. In this perspective, Sherman's language on the assignment sheet miscued the student, evoking her view of herself and her classmates as baseball fans. Certainly she and other students seemed eager to learn to be business decision makers and to adopt the roles and strategies that would meet Sherman's expectations.

It would be possible, however, with the use of other perspectives, to explore Harrington's story as a conflict of gender and power or as her struggle to reconcile various roles or selves. Each interpretation, we recognize, would allow a different insight into this very complex difficulty that occured as Harrington and others tried to construct an audience and a self.

DIFFICULTIES WITH STATING A POSITION

THE NATURE OF THE DIFFICULTIES

All three of Sherman's assignments asked students to state a position— which stadium site or restaurant was best, or what was the best way to improve U.S. productivity. However, a number of students did not do so. In the stadium paper, for example, 16 percent of the students failed to state any position, and another 11 percent tacked on a decision that had a loose relationship at best to the rest of the paper, which was a textbook summary.

In a study by Voss and his colleagues (1983), undergraduates seemed perfectly capable of stating a position on an issue similar to Sherman's papers. The researchers, in a laboratory setting, asked ten undergraduate students ("novices") to solve orally (without recourse to written texts) the problem of how to improve Soviet agricultural productivity— a problem similar to Sherman's productivity term paper. The students' problem-solving processes were then compared to those of "experts." In Voss's laboratory setting, all ten students proposed a solution. But low-success students in Sherman's class showed a novice approach that did not turn up in Voss's laboratory setting—they did not pose any solution at all.

TEACHER'S METHODS AND STUDENTS' STRATEGIES

In light of Voss's success in getting all students to state a position, what encouraged Sherman's students not to state a position, even when they were explicitly asked to do so? Three important differences between Voss's and Sherman's settings may provide clues: (1) In Sherman's class, students functioned as students in a regular classroom, (2) they worked directly from written texts, and (3) they produced texts. Factors that appeared to contribute to students' failure to state a position were related to students' roles in the classroom and to their notions about the use and production of *written* texts.

Sherman's and the Students' Differing Approaches to the Textbook and Source Texts

Stadium and Restaurants as Examples of the Text

The students' view of the texts they used was often different from the one that Sherman wanted. When a freshman interviewer asked one of Sherman's students what had been the most difficult aspect of the stadium paper, he replied, "The hardest part was figuring out how to make the assignment fit the textbook." Many other students said in their interviews, tapes, or logs, that the stadium or the restaurants were "examples" of the textbook. Dawn Shale (p. 67), after summarizing the factors listed in the textbook chapter, wrote, "These factors are many of the factors that are involved in finding a location for the new stadium in Baltimore." After summarizing the textbook, she merely tacked on the stadium as an example.

Note Taking Focused On the Textbook

In the first two papers, students who adopted the text-processor role took notes primarily about the textbook, not about the stadium sites or the restaurants, and as they wrote their papers they continued to work closely from the textbook. They seemed to have difficulty with the notion that "real" information should or could be gathered from sources other than texts. For the productivity term paper, text-processor students focused on gathering information from library sources, using one of two strategies:

The Main-Article Strategy: Some students, rather than focusing on finding a solution to the problem, looked in the library for what one of them called "my main article." Then they adopted the stance and arguments of that article. Some students skillfully integrated material from other sources into their main article summary, but their focus still remained on processing texts.

The Stretch Thesis Strategy: The second strategy was to combine a number of library sources and then compose a very broad thesis to cover the sources. The thesis might read something like, "Problems in productivity are caused by A, B, C, D, E, and F, and should be addressed by doing G, H, I, J, K, and L." This "stretch" thesis could expand infinitely to incorporate the various sources that students found, and it related the various sources in a loose, additive fashion. This approach was more creative and less anchored to a single text than the main-article strategy, but the student still seemed primarily focused on synthesizing texts and not on deciding what to do about productivity.

Students' Use of Models from Other Settings

Students who stated no clear position in their productivity term papers appeared to draw on familiar notions of what a term paper or research paper was: notions that did not include independent decision making about a problem. Schwegler and Shamoon (1982) have suggested that students believe the research paper to be primarily informational, not argumentative or analytical. "The paper is viewed as an exercise in information gathering, not an act of discovery" (819). Applebee (1984) found that in most high schools he studied, writing most commonly tested the ability of students to recall or transcribe newly acquired information. When Flower (1990), with deliberate vagueness, instructed students in a freshman reading and writing class to write a "research paper," many students generated plans merely to summarize text or to review and comment on texts—evidently calling on models of the research papers they had used in other settings (44–47). The data from Sherman's class suggests that when a teacher in a discipline-based classroom gives direction for a specific task, students may employ models from other settings if they do not fully understand, or cannot use, or do not consider it advantageous to use, the new models they are being taught.

Sherman's Use of Familiar Topics and Settings for an Assignment

Despite some students' failure to state positions, one teaching method that seemed to help other students adopt the decision-maker role was selecting a "hot" topic, like the stadium site, that was the subject of debate in the students' familiar environment outside the class. The student data reveal students getting involved and interested in selecting and defending a stadium site. Though the question "Which stadium site did you choose?" was not on the list of questions the freshman student interviewers were to ask, many interviewers added that question, and with great interest.

In one taped interview, a text processor who had not announced a decision at all in her stadium paper, but had skillfully summarized the textbook, was asked by her freshman interviewer, "Which site did you pick?" Her answer was "hmm." When asked again, she hem-hawed a bit and finally named a site, hiding from her interviewer the fact that she had written a paper on the stadium and not named a site. Clearly, in the peer environment created during the interview, if you're going to talk about the stadium, you state your position—which site are you defending? However, if students merely adopted the layperson role of streetcorner arguers defending their chosen positions, problems arose, as we have already seen in our discussion of ethos, and as we will now see further as we examine just *how* students who stated positions went about arriving at them.

TWO INTERRELATED DIFFICULTIES: USING DISCIPLINE-BASED METHODS TO ARRIVE AT (AND SUPPORT) A POSITION; MANAGING COMPLEXITY

THE NATURE OF THE DIFFICULTIES

Sherman's Expectations

Using discipline-based methods of reasoning and managing complexity were inextricably linked in Sherman's class because a major function of the methods he taught was to manage the complexity of business decisions. Sherman's version of the five tasks of good/better/best reasoning (p. 12) appeared in his expectations that students would use the define/analyze/prescribe rubric. He also expected that his students would use "factor rating"; would treat the define/analyze/prescribe process as recursive; and would link the definition, analysis, and prescription. We will explain each of these expectations.

Factor Rating

Factor rating, as explained in the textbook chapter that students read for the stadium paper, helps the decision maker perform the five tasks of good/better/best reasoning. To conduct factor rating, one first identifies the important factors that will comprise the definition of "good" (Task 1). Individual feelings and values and an element of rationale-building (Tasks 4 and 5) enter the process as the student decides what factors he or she thinks are important for the particular situation. For the stadium site the student might decide to consider taxes, transportation, availability of raw materials, and so forth. The student then assigns to each factor a percentage of the total weight. For the stadium, the student might decide that taxes will weigh 10 percent, transportation 40 percent, raw materials 2 percent, and so on. The sum of all weights must equal 100 percent.

Next, the student analyzes each site (Task 2), assigning a number from 1 to 100 for each factor in that site. Camden Yards might have excellent transportation, so it would get 100 points in that category. Catonsville might have middling transportation so it would get only 50 points in transportation. This procedure offers a way of "seeing" the site and concentrating only on the factors one has chosen, thus controlling the otherwise endless flood of information one might collect about a proposed site. The resulting chart brings the student's definition of "good" and the information about sites into disciplined relationship with one another so that a single judgment can result (Task 3). A factor rating chart for the stadium might resemble Table 3.3.

To make a judgment (Task 3), the student multiplies the number of points given to each factor by the percentage awarded to that factor (listed on the top line) and calculates a final score for each proposed location. To get Catonsville's score on transportation, multiply 50 x .40. Add all the scores together to get a total score for Catonsville. The location with the highest total score is the one that best fits the definition of "good" that was established by choosing factors and their weights.

Sherman did not necessarily expect students to use factor rating formally in their stadium papers, but did expect them to select relevant

Table 3.3   Factor-Rating Chart (Stadium Paper)

	Taxes	Transportation	Etc.
Percentage awarded[a]	10%	40%	Etc.
Catonsville (points)[b]	80	50	Etc.
Camden Yards (points)	40	100	Etc.

[a]Weights of all factors must equal 100%.   [b]Allocate maximum 100 points for each factor

factors, indicate those they believed to be most important, and then link the factors to their chosen stadium site. These three expectations were the most common topics of Sherman's comments on the stadium papers during the course, as the student strategy sequence (p. 38) revealed.

Define/Analyze/Prescribe as a Recursive Process

Sherman's way of handling Task 5—relating the solution-searching and rationale-building elements—was to see the define/analyze/prescribe process as recursive, not linear. If viewed as a linear, solution-searching process, the define/analyze/prescribe formula seems to lead from definition through analysis to prescription. However, the recursiveness of the process makes it also a rationale-building process because one may also start with a prescription and build the definition and analysis to fit. Sherman embodied this notion in an interview shortly after the course had ended:

> Students' definition of productivity should have been dictated by where their paper was going, even though that sounds kind of backwards. Once you find out what you're going to be able to do in your paper, you define productivity narrowly or broadly in that context.

Linking Definition, Analysis, and Prescription

Definition and analysis, in Sherman's class, served as the needed rationale to support the students' prescription. It was not sufficient simply to summarize the textbook or to present a definition or analysis without relating that material to the decision the writer made.

Low-Success Papers

Some students fell short of Sherman's expectations for using discipline-based methods and managing complexity. The three most common types of low-success papers were (1) automatic defense of a previous position, (2) the "find reasons" paper, and (3) comparison/contrast instead of evaluation.

Automatic Defense of a Previous Position: In the stadium papers, many students automatically defended their hometowns rather than judiciously considering various sites. In other words, for Task 5 they adopted a rationale-building strategy that was not integrated with solution-searching. Early in her think-aloud planning, Marsha Harrington announced as a foregone conclusion that Catonsville—her own hometown—was the best stadium site. (She had lots of company in defending a hometown site, as our check of students' home addresses revealed.) Sherman had nothing against students defending their hometown because personal values might play a role in decision making, but he wanted them to keep an open mind and be guided by the decision-making methods he was teaching—in other words, to combine solution-searching with rationale-building.

The *"Find Reasons" Paper*: Some students only listed the reasons or advantages for their particular solutions, without considering alternatives or counterarguments.

Comparison/Contrast Instead of Evaluation: On the McDonald's-Popeye's paper, some students made decisions about what the differences and similarities were between the two restaurants, but did not make the evaluative decisions (Task 3) concerning how the restaurants' layout and work designs met the restaurants' goals.

TEACHER'S METHODS AND STUDENTS' STRATEGIES

Familiar Setting and Topic

Although Sherman's use of a familiar topic and setting for his stadium assignment helped students state a position, it also proved problematic. Marsha Harrington's automatic defense of her hometown may have happened in part because the assignment evoked a familiar issue for which many students already had loyalties. Had he given them a traditional business "case" involving an issue unfamiliar to them, they would have had to consider the wider range of evidence as a basis for their decisions.

Reading Comprehension

The Textbook's Dense Language

The dense language of some of the textbook's description of the decision-making process and students' strategies for handling that difficulty may have hindered their efforts in following the decision-making processes Sherman wanted. For example, the book's explanation of factor rating is couched in the bureaucratic language that Richard Lanham (1979) loves to hate, and that Sherman, in an interview, called "boring." It reads, in part:

A typical location decision involves both qualitative and quantitative inputs, and these tend to vary from situation to situation depending on the needs of each particular organization. *Factor rating* is a general approach which is useful both for evaluating a given alternative and for comparing alternatives. The value of factor rating is that it provides a rational basis for evaluation and it facilitates comparison among alternatives by establishing a *composite* value for each alternative that summarizes all related factors.

The textbook includes a factor rating chart more complex than the one we included for Table 3.3. Only a few students read and understood the textbook's discussion of the factor rating method and used it to reach a decision. No student constructed a quantitative chart as the textbook illustrated.

An earlier part of the chapter, however, has a simpler discussion and a clear, easily readable chart (reproduced here in shortened form) which summarized the factors that generally affect location decisions:

> Factors Which Affect Location Decisions:
>   Regional Factors
>   Location of Raw Materials
>   Location of Markets
>   [etc.]
>   Community Considerations
>   Facilities
>   Services
>   [etc.]
>   Site-Related Factors
>   Land
>   Transportation
>   [etc.]

The ease and visibility of this chart compared to the density of the factor rating explanation seems to have shaped some students' decision-making processes in problematic ways. For example, one student reported in her log that she read and highlighted the textbook chapter, reread the highlighted parts, but finally,

> I found I did not understand most of what I read. I basically used a chart in the book outlining factors that affect location decisions. I took points from this chart and used them as points in my paper.

Students' Textbook-Items-as-Points Strategy

We have seen this "points" language before—when Kelly Rice lacked information and a theme about the two fast-food restaurants (p. 65). Now, again, a lack of information (the inability to comprehend the textbook) has led a student to adopt the text-processor role, merely summarizing textbook "points" rather than using the textbook as a resource for decision making about the stadium. This story reinforces our earlier conclusions that a text-processor role is not necessarily a low-investment approach but may be the result of complex factors (p. 11).

Students' Use of Procedural Information from the Textbook

Carla Stokes's difficulty involved a complex form of reading comprehension in which she tried to *use* the decision-making process she read in her textbook. The process was explained in what to us seems clear and simple language near the beginning of the chapter, and the steps of decision making were set up in list-like form to make reading easier. In the following excerpt from one of her tapes Stokes begins to read aloud the steps of the decision-making process from the textbook (notice that the steps are a version of define/analyze/ prescribe):

> The procedures for making location decisions are [begins writing, working closely from the textbook in front of her] one, you determine the criteria used to evaluate the alternatives, identify the important factors, develop uh location alternatives—general, region, or community site alternatives—and lastly evaluate and make a selection [stops writing]. Um, different locations that I've heard of are. . . .

Stokes, who was well acquainted with the stadium controversy, immediately went through five possible stadium locations, jotting characteristics of each. She had stated the steps in order, beginning with definition, but her actual decision making began with the third step—developing and comparing location alternatives.

Omitting definition was disastrous for her: Since she had not first articulated the factors to consider nor weighed their relative importance (factor rating), she had no definition of a "good" stadium site, and hence no way to control the flood of things she knew about the five locations. Her discussion of the sites implied and assumed a number of factors, but the factors were not prioritized or consistently applied. Though the textbook description told Stokes how to do the good/ better/best reasoning tasks, and though she attended to that information as she began to make her decision, she did not translate that description into an appropriate procedure.

Distinguishing the Decision-Making Sequence
from the Organizational Sequence of the Paper

In writing her draft, Stokes tried to follow the same organization as her planning—taking each of the five sites in turn and discussing its pros and cons. Understandably, her draft got out of control. It's "too long," she said, and so she abandoned it. She seemed unable to see that her list of five sites could be viewed as a planning document which, though long, might help her in making a decision, and that her decision could be stated and defended in a paper that had a different organization and length.

No students in this class, as far as our evidence shows, produced any planning document for the stadium paper that was deliberately different from the final paper in its organization, or that was longer than what the student estimated would be the length of the final, one-page, typed paper. Flower and Hayes (1981a) have found some students whose "plans for producing a paper take precedence over any plans for exploring the topic" (54) and who "stop productive idea generation because it doesn't look like a finished paper" (56). Flower and Hayes suggest, rightly we think, that the problem lies partly in students' failure to realize that at times expert writers maintain a distinction between generating ideas and constructing a paper (56).

Text Processing as a Fallback Position

After abandoning her draft, Stokes turned to the textbook and produced a low-success, text-processor paper: a close summary of the textbook followed by a decision stuck on the end, seemingly as an afterthought unrelated to the factors she had discussed throughout most of the paper. We have earlier seen the text-processor role linked to insufficient information and a sense of not understanding the textbook. Now we see another possible factor in students' choice of that role: their inability, even in a good-faith effort like Stokes's, to make the new approach work, or to make it consonant with the other constraints (such as length) they perceived for the task.

Students' Find-Reasons Strategy for Idea Generation

A number of students began the stadium assignment with an automatic decision and then used the textbook's factor chart to help them think of reasons (advantages) for their chosen site. One student even called the factors "reasons," then crossed out "reasons" and substituted "factors" in her final draft. The factors that should have been used to help *determine the decision* served solely to suggest a list of advantages to *support an automatic decision* based on previous loyalties. In Voss's terms, rationale-building was not combined with solution-searching. In an interview, Sherman explained his disappointment when students automatically chose a position and then defended it merely by listing reasons or positive advantages:

> If they start with a solution and reasons—the stadium should be here for these reasons—students don't have the perspective of what they're *sacrificing* in choosing that particular stadium site.

Students' Use of the "Thesis" Concept

Thirty-six percent of our focus group of students used the word *thesis* at least once in their data, though Sherman never specifically mentioned the term (he did use the term *theme* in reference to the McDonald's-Popeye's paper, however). The "thesis" term had been heavily emphasized in the freshman composition course that most of Sherman's students had taken. Three problems were sometimes linked to students' notions of thesis. Marsha Harrington, who relied heavily on her concept of "thesis" and "subs" for all her papers, reflects two of the problems—the premature automatic decision and the find-reasons strategy.

Harrington, the student who interpreted her stadium paper audience merely as baseball fans, and who automatically assumed she would defend her hometown of Catonsville, announced early her "thesis" that Catonsville was the best stadium site and immediately said on the think-aloud tape, "Then just go through and list my reasons." She identified these reasons as "subs" or "subtheses," a common term in freshman composition. She exhibited traits that Walvoord, as a composition teacher at Loyola, knows that teachers face in the composition classes—students' notions that generating the thesis is the first act of the writer, and that subtheses are merely reasons why the proposed thesis would be advantageous.

Student Kurt Larson illustrates a third problem—he gave the term "thesis" to the definition of productivity that opened his term paper, not seeming to realize that the thesis is not necessarily whatever comes first in the paper, but the main idea—in this case, his solutions to the productivity problem.[5]

Use of "Thesis" and Students' Success

Despite problems with "thesis" in Sherman's class, we were surprised to find that 60 percent of the focus group who received course grades of "A" or "B" used the word *thesis* at some point in their data, while none of the focus group who received "C" or below used it. That suggests several possibilities: (1) Although students have some difficulties using the concept of "thesis," it may be a useful tool for those who employ it, or (2) those who employ it may have other qualities that help them achieve success—perhaps an appreciation for organizational structures. It is also possible that (3) the frequency of the word "thesis" in the 14-student focus group has no significance, since our sample is so small.

In any case, we were reminded again that students brought with them models which they had learned in other settings—models of which Sherman, during the course, was not aware, and which might influence how students thought and wrote. The writing-across-the-curriculum program at Loyola College, partly on the basis of these findings, has tried to make all instructors aware of the thesis and subthesis terminology used widely in freshman composition classes, and to encourage both composition teachers and teachers across the disciplines to counter students' premature closure on thesis, their find-reasons strategy, and their confusion of thesis with whatever comes first in a paper, and to explain to their students how the thesis concept may or may not be useful in other classes.

Sherman's Emphasis on Defining "Good"

Sherman's emphasis on defining "good" as part of good/better/best reasoning had a strong impact, helping students to meet his expectations. His assignment sheets emphasized the importance of beginning with a definition of "good," and his definition/analysis/prescription formula made "definition" highly visible as the first necessary element. Virtually every day between the time he gave the assignment and the time it was due, he spent at least some minutes in class discussing the assignment and answering students' questions about it. The student-observers' notes and Sherman's daily class log reveal that these discussions often focused on helping students with defining "good." The textbook, too, as we have seen, described a decision-making process that began with defining what a "good" location would be. The in-class discussion on the productivity paper, as we have seen, was actually divided into definition, analysis, and prescription. All these methods seemed influential in the fact that most students at least began their papers with a definition, as Sherman requested. In the good/better/best assignments in other classes, where the definition of "good" was much less visible, this was not at all the case.

The Assignment Sheet

Though most students included a definition of "good," problems arose as they integrated the definition into the decision-making process. Sherman expected, as we have said, the three activities of definition/ analysis/prescription to be recursive, and the decision-making process to combine solution-searching with rationale-building. But in Sherman's communications to students, the recursiveness of the decision-making and the composing processes was not always explicitly separated from a linear plan for organizing the paper, in which the definition appeared first, then the analysis, then the prescription. For example, Sherman's assignment sheet for the productivity paper states:

> Define "productivity" in a useful way, present a sense of why conditions exist that restrict the growth of the quantity and quality of our output, and present a strong case for an appropriate way to redirect our nation toward higher productivity.

Many students interpreted this as a chronological sequence for decision making and composing. They began by looking for a definition of productivity—any definition. Once that was "out of the way," as one student put it, they fashioned their analysis and prescription, but never came back to reshape the original definition to fit.

Structure of the In-Class Discussions

The structure of in-class discussions may inadvertently have contributed to the problem of students treating the process as linear. In the in-class discussion on the productivity paper, for example, Sherman had first asked students to generate definitions of "productivity," then to suggest causes of the problem, then to name the various prescriptions that they had defended in their papers. Sherman's blackboard list was a brainstormed list of components from various students' positions and therefore did not show the recursiveness of the process, where the writer would return to reshape the definition to fit his or her particular prescriptions.

Sherman's Emphasis on Evaluation

In the McDonald's-Popeye's paper students were to "evaluate" (a word Sherman used twice on the assignment sheet) the two local fast-food restaurants. In class, during the days when students were working on the papers, Sherman recorded in his log that he emphasized his expectations that mere comparison/contrast was not enough. He told students that they needed a theme that would evaluate the layout and work design in terms of the restaurants' goals. That language and those concepts got through to the students, at least in the sense that their class notes and logs often contain the words "evaluate" and "theme." A paragraph from a successful paper illustrates the qualities that Sherman wanted.

Brian Smith's opening paragraph states that both restaurants have the same basic goals—promptness and efficiency in serving large numbers of customers. A later paragraph discusses how well each restaurant achieves promptness and efficiency in line balancing (distributing work efficiently so that each worker is busy all the time and the product moves at maximum speed):

> Line balancing at [fast-food restaurants] is very important. At McDonald's there seems to be a lot of time wasted. There are too many counter people. When they are not busy, they just stand around. . . . At Popeye's, line balancing is *more efficient*. When it is slow . . . the counter people clean the restaurant. [Italics ours]

In his paragraph, Smith does not merely compare the restaurants, he evaluates them against their goal of efficiency. Sherman's ways of emphasizing evaluation worked for Smith and others.

Students' Use of Models from Other Settings

Treating the McDonald's Paper as Comparison/Contrast

Instead of the *evaluation* that Smith conducted, however, many students on the McDonald's-Popeye's papers wrote mere comparison/contrast: The assignment sheet's opening instructions to "compare and contrast" the two restaurants may have evoked for students this familiar mode. The day after Sherman's in-class discussion of the need for finding a theme rather than merely comparing and contrasting, one of our paid student observers, who was also a student in the class, referred to the assignment in her written class record as "Comparison on McDonalds and Popeyes."

Once again, models from other settings—the "reflection" paper, the "term" paper, or the comparison/contrast paper—may be powerful influences on students' writing and thinking strategies, overriding other instructions from the teacher.

Students' Ways of Interrelating Different Types of Information

Moving from Comparison/Contrast to Evaluation

In addition to using models from other settings, another possible reason for students to treat the McDonald's-Popeye's paper as mere comparison/contrast is that they did not make a crucial distinction between a restaurant's goals and its layout and work design. For example, Kurt Larson's pre-draft writing on the McDonald's-Popeye's paper (Figure 3.3) combines in a two-columned list his observations about the restaurants' goals and their layout and work design (line balancing and processing)—but he could not transcend mere comparison/contrast until he used the restaurants' goals as a standard *to evaluate* other differences.

Thirty percent of the students also used a two-columned comparison/contrast chart like Larson's. Though such charts helped them to line up the similarities and differences between the restaurants, again the charts did not help them evaluate the layout and work design on the basis of how well those factors met the restaurants' goals.

Students' Types of Pre-Draft Writing

Students' pre-draft writing did not help them to evaluate or to use the decision-making processes Sherman wanted. Instead, as Table 3.4 for the stadium paper shows, students focused on pre-draft writing

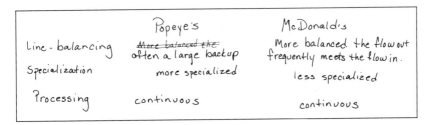

Figure 3.3. Kurt Larson's notes on McDonald's and Popeye's.

Table 3.4   Pre-Draft Writing (Stadium Paper)

Type of Writing	Number of Pre-Draft Writings
Notes on text	7
Information about sites	3
Decision-making procedures	
Factor rating	0
Freewriting*	4
Plans for final paper	
Thesis statement	1
Introductory paragraph	3
Outline	3

* Freewriting: Any list or full prose not directly based on reading/observation, and not related to an organizational plan for the paper. For a discussion of how the term freewrite has been used by other researchers, see Hillocks 1986, 176.

N = 21 pieces of pre-draft writing produced by 16 students on whom we were reasonably sure we had full pre-draft writing data. Four students produced no pre-draft writing; others produced more than one specimen.

that summarized the textbook, compared/contrasted, and organized the final paper.

What is missing are forms of writing that would facilitate evaluation and factor rating. No student used the kind of factor rating chart modeled in their textbook. For the stadium paper, such a chart might have resembled Table 3.3 (p. 75). The factors, each with its weighted importance, together form a definition of a "good" stadium site. The chart shows a visible and quantitative way to measure the characteristics of the various sites against the student's definition of "good."

Table 3.5 shows a factor rating chart for the McDonald's-Popeye's paper.

The chart distinguishes between differences in the restaurants' goals and differences in their layouts and work designs. It visibly places the layouts and work designs in an evaluative relationship to the goals.

We have seen two students who desperately needed a decision-making structure that factor rating charts could have provided. Carla Stokes made a long list of five stadium sites but had no definition of a "good" stadium to control that list, and no way of bringing what she knew about the alternative sites into disciplined relationship with a definition of "good" site. Kurt Larson merely listed similarities and differences among the goals and the other characteristics of the restaurants with no way to evaluate the differences in layout and work design in relation to the goals.

Table 3.5   Sample Factor Rating Chart (McDonald's-Popeye's Paper)

	Restaurant Goal 1	Restaurant Goal 2	Etc.
Percentage awarded[a]	%	%	%
McDonald's			
Layout:			
Line Balancing[b]			
Etc.			
Work Design			
Specialization			
Etc.			
Popeye's			
Layout:			
Line Balancing			
Etc.			
Work Design			
Specialization			
Etc.			

[a]Weights of all factors must equal 100%.   [b]Allocate maximum 100 points per each factor.

In sum, complex difficulties arose as students tried to use discipline-based methods and to manage complexity. The familiar stadium topic encouraged them to state positions. Sherman's emphasis on evaluation and on the role of definition appeared to help many students. However, the familiar topics and settings also suggested models of decision making Sherman did not want. Understanding and using the textbook's description of decision-making procedures proved difficult. Students confused the sequence of decision making with the organizational sequence of the paper and, accordingly, they did not produce pre-draft writing that specifically helped them with the decision-making process as distinct from composing the paper—pre-draft writing that would help them bring different types of material into disciplined relationship to one another so that a single decision could be made. Searching for a way to structure their work, some students used the notion of "thesis" from their freshman composition classes, but did not always know how to apply it. We concluded that Sherman might:

1. clarify in the assignment sheet the importance of following appropriate decision-making procedures
2. teach the decision-making process procedurally, actually guiding students through it, rather than relying on the textbook's description

3. clarify the relevance of "thesis" within his own decision-making and composing structures

4. teach modes of pre-draft writing that would facilitate decision making and that would help students:

   • distinguish between the decision-making process and the organization of the paper

   • distinguish among various types of material

   • bring various types of material into disciplined relationship to one another so a single decision could be made.

DIFFICULTIES WITH ORGANIZING THE PAPERS

THE NATURE OF THE DIFFICULTIES

Students' choices of organizational patterns were linked to their roles and their other strategies. We have seen the text processors take textbook items as points of their papers, and the layperson baseball fans merely list advantages of their chosen sites. This section focuses on a particular difficulty not yet discussed: students who chose define/analyze/prescribe as an organizational plan often did not create the tight "fit" that Sherman wanted among these three elements.

TEACHER'S METHODS AND STUDENTS' STRATEGIES

Sherman's and the Students' Differing Approaches to Definition

Sherman's instructions on the assignment sheet to begin with a definition of productivity, and his emphasis of that point during in-class discussions, ensured that virtually all students included such a definition. Sherman specifically warned them against using a dictionary definition, and none did. However, some students treated a definition they found in a library source or their textbook like a dictionary definition, not understanding that Sherman was inveighing against using external definitions with which to shape the paper instead of deriving definitions from the context of the students' own work.

Instead of dictionary definitions, Sherman's assignment sheet told students to formulate a "useful" definition. He explained in class and in interviews that a useful definition was one that was "dictated by where the paper was going." This instruction appeared to help a number of students, but many others still found it difficult to grasp this new way of deriving a definition.

After reading library sources, Kurt Larson, for example, decided that he wanted to defend the notion that raising productivity involved meeting the needs of workers rather than establishing a system that ignores their needs and morale. His definition of productivity, in Sherman's view, should likewise have focused on workers as the key. In his notes, Larson included several definitions of productivity copied or adapted from his reading; for example,

> productivity is the measure of how an employee perceives the quality of the product he/she is producing and how hard he/she is willing to work to achieve that quality.

According to Sherman, "result" would be a better word than "measure," but the definition is nicely worker-centered. Unfortunately, however, Larson did not use it. Instead, he used a definition that focused on "efficiency":

> Productivity is a measure of the efficiency with which a product has been produced and the extent to which that efficiency leads to the quality of the output.

Larson's analysis and prescriptions, which focused on meeting workers' needs as the key to productivity, did not therefore follow from the definition with which he had begun his paper.

After his paper had been handed in, Larson's final log entry shows his realization that he had not achieved a good fit, and that his choice of definition was one of his primary problems:

> Upon reflection of the paper I don't think I ever fully grasped the right definition of productivity.

Students' Attempts to Use Transitions

Larson's paper used transitions that promised more "fit" than the paper actually delivered. He began the prescription section of his paper by stating that a close fit should exist between analysis and prescription, and also by trying to weave his efficiency-centered definition into his concern for workers:

> Since the main problem lies in the efficiency of the workers, it is only natural to say that, to correct the problem it must be addressed on the same level.

After this promising transition sentence, however, Larson said on the think-aloud tape, "I can lead into how the Japanese do it versus how we do it"—and he lost his focus on the "efficiency of the workers."

Sherman's and the Students' Differing Approaches to Source Texts

Sherman expected students to use source texts within their own define/analyze/prescribe framework; however, one reason Larson was so eager to "lead into how the Japanese do it versus how we do it" is that he had good notes from his source texts on the Japan–U.S. comparisons. Larson yielded to the temptation to elevate the source text's contrast/compare mode so that it obscured the fit between his analysis and his solutions. Larson appeared to be on the verge of a better understanding of the fit that Sherman wanted, as his transitions show, but his failure to shape an integrated definition and his over-reliance on the organizational plans of his source texts prevented a full achievement.

PRE-DRAFT WRITING

Having completed our discussion of the six areas of student difficulty, we take up two topics that transcend any particular area of difficulty: students' pre-draft writing and the effectiveness of Sherman's draft response on the productivity papers.

We have seen that pre-draft writing served many functions in students' writing and thinking (pp. 63–64). We have also noted that students' organization of pre-draft writing was similar to the organization of their final papers, and thus did not help them achieve Task 3—relating information about the alternatives to the definition of "good" in a disciplined way so a single judgment could be made (pp. 85–86).

What remains to be said is that students who received high course grades did *more* pre-draft writing (Table 3.6), and they did *different kinds* of pre-draft writing from those who received low course grades (Table 3.7).

Table 3.7 shows that 80 percent of focus group students who received "A" in Sherman's course made notes *on separate pages* about their readings or observations, as opposed to 50 percent of students who

Table 3.6   Amount of Pre-Draft Writing and Grade Success
(All Three Assignments)

Course Grade	Mean Number of Pre-Draft Writings per Assignment
"A"	3.5
"C"	1.9

Note: A pre-draft writing is one continuous piece of one type of writing, such as a set of notes from reading, an outline (together with any revisions marked on it), a new outline.

N = All "A" and "C" students from the focus group, except for one student for whom we were not sure we had full data: 5 "A" students (15 papers); 4 "C" students (12 papers).

received course grade "C." Moreover, 53 percent of "A" students created notes that had somewhere within them two or more levels of hierarchy, as opposed to 17 percent of "C" students.[6] Sherman's "A" students also made drafts of less than two-thirds of the paper more frequently than "C" students did. Usually these were drafts of the introduction, serving to set up the rest of the paper.

The students who earned course grades of "C," on the other hand, created more of what we classified as *freewriting*—that is, lists or full prose not directly based on reading or observation and not reflecting a plan for the organization of the paper.

Hillocks's (1986) summary of research on freewriting indicates the term has been used primarily in research on teaching strategies, and is thus linked to a *teacher's* instructions to write whatever the student thinks, or to write anything the student wishes about topic X (sometimes called the "focused" freewrite). In our definition, the term freewrite refers to a *student*-generated piece of writing; nevertheless, Hillocks's findings are relevant to ours. Summarizing empirical research, Hillocks contrasts the mixed results of teaching freewriting with the more uniformly positive results of teaching "inquiry strategies"—that is, more focused exercises designed to guide students through a specific type of inquiry process. He speculates that the studies "point to a hitherto largely unrecognized aspect of the composing process—the ability to process data using strategies required by particular kinds of discourse" (186). Our study appears to support that hypothesis. Sherman's high-success students used more structured forms of pre-draft writing. Freewriting did not help Sherman's students do the five tasks necessary to good/better/best reasoning, particularly Task 3—bringing ideas and facts about a problem and its alternative solutions into a disciplined relationship to one another and to the decision maker's

Table 3.7   Types of Pre-Draft Writing and Grade Success
              (All Three Assignments)

Course Grade	Underline Reading	Notes on Reading and Obser-vation[a]	Freewrite[b]	Outline	Draft of Less Than Two-Thirds of Paper
		Percentage of Papers That Used Each Type of Writing			
"A"	33	80 (53)[c]	13	33	33
"C"	33	50 (17)[c]	50	33	08

[a]Any note directly based on the text or scene observed and written on separate pages (not margins of the reading selections).

[b]List or full prose not directly based on reading/observation and not reflecting a plan for the organization of the paper.

[c]A note that, somewhere within it, delineates two or three levels of hierarchy by, for example, indenting or numbering subordinate points.

N = All "A" and "C" students from focus group, except for one student for whom we were not sure we had full data: 5 "A" students (15 papers), 4 "C" students (12 papers).

definition of "good." For that task, students needed more disciplined forms.

Further, we have suggested that neither outlines nor drafts of the paper help with Task 3 in complex situations as effectively as would forms like the factor rating chart we discussed earlier, forms which no students in Sherman's class produced. In the next chapter, we will see how high-success students in Breihan's class produced such forms of pre-draft writing.

SHERMAN'S RESPONSE TO DRAFTS

After having attended a workshop in writing across the curriculum the previous summer, Sherman initiated in this class his own written response to each student's draft of the productivity paper. He wrote marginal comments primarily concerning content and organization, occasionally circled grammar and punctuation errors he noticed, and wrote an end comment of, typically, a few phrases or sentences. Students then revised the papers to receive their final grades. With 44 students each producing an eight- to ten-page draft, Sherman's responses involved a significant time investment for both himself and his students. One of Sherman's questions as we began our research was, "Was draft response worth my and my students' time?"

One conclusion we drew from our study of Sherman's class was that giving draft response on the earlier stadium and restaurant papers rather than on the last paper might have better served Sherman's goal of getting his students involved in the complexity of business decision making. One reason is that students could then benefit in later papers from Sherman's draft response and his encouragement of revision. Second, working from observation and from media accounts in the earlier analytical assignments was more difficult, more challenging, and also more akin to actual business problem solving than using library sources, as for the productivity term paper, where many students paraphrased heavily from print sources.

We also learned that students did pay close attention to Sherman's responses on their drafts: In a sample of twenty papers, 96 percent of Sherman's meaning-changing suggestions resulted in some sort of revision by the student.[7]

Table 3.8 shows that in our sample, 82 percent of Sherman's meaning-changing comments resulted in a student revision that improved the paper.[8] In their improvement of their papers there was no meaningful difference between students who earned course grades of "A" and course grades of "C."

Our way of measuring the improvement of the draft as a result of Sherman's comments puts teacher response and student revision into an admittedly narrow frame that Herrington (1988) has called "stimulus-response." That students could improve a draft in response to

Table 3.8   Sherman's Meaning-Changing Comments and Student Improvement (Productivity Paper)

	Percent of Total Comments
Improvement	
Revised as asked	38
Revised at a lower level than asked	27
Deleted	17
Total	82%
No Improvement	
Revised at a lower level than asked	10
Deleted	04
No change	04
Total	100%

N = 20 papers (10 from focus group; 10 representing a range of course grades).

Sherman's comments does not therefore indicate what they learned from the experience. In a previous study of a business class taught by another teacher at Loyola, Singer and Walvoord (1984) found that when business students revised case analyses after teacher response, they improved their ability to write case analyses on their own. Even more broadly, Herrington (1988) has noted that in the classroom she studied, peer review changed the power relationships in the class, giving greater authority to students. In sum, then, our report on the improvement of the papers presents only one aspect of the multiple effects that draft response may have in the classroom.

SHERMAN'S AND WALVOORD'S CONCLUSIONS

In this chapter, we have discussed how Sherman tried to help his students learn to adopt the role of professional-in-training, to "get involved in the complexity of business decision making," rather than merely play the role of text processor or layperson. We have discussed the six areas of difficulty that we constructed from our data. We have explored how difficulties were influenced by the teacher's methods and students' strategies. We have examined students' pre-draft writing and their responses to Sherman's comments on their productivity paper drafts.

Our studies showed us that the writing-across-the-curriculum workshop had been only a beginning, and that effective teaching for Sherman had to be based on his knowledge about his own students and his own classroom. Our collaborative study was a powerful impetus for change for both of us—Sherman in teaching business and Walvoord in teaching composition. We were strongly impressed by the usefulness of considering the roles that we expected from our students, that we modeled for them, that we helped them assume. We concluded that Sherman's ways of treating students as decision-makers-in-training during his in-class discussions, and his choice of familiar "hot topics" such as the stadium helped his students act as decision makers. Also, there were positive gains from Sherman's modeling of the define/analyze/prescribe rubric, and his emphasis on definiton and evaluation. Sherman's draft response we judged well worth the time he and his students spent.

Further, we learned how students used his assignment sheet, how they approached textbooks and source texts, how they assigned value to his assignments, how they used peers, how they arrived at and used categories for their observations, and how they defined themselves and others. We were surprised at the extent to which they used models from other settings, including the "thesis" concept. Particularly, we wanted to help them avoid some strategies that were not helpful—their textbook-items-as-points strategy, their equation of the sequence of decision making with the organizational sequence of the paper, their "find reasons" strategy, their reliance on a textbook chart to find reasons, their linear decision-making process. We wanted to help them create a "fit" between the various parts of their papers and expand their strategies for pre-draft writing. After our analysis of the data, we believed that the most important thing Sherman might do to help his students was to expand and clarify his assignment sheet, to institute better guidance for students at the beginning of the writing and thinking processes, and to help them use procedural knowledge.

In her composition classes, Walvoord has tried, since our study, to suggest to students what features to look for, what questions to ask, and what common pitfalls to avoid, as they enter classes in other disciplines. Walvoord has tried to address some of the uses and limitations of the thesis concept in other settings and to show students that definitions may in some instances be shaped to fit the demands of a particular argument or problem.

In a class of students that represented different genders, backgrounds, test scores, learning styles, and interests, our study led us to believe in the power of teaching to help students become competent communicators in the community of the classroom, the discipline, and the academy. Our investigation of the "difficulties," we believe, has helped us and our students to bridge the distances that separate us and to form a community of scholars.

Notes

1. The five tasks for good/better/best reasoning are:

Define "good" so as to accommodate a number of variously weighted factors and address the issue of "good for whom?"

Observe and analyze causes of the problem, aspects of the situation, and/or alternative solutions to the problem.

Bring the information into disciplined relationship with the definition of "good" so a single judgment can be made.

Integrate values/feelings with reasoning so as to reach a defensible position.

During the process, conduct simultaneously the processes we term "solution-searching" and "rationale-building" (see pp. 12–13).

2. Bransford et al. 1986; Perfetto, Bransford, and Franks 1983; Simon 1979; Greeno 1980; Larkin, Heller, and Greeno 1980.

3. Our term encompasses what Rohman (1965) terms "pre-writing"; however, we want to avoid the confusion of giving that term to the actual writing of notes and plans.

4. Aristotle 1954, pp. 1377–1378; Ede and Lunsford 1984; Ong 1975; Park 1982.

5. McCarthy's 1987 study, which follows a single Loyola College student through freshman composition and successive courses into his sophomore year, also illustrates some difficulties one student faced in trying to transfer to later courses what he had learned about thesis and subs in freshman composition.

6. Kennedy's 1985 study is similar: three college students who were "fluent readers" took more notes on their reading in preparation for writing a paper than three "not-so-fluent readers."

7. The sample, which included the ten focus-group students who revised their productivity papers plus ten other students with a range of course grades and paper grades, was analyzed as described on pp. 40–41.

8. Using the same 20-student sample described in Note 7, we analyzed whether Sherman's meaning-changing comments had resulted in student revisions that improved the paper. We used the analytic technique described on p. 41. Sherman's comments on the revised paper usually indicated whether he thought the student had improved the paper. When Sherman did not comment, Walvoord made a judgment based on her knowledge of Sherman's expectations and his comments on the other papers.

4 Arguing and Debating: Breihan's History Course

Barbara E. Walvoord
Loyola College in Maryland

John R. Breihan
Loyola College in Maryland

This chapter continues the exploration of the "difficulties" (p. 5) that arose as students tried to meet their teachers' expectations, and the teachers' methods and students' strategies that appeared to affect those difficulties. Our special focus (p. 16) in this chapter is students' development across the semester and how John R. Breihan's teaching methods nurtured that development.

Breihan's "Modern Civilization" course was a 100-level, required CORE course enrolling 27 students (mostly freshmen) at Loyola College in fall, 1985. Characteristics of the class, the college, and the students appear on p. 18 and in Appendix B. "We" in this chapter refers to Walvoord and Breihan, who collaborated in gathering the data and writing this chapter.

In Breihan's class, difficulties arose in all six areas we constructed for the four classes (p. 14). However, we chose three areas of difficulty— stating a position, managing complexity, and using discipline-based methods to arrive at and support a position. We chose these three, first, because they were the main focus of Breihan's and his students' attention: 76 percent of Breihan's meaning-changing comments (p. 40) on students' essay drafts involved these three areas. Second, these three areas have seemed important to teachers and difficult for students, not only in our four classes but in other academic settings as well (Applebee et al. 1990; Connor 1990; Connor and Lauer 1985; Cooper et al. 1984; Perkins 1985).

We chose to focus on the effects of Breihan's teaching methods because those methods had been carefully crafted over a period of years and influenced by his extensive experience in writing-across-the-curriculum workshops (Breihan 1986; Mallonee and Breihan 1985;

Walvoord and Dowling 1990). Further, Breihan's methods conformed to the "environmental" mode that Hillocks's (1986) analysis of empirical research on writing instruction has shown to be the most effective. Rather than merely presenting information (the "presentational" mode), Breihan's environmental mode structured ways for his students to learn to use information. Breihan's course also contained the characteristics that Kurfiss (1988), after a survey of the literature, lists as being common to courses that successfully support critical thinking:

- Critical thinking is treated as a learnable skill, with instructor and peers as resources for learning.
- Problems, questions, or issues are points of entry into the subject and a source of motivation for sustained inquiry.
- Challenges to think critically are balanced with support for students' developmental needs.
- Courses are assignment-centered rather than text- and lecture-centered. Goals, methods, and evaluation emphasize using content rather than simply acquiring it.
- Students are required to formulate and justify their ideas in writing or other appropriate modes.
- Teachers make standards explicit and then help students learn how to achieve them. (88–89)

Breihan's specific teaching methods most notably included:

1. An issue-oriented course plan, using issues as points of entry into the course.
2. Three major argumentative essays about those issues; these essays formed the central assignments toward which much of the other course activities were pointed.
3. A checksheet for evaluating/grading the essays that made his expectations very explicit.
4. Daily, focused writings ("exercises") explicitly planned both to develop needed skills and information and to serve as pre-draft preparation for the essays.
5. In-class discussions in which Breihan led his students through the modes of argument he wanted them to learn.
6. Seven in-class debates on historical issues that also served as pre-draft preparation for the essays.

7. Responses by Breihan on drafts of the essays, after which students revised.

But more important than the individual methods, to Walvoord the striking characteristic of Breihan's classroom was the consistent, focused, deliberate amassing of various activities, both written and oral, that all pointed toward the central course goal—teaching students to argue about issues by using historical evidence.

BREIHAN'S EXPECTATIONS

A student we call Bonnie Kraft recalled, in an interview by Walvoord three years after having taken Breihan's class, her surprise as she began to comprehend Breihan's expectations:

> I remember going in there thinking, O.K., this is just a basic history course, you know, it's not going to be a lot of work, you know what I mean, it's just going to be basically all lecture and then I'm going to have to restate what he told me on an exam. But Dr. Breihan was saying, "I'm not a history teacher; I'm a historian who teaches history." And right there I knew the outlook that I had was WRONG! [As I looked through the course material] I remember thinking, this is going to be different than what I thought.

Breihan describes what history courses, in his opinion, should do:

> The difference between basic historical study, of the sort that ought to go on in high school, and history as what historians actually *do*—is argument. History textbooks, for example, attempt balanced, comprehensive narratives of past events. Historians don't read them. They read (and write) opinionated arguments about what the past was like, and they often say why contemporary eyewitnesses and even other historians had it wrong. College history courses should introduce students to the world of what historians actually do. This usually involves introducing them for the first time to the concept of conflicting opinions in print, which is often difficult for them to grasp, and teaching them to recognize and adopt a critical approach to the opinions of others. This is combined with assigning them to develop their own opinions and to argue them against opposing points of view.

Breihan's history department had specified a goal of cultural literacy for this course as well, and the readings and lectures accordingly contained a great deal of factual material. But Breihan felt that this material was best learned by being used in argument.

THE ARGUER/DEBATER ROLE

The professional-in-training role (pp. 8–9) that Breihan wanted was the role that during data analysis we came to call "arguer" or "debater." It was different in emphasis, as we will see, from Sherman's expected role of business decision maker, though Breihan, like Sherman, tried to move students from mere text-processor or lay roles into the appropriate professional-in-training role.

Because few of Breihan's freshman and sophomore CORE students would major in history, he expected them to use historical material as evidence to argue questions of concern to citizens involved in the public life of the nation. Many of Breihan's essay questions therefore cast students in the role of politician (senator, advisor to a ruler) or of citizen/analyst who applies historical knowledge to current world concerns. The titles of the three main units of Breihan's course were phrased as questions on such concerns:

Unit 1: Political stability—What is it worth?
(16th–18th centuries)

Unit 2: Economic growth—What does it mean?
(Industrial Revolution)

Unit 3: Why arm? Why fight? (World Wars and the Cold War)

The "Loyoliana" question is one of the options for Essay 1 at the end of Unit 1 (see Figure 4.1).

BREIHAN'S EMPHASIS ON GOOD/BETTER/BEST REASONING

Seventy-seven percent of Breihan's essay questions, like all of Sherman's, were in the good/better/best mode—here, for example, he asks what kind of government would be "best" for Loyoliana. Other questions involved actual historical situations: he asked the writer to be a U.S. senator who must decide whether to vote for ratification of the N.A.T.O. treaty and then must explain that decision in a letter to constituents. In still others, the student as historian/citizen-in-training argued a position to the teacher on, for example, whether Burke's or Paine's theories of government were more "valid."

BREIHAN'S EXPECTATIONS FOR FINISHED ESSAYS

Figure 4.2 summarizes Breihan's expectations for the finished essays. Our analysis relies on the various handouts Breihan used to explain

---

You have been approached by General Perez, dictator of . . . Loyoliana, for advice about politics. General Perez would like to bring about reform in his . . . country, where the relative positions of the relatively small landowning elite and the majority of impoverished inhabitants resemble France in 1789. He is willing to leave office peacefully and hand over his powers to a constitutional government. Yet he fears anarchy—Loyoliana had a serious civil war 40 years ago that killed thousands. He is also a keen student of European politics, 1500–1800, and is worried that reform might go too far and become a bloody revolution like the one in France. That is why he has come to you. He knows that you were a good student in the early part of History 101 at Loyola College, where you studied such matters with great intensity. He will not be convinced by any arguments or facts about other political systems (like those of the U.S.A. or U.S.S.R. today); he wants you to draw your arguments about government and examples to prove them entirely from the record of the European past during the three centuries between 1500 and 1800. He also requires that you answer any possible counterarguments against your recommendations. Prepare a report to General Perez along these lines. Be careful—the fate of millions may be at stake!

Figure 4.1. The Loyoliana Assignment.

Key words
used in class: **The essay should:**

issue	address the issue stated or implied in the question
opinion	by stating the student's opinion or
thesis	thesis that has been reached by
feelings	evidence from the standpoint of the student's feelings and values.
values	
	The student's opinion should be supported by specific, accurate
fact	facts/opinions found in the primary and secondary sources students read.
evidence	These facts and opinions should be used as evidence—that is,
connect	the student should connect the historical material to his/her
subtheses	own opinion by stating warrants and by using subtheses.
	The student should draw material from all or most of the relevant lectures and readings.
alternatives	In the argument, the student should acknowledge alternative
counter-	solutions/outcomes and should raise and answer the counter-
evidence/	evidence or counterarguments that would be expected from
argument	course readings or common sense.

Figure 4.2. Summary of Breihan's expectations for the essays.

his expectations to students, his statements in class as recorded by Walvoord and the student observers (p. 23), the checksheet he returned to students with drafts and final essays, the comments and grades he assigned to essay drafts and final papers during the course, the log he kept during the course, interviews and discussions between Walvoord and Breihan both during and after the course, and Breihan's post-course primary trait analysis (p. 35).

We turn now to explore three areas of difficulty that arose as students tried to meet Breihan's expectations. In each area, we focus on how students developed across the semester and on how Breihan's teaching methods appeared to structure and nurture that development. In the third area—using discipline-based methods to arrive at a position and to support it with evidence—we also explore some differences between good/better/best reasoning in Breihan's and Sherman's classes, as well as aspects of Breihan's teaching methods that, on the basis of our study, he decided to change.

DIFFICULTIES WITH STATING A POSITION

THE NATURE OF THE DIFFICULTIES

When they entered the class, Breihan's students generally expected to play the text-processor role (p. 9), not to state intellectual positions of their own. In the fourth week of the course, a freshman we call Tracy Wagner wrote in her log,

> I haven't done things like this before. In high school we took the answers straight from the book. I am not in the habit of developing arguments.

Stating a position has seemed hard for students in other academic settings. Though Sherman specifically asked students to defend a stadium site, 16 percent of his class of junior and senior business majors stated no stadium location, and another 11 percent tacked on a decision only as an afterthought to their textbook summaries (p. 71).

In the 1988 National Assessment of Educational Progress, when eleventh graders were asked to take a stand and argue their position against an opposing point of view, nearly 33 percent did not state a position (Applebee et al. 1990).

STUDENTS' DEVELOPMENT

Breihan had good success in teaching his students to state a position. By the seventh week, when they drafted Essay 1 in class, every student in the focus group of nineteen students stated a position and then tried to support that position with evidence (for focus group see p. 40 and Appendix B). Further, all but one of the nineteen students stated the position in the first paragraph or two of the essay. The one student who did not—Tracy Wagner, who was "not in the habit of developing arguments"—devoted the first 40 percent of her draft to an encyclopedia-like report that began "Edmund Burke was born in . . ." But even she eventually got to a statement of her position on the issue.

HOW BREIHAN'S TEACHING METHODS HELPED STUDENTS LEARN TO STATE A POSITION

Our data suggest that Breihan's teaching methods helped students learn to state positions in the following ways:

Visible Issue Orientation

Breihan titled each unit with an issue-oriented question that implied a position (e.g., "Unit 1: Political stability—what is it worth?"). These issues were printed in the syllabus and at the head of the lecture outline that Breihan gave his students at the beginning of the semester. Walvoord observed that most students kept the outline in front of them during the class session, and many made notes directly on it; thus the issues were constantly before the students' eyes.

Daily Focused Writing

Many of the daily, in-class writing exercises focused on issues. For example, Breihan's instruction sheet for a number of the exercises began with the question, "What is the issue at stake in this chapter?" Only then would succeeding questions on the sheet address the specific readings for that day. Several students remarked in their logs or on their tapes that these questions about the "issue at stake" became habitual for them whenever they began a reading assignment for Breihan's course. The focus on issues, then, pervaded those areas—

readings and class sessions—where students might otherwise have expected merely to be acting as text processors, storing up facts. The exercises directly guided the way students approached their textbook—one of the sources of difficulty in Sherman's class.

Further, the daily writings gave students practice in stating a position before they wrote their essays. One daily writing assignment shortly before Essay 1 asked students to state in a single paragraph which solution to 17th-century anarchy—the English or the French type of government—they personally found most reasonable and attractive. This exercise served as a direct preparation for Essay 1 where, for example, the Loyoliana question asked students to recommend a type of government to General Perez.

Finally, the daily writings, coupled with a series of debates, gave students the time, information, and experience that made them ready to adopt positions. Before the in-class draft of Essay 1, students had written and debated a number of times and from different angles 17th-century French absolutism and the Glorious Revolution in England. Their logs and tapes show them reacting to the issues, expressing likes and dislikes, hashing over various positions, and getting ready to take a stand.

In-Class Debates

The seven in-class debates held at various points in the semester also reinforced the process of taking a stand on an issue. For example, shortly before they wrote Essay 1, students participated in a debate in which half the class argued that Louis XIV was a "good king" and half the class argued that he was not. (Breihan consciously sacrificed subtlety of historical interpretation in order to emphasize the importance of taking a clear stand on an issue.) The debates were a visible and prominent feature of the course for students, who mentioned them frequently in their logs, notes, and dormitory study groups. Students in two dormitory study groups who taped their sessions for us discussed who said what in specific debates, weighed the relative merit of various debate teams, and redebated some of the issues. The seven debates cast students visibly and physically in the role of arguer/debater (not of text processor) and encouraged them to read their assignments with the goal of preparing for the upcoming debates.

In-Class Discussions

The in-class discussions likewise emphasized the importance of taking a stand. Quoted below is an excerpt from a class Walvoord visited during the fourth week. First, notice that the written exercise students have brought to class is the basis for the discussion—the course is assignment centered; writing directly relates to what happens in class and to the central goals of the course. Second, note how Breihan emphasizes "turning the corner" from mere summary to taking a stand. (The discussion contains other lessons as well—about how to raise and answer counterarguments and how to support a position with evidence, which are the topics of the last two sections of this chapter.)

At the point where the classroom discussion begins, Breihan asks the same question as the exercise sheet students have just submitted:

> *Breihan*: How can the letter by Colbert be used as evidence on the issue of whether Louis is a good or a bad king?
>
> *Vicky Ware*: [summarizes the reading]
>
> *Breihan*: [reinforces her, but pushes her further] Everything you've said is right, but you need to turn one little corner.
>
> *Ware*: [hesitates]
>
> *Breihan*: [rephrases his question]
>
> *Ware*: He [Louis XIV] was good.
>
> *Breihan*: [exults] YES!

The "corner" is to move from merely summarizing Colbert's letter to saying that the material can be used to support an argument that Louis was a good king. Breihan tells the class he wants them to state their positions ("opinions") boldly: "be *that* heavy-handed in your writing." They must take a stand; then they must "make the connection" that links the historical material to their opinion about Louis, so that the historical material is not merely included, but acts "as evidence" to support the student's opinion. Breihan also suggests that, to make the connection between specific information and their own opinions, students can say, *"Louis XIV was a good king because...."* (Later in the chapter, we will see how Bonnie Kraft adopted this linguistic formula as a key to her reasoning about good/better/best issues.)

Further lessons about how to form and support opinions emerge in a multi-student exchange which Breihan orchestrates later in the same class period:

> *Bonnie Kraft*: [summarizes part of a reading selection in response to Breihan's question]
>
> *Monica Rhodes*: [summarizes another part of it]
>
> *Breihan*: How does it go, this dispute? Mr. McConnell?
>
> *Jim McConnell*: [answers with summary of the argument]
>
> *Breihan*: So how would you use this as evidence [on the central issue of the day's discussion]?

The same question about evidence has been asked on that day's exercise sheet. The lesson is that readings are not merely to be summarized, they are to be used as evidence for a position.

> *McConnell*: [responds satisfactorily]
>
> *Breihan*: Anybody look at it differently? Mr. Nessay?
>
> *Jerry Nessay*: [responds]

Breihan has introduced counterargument, a necessary part of any successful essay in his course. He is also emphasizing that various opinions may arise in the class, even though students are all reading the same material.

> *Breihan*: Yes, but you've made some very general statements. Get to *this* document. Miss Ware?
>
> *Ware*: [begins, but stops]
>
> *Breihan*: How do you know Louis was bargaining here—let's get specific. Let's get to the document.

Breihan pushes for specificity and for reference to the day's readings—both important lessons for success on the essays.

> *Ware*: [silence]
>
> *Sharon Drake*: [bails her out]
>
> *Breihan*: [leads Drake, as she makes the argument that Louis was autocratic]

Again, Breihan is insisting that students take stands and construct arguments in the class, not merely summarize readings.

> *Breihan*: Look at the dates. It takes three years of dickering before he [Louis] dismisses the deputies. We have absolutism here, *but*. When he did go in, he didn't send the army in, he took just ten guys. This is the importance of information [i.e., the little piece of information about how long it took for the king to act and how few men were involved allows one to make a point]. So you could use this as Miss Ware and Miss Drake

did [to support the point that Louis was autocratic], *but* [he explains how the same reading selection could also be used to support a different point—that Louis was restrained in his use of absolute power].

Throughout this and other in-class discussions Breihan led his students through the process of taking a stand, supporting it with evidence, and defending it against counterargument—all part of the professional-in-training role of arguer/debater he expected from them.

Comments on Essay Drafts

Notice Breihan's last comment: Even Vicky Ware, who had made a beginning and then had to be bailed out, shared the credit for having made the point that Louis was autocratic. Breihan credited students with stating positions even when they had needed help in articulating those positions. He did the same in his responses to their essay drafts. The comments Breihan wrote at the end of a draft always began with a summary of the student's thesis and main points. Here is the opening of a typical comment:

> Mr. Carter:
> This essay puts forward a very clear thesis that a "strong government" is needed to end anarchy. After reviewing several alternatives, you end by saying that a mixed government on the English model would work best for Loyoliana.
> What is missing here is argument and evidence in favor of the thesis that you state so clearly. WHY would this system work so well? [The comment continues with further questions and suggestions for revision.]

Breihan's habit of addressing students by their surnames and crediting them with positions was intended to help them act like mature adults and scholars who take positions and defend them. His comment to Carter opened in much the same way he would open a published article in which he first stated the argument of another historian, then addressed the strengths and weaknesses of that argument. Thus the conversation between Breihan and his students took on the cast of professionals participating in a dialogue about historical issues.

Breihan's practice of identifying an argument with the student who had made it also reinforced the concept that argument in history is made by individuals who may be more-or-less accurate and astute, and who work from various biases, and that in their own writing students were expected to cite the authors of arguments they included.

Checksheet

Another teaching method that emphasized the importance of assuming a position was the checksheet that Breihan gave students at the beginning of the semester (Figure 4.3).

Breihan had constructed the checksheet based on his observations of students' essays over several years. Each item on the checksheet described a type of paper Breihan actually received, beginning with the least successful and going up to the most successful. Rough grade equivalents were:

Items	Grade
1–4	F
5	D
6–9	C
10	B
11	A

On the checksheet, stating a position appears as the first characteristic in every item from 7 to 11. The breakdown of grade values above also shows that students, in order to get a "C" or above, had to state a position. The checksheet, then, was one way Breihan did what, as we have mentioned, Kurfiss (1988) found in her survey of successful courses that teach critical thinking: the teacher makes expectations clear (pp. 88–89).

Breihan took pains to make this sheet highly visible to students. A copy of the checksheet was included in the packet of materials they received at the beginning of the semester. Breihan marked a copy of the checksheet and returned it along with his written comments and the draft. Later, each student resubmitted the revised essay together with the draft and checksheet, and Breihan made another check on the checksheet to represent his evaluation of the revised essay. Usually the student had improved, and the second check was higher on the scale. The checksheet, as well as Breihan's other methods, embodied another characteristic Kurfiss (1988) notes—critical thinking is treated as a learnable skill, and the teacher offers support for students' development (pp. 88–89).

Breihan's Use of "Thesis" Terminology

Notice that the checksheet mentions the word *thesis*. Breihan frequently and deliberately used that term. He was consciously relating his course to the required freshman composition course, which his students would

An assessment of your essay is marked on the scale below. The scale describes a variety of common *types* of paper but may not exactly describe yours; my mark on the scale denotes roughly where it falls. More precise information can be derived from comments and conferences with the instructor.

_____ 1. The paper is dishonest.

_____ 2. The paper completely ignores the questions set.

_____ 3. The paper is incomprehensible due to errors in language or usage.

_____ 4. The paper contains very serious factual errors.

_____ 5. The paper simply lists, narrates, or describes historical data, and includes several factual errors.

_____ 6. The paper correctly lists, narrates, or describes historical data, but makes little or no attempt to frame an argument or thesis.

_____ 7. The paper states an argument or thesis, but one that does not address the questions set.

_____ 8. The paper states an argument or thesis, but supporting subtheses and factual evidence are:

　　_____ a. missing

　　_____ b. incorrect or anachronistic

　　_____ c. irrelevant

　　_____ d. not sufficiently specific

　　_____ e. all or partly obscured by errors in language or usage

_____ 9. The paper states an argument on the appropriate topic, clearly supported by relevant subtheses and specific factual evidence, but counterarguments and counterexamples are not mentioned or answered.

_____ 10. The paper contains an argument, relevant subtheses, and specific evidence; counterarguments and counterexamples are mentioned but not adequately answered:

　　_____ a. factual evidence either incorrect or missing or not specific

　　_____ b. linking subtheses either unclear or missing

　　_____ c. counterarguments and counterexamples not clearly stated; "straw man"

_____ 11. The paper adequately states and defends an argument, and answers all counterarguments and counterexamples suggested by:

　　_____ a. lectures

　　_____ b. reading assignments: specific arguments and authors are mentioned by name

　　_____ c. common sense

Figure 4.3. Breihan's checksheet for essays.

take the following semester, and in which "thesis" was heavily emphasized. By encouraging the thesis/support format, Breihan also forefronted the student's position.

Breihan's method here contrasted with Sherman's, which emphasized define/analyze/prescribe. Each format brought corresponding difficulties. The define/analyze/prescribe format offered a process for arriving at a position, but, if students used it as an organizing pattern in their papers, it postponed the student's position statement until the end. This sometimes invited students' difficulties with stating any position at all, or with linking a stated position to the definition and analysis that had preceded it (see Kurt Larson, p. 89). The thesis-first format, on the other hand, forefronts the students' decision but might encourage the view that forming a thesis is the first act of a writer, rather than the result of evolving investigation, planning, drafting, and revising. Breihan countered this danger by the daily, focused writing and the frequent debates which prepared students to state a thesis for each essay.

Essay Assignment Sheets

Breihan's Loyoliana essay assignment sheet (p. 101) does not begin with advice to the student to read the textbook, but rather with General Perez's dilemma. Breihan uses the words *advice* and *recommendations*, and, twice, the word *argument*, which he also used frequently in class, and which appears frequently in students' logs and tapes—they get the message that this class is about argument. The word *report*, which might imply mere textbook summary, appears at the very end, where its meaning has already been established by the earlier framework of "argument." Explicit instructions to answer counterarguments further define the students' position as arguer/debater.

Further, the assignment sheet does not specify a limited body of information that students could summarize, but only refers to "European politics 1500–1800." There is little on this assignment sheet that could possibly mislead students into thinking that they should summarize a portion of historical material they had studied. Everything drives toward the message that they are to assume the role of arguer/debater.

After analyzing all these teaching methods, it seemed to us that what helped students learn to take positions was not only the number and type of teaching methods Breihan used, but their consistency in reinforcing the arguer/debater role and in addressing students' approaches to textbooks, their use of the "thesis" model, and their pre-draft writing.

Joe Walker's log entry from the third week of the course shows how Breihan's teaching methods were helping students learn to state a position:

> I feel pretty good about the work done so far. It teaches you to think in a new way, which is somewhat difficult to adapt to after spending many years doing things the other way—that is spitting out facts instead of arguing opinions with support of factual evidence. Dr. Breihan explains things well, which is a big help.

As students adopted the arguer/debater role and learned that they must state a position, they began to confront two other areas of difficulty—managing complexity (primarily through raising and answering counterarguments) and using discipline-based methods to arrive at a position and to support it with evidence.

DIFFICULTIES WITH MANAGING COMPLEXITY: COUNTERARGUMENT

THE NATURE OF THE DIFFICULTIES

Breihan, like Sherman, expected that students would not merely use a "find reasons" strategy—listing advantages or reasons for their own positions—but that they would consider the complex aspects of an issue, entertain alternative solutions to a problem, and raise and answer counterevidence and counterarguments to their own positions. Breihan often used the term *counterargument* generically to refer to both counterevidence and counterargument, and we follow his practice.

In other academic settings researchers have found raising and answering counterarguments both rare and difficult for students. In the 1988 National Assessment of Educational Progress, when eleventh graders were asked to take a stand and argue their position against an opposing point of view, only 21 percent even briefly refuted some aspects of the opposing ideas (Applebee et al. 1990, p. 34). In a study by Perkins (1985), high school and college students offered only a few lines of argument to support, and far fewer in opposition to, their oral arguments on current issues. Cooper et al. (1984) asked a group of 400 SUNY at Buffalo entering freshmen to write persuasive essays during orientation week, then asked a group of SUNY teachers to rate those essays holistically. In a sample of 50 essays, only 16 percent of the students addressed an opposing point of view on the issue. Yet counterargument was important to the raters.

STUDENTS' DEVELOPMENT

In contrast to these other settings, 58 percent of Breihan's students, by the final essay in his class, raised at least one counterargument relevant to a stated position and responded to that counterargument with further argument and specific evidence.[1] Even by Essay 1, in the seventh week of the course, 47 percent of the students met that standard. Data from early logs and exercises indicate that this was not because Breihan's students expected or knew how to raise and answer counterarguments when they entered the course; on the contrary, as we have seen, most expected to "take answers out of the book." Rather, Breihan's teaching methods very early impressed upon students the importance of counterargument. And Breihan's methods taught students how to raise and answer counterarguments. Larry Crane, for example, got the message very early. In the third week of the course, he recorded in his log:

> As I read the selected passages, I tried to discern the writer's opinion (thesis) of Louis XIV. I looked for evidence in support of his opinion and *evidence in support of the opposite*. [Italics ours]

In the sixth week, preparing for the Loyoliana essay, he recorded that he jotted down "any ideas at all I had about the various aspects of the question, possible solutions, *counterarguments*, strategies, areas I need to investigate further, etc." (Italics ours). Like many other students, Crane early realized that, as he observed in his log on November 11, "counterarguments really thrill the professor!"

HOW BREIHAN'S TEACHING METHODS HELPED STUDENTS LEARN TO RAISE AND ANSWER COUNTERARGUMENTS

Choice of Texts

Breihan used four textbooks, one of which was a traditional, chronological account of events. A student who clung to the text-processor role and who received a "C" in the course wrote in her course evaluation at the end of the semester that this text was "straight facts stated out, easy to understand. We didn't use it enough." As the student noted, Breihan placed his major emphasis on other texts that modeled and encouraged counterargument. One such text was a collection of primary and secondary readings arranged by issue—for example, evaluating Louis XIV. The other two texts were writings of Edmund Burke and Thomas Paine. Thus Breihan chose and heavily emphasized textbooks that presented conflicting viewpoints on issues, making it difficult for students to see one book as a single, monolithic "right" representation of historical facts. Moreover, many of the authors in the textbooks themselves raised and answered counterarguments, thus providing further models for Breihan's students.

The Language of the Assignment Sheets and the Checksheet

Assignment sheets specifically mentioned the need for counterarguments, as we saw in the Loyoliana question. Further, Breihan's checksheet (Figure 4.3), which students had from the first day of class and which Breihan used as part of his response to their drafts and final essays, featured counterargument as the final, crowning trait that distinguished an "A" paper from all the rest (item 11).

Response to Drafts

Twenty-one percent of the meaning-changing comments (p. 40) Breihan wrote on students' essay drafts concerned counterarguments.[2] Breihan both praised counterarguments when he found them and suggested them when he did not. He frequently mentioned specific authors or positions that the student should answer; for example, on one essay he suggested that

> You need to answer the counterarguments contained in Ashton.

To a student who had included a number of counterarguments but not answered them very fully, he wrote:

> You might also elaborate on the game laws counterargument and do more to counter Bossuet than simply to bring up St. Simon (who says St. S. is right??)

Our data reveal that 93 percent of Breihan's meaning-changing comments on essay drafts resulted in some kind of revision.[3] Breihan's draft response then led students to consider counterarguments as one of the chief issues in their revisions.

In-Class Discussions

The in-class discussions, often based on the daily writings, aided comprehension and reinforced the notion that the readings were arguments on an issue. In the in-class discussion reproduced earlier, Breihan had asked for a summary of some readings by saying, "How does it go, this *dispute?*" In the class discussion, as we saw, Breihan led his students through a dialogue of argument and counterargument.

Debates

The seven in-class debates helped students in many ways. On a basic level, they helped with reading comprehension—not only with understanding the meaning of statements in the readings, but also with understanding that the readings were themselves debates, answering other voices, and that they could be used as ammunition for the students' own debates. Bonnie Kraft, reading the assignments in Burke and Paine, recorded in her log:

> The readings were difficult and confusing. I spent much time rereading passages to make sure I understood what each man was arguing. This assignment took about 6 or 7 hours.

During the Burke-Paine debate, still unsure of herself, she sat silent, allowing her classmates to carry the argument, remarking in her log later:

> Today's debate was a good experience and turned out exactly as I thought. I [had] missed some major points in the readings of Burke and Paine. I left class with a better understanding of the assignments.

After this debate, another student recorded the insight that "Burke and Paine are counterarguments to each other!!"

Debate as an Aid to Dialogic Thinking

In the high-success students' essays, argument and counterargument proceed in a constant, seesaw pattern of dialogue on both the macro and micro levels. For example, Larry Crane's in-class draft of the Loyoliana essay begins by arguing that the "English plan" of constitutional government has strong features that Loyoliana should adopt. Then, addressing the counterarguments, he acknowledges that this English plan has shortcomings, thereby setting himself up to argue that it should be modified with some features of the "French plan"—absolutism—and some additions of his own. (In a wonderful adoption of the professional-in-training role, he calls this amalgam by his own name—"the Crane Plan.") At the macro level, the overall organization of his paper is thus a dialogue of argument, counterargument, and answer. But such dialogue is also integrated at micro levels in every section of his paper. An example is this section, in which he addresses the kind of executive that Loyoliana should have (labels at left are ours):

Argument	Another shortcoming [of the English plan] was the succession of the monarch through heredity. Paine is right in saying that talents and abilities cannot have hereditary descent. An heir to the throne may have no desire or talent to rule. What is worse, kings sometimes have congenital birth defects. Charles II of Spain was unable to father a child and the result was the War of Spanish Succession. Louis XIV was a child when he inherited his title and the Fronde ensued. The crown may even fall to a foreigner.
	For Loyoliana, a non-hereditary executive possessing talent and abilities and acceptable to a majority of legislators is clearly called for.
Counter	Hume argues, however, that such an "elected monarch" would be motivated to accumulate as much wealth as possible before giving way to his successor. Also, any elected monarch would still harbor friendships and animosities and use his position to address them. But Hume
Answer	also writes that people voting by their representatives form the best democracy. Could not those representatives then be counted on to elect a leader of limited powers who had the interest of the nation and the people at heart?

Other paragraphs and sections of essays proceed similarly in Crane's and other students' essays. The frequency and importance of the dialogue at macro and micro levels are shown by a count of the types of connections that link ideas to one another in a sample of Breihan's students' essays.[4] (We used Bonnie Meyer's categories to classify types of connections, p. 42.) As Figure 4.4 illustrates, the kinds of connections that introduce counterargument or answers to counterargument are second highest in frequency. Further, the "A" essays have substantially more such connections than the "C" essays.

This dialogic pattern of argument, counterargument, and answer was a unique feature of Breihan's class, different from the other classes we studied. It appears to us that Breihan evoked it because he made very clear that he wanted it and he taught students how to do it.

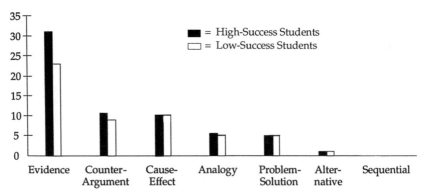

Figure 4.4. Types of connections among ideas in first three levels of hierarchy of high-success and low-success student essays. Evidence: Facts and opinions from course readings, presented as evidence (Meyer's "descriptive"). Counterargument: Counterargument and counterevidence, and answers by the writer (Meyer's "adversative"). Cause-Effect: Causes or effects (Meyer's "causation"). Analogy: (Meyer's "analogy"). Problem-Solution: (Meyer's "response"). Alternative: Any alternative not presented as a counterargument (Meyer's "alternative"). Sequential: Sequence is the only connective (Meyer's "sequential"). N = 10 essays: one high-success and one low-success essay (randomly chosen) on each of five topics spaced across the semester.

The debates seemed particularly effective in modeling the dialogic pattern of constant argument, counterargument, and answer. The teams in the debate did not simply each speak once or twice in a pro-con, one-side–other-side fashion. Instead, they contributed points in a basketball-like fashion, each side making a point, then yielding the floor to the other side, who could counter the point or begin a new one. In the debate about Louis XIV, for example, a student on one team might make the point that Louis built Versailles—a cultural and artistic landmark still admired for its elegance and beauty. Someone from the other side, however, might counter that Versailles was financed on the backs of desperately poor peasants cruelly taxed. Then the first side countered that or raised a new point.

Successful students' planning, as revealed in their logs and tapes, often exhibited a debate-like dialogue. One student described his habit of "arguing with myself" while planning a paper. Bonnie Kraft shows this dialogic way of thinking in an oral planning session for an exercise just after the Louis XIV debate, in the fourth week. Students were to make a one-paragraph statement and defence of what they thought was the best solution to 17th-century anarchy—the absolutism of Louis XIV or the limited monarchy of Britain. As she generated reasons why the English solution was better, she immediately addressed counterarguments, as these excerpts from her think-aloud tape illustrate:

Argument	This leads to another reason I think the English solution was better, because, um, because um, there were checks and balances. [she talks through some evidence and explanation] But under the absolutism in France, Louis could do or make the decisions that he wanted; he didn't have anybody to regulate him or to tell him that that was wrong and that wasn't a good thing to do. He just did what he wanted to do.
Counter	I'm not saying that Louis didn't do good for the people or what he thought was good, but
Answer	no one was there to regulate what he did. . . .
Counter	The English solution didn't go without any problems. I mean there was a problem in finding someone that would succeed William and Mary and, um, and/or the Prince of Orange.
Answer	But the system is so much more democratic. . . . I wonder if I could include, or to say that the English wasn't perfect, but the good points outweighed the bad. I think that would be a good way to present this essay—to say that the English were good because they were doing good for the people.
Argument	They did set up a framework of government and looked toward the future.
Counter	But then again there was always the problem of succession.
Answer	But they solved that problem [3 second silence] with the, uh, with the Hanoveria- Han, Ha-, um, HanOverian succession, HanoVERian, I guess, HanoVERian succession.
Counter	Or that, um, there was a problem with the title *prime minister,*
Answer	but rather Walpole worked out the system for that.

Kraft's planning and that of a number of other high-success students was characterized throughout by this dialogic pattern. Other researchers have also noted the role of dialogue in argument. Basseches (1980) argues that mature critical thinking is "dialectical," that it moves beyond Piaget's formal operations to the ability to examine critically one's own ideas from an opposing point of view. Hays, Brandt, and Chantry (1988) suggest that this dialectical ability originates as literal internal dialogues between the thinker and one who might question or oppose the thinker's position. Our study of Breihan's class suggests that internal dialogues may be taught or evoked for students in a class where, over and over, in a number of ways, language is employed in a debate-like pattern.

Debate as an Aid to Pre-Draft Writing

Breihan used the debates also to help students with pre-draft writing. On the blackboard, he jotted down, in columns, the points the teams made, then drew chalk arrows between an argument in one column and its counterargument in the other. Similar arrows appeared in students' pre-draft writing, helping them to transcend a mere pro-con or one-side–other-side organization and to achieve dialogue on both the macro and micro levels. Pete Lane was a student who lacked counterargument in Essay 1 but achieved it by Essay 2. In the interim he had begun to use arrows in his notes in imitation of Breihan's blackboard models (Figure 4.5). A number of students likewise used arrows to make pros and cons talk to each other, some writing in the margins of their reading notes *counterarg* with an arrow to the argument under attack.

Jim McConnell combined pro/con with argument/counterargument in his written plan for Essay 3:

Reasons For

Arguments   Counters
[He lists them]   [He lists them]

Reasons Against

Lane's and McConnell's pre-draft writings use the two axes—horizontal and vertical—to bring different types of information into a disciplined relationship in order to arrive at and support a decision—the third task of good/better/best reasoning (p. 12). A related form of dual axis pre-draft writing—the factor-rating chart—was described in Sherman's textbook, but students did not use it (p. 75). In Breihan's class, the

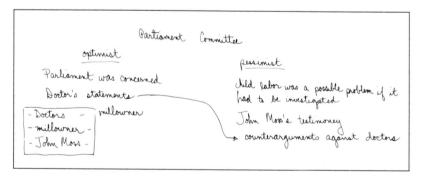

Figure 4.5. Pete Lane's notes (*Optimists held that the Industrial Revolution was good for workers; pessimists held that it was harmful.)

dual axis forms students used were actually written on the board and they grew from a dialogic in-class debate.

Even more flexible than dual axis arrows or charts was the system of pre-draft writing Bonnie Kraft used for Essay 1. She noted "counterarg" in the margins of her reading notes, then cut up the notes and taped them back together to form a very detailed outline in which arguments and counterarguments were interspersed in a dialogic pattern. This pattern then governed her essay draft.

Once Pete Lane had begun to use arrows in his notes, he began to write essays that raised and answered counterarguments and even to help other students to do so. Here is such an exchange within a dormitory study group the night before the in-class draft of Essay 2. Notice that the other student, Sara James, envisions counterargument as the admission of weakness by the writer, while Lane portrays it as an actual dialogue among opposing voices. Lane also uses the word *sceptical*, which Breihan often used to describe the way students were to approach their sources.

> *Sara James*: [What about counterargument in Essay 2?]
>
> *Pete Lane*: That's like saying, England was a good government, look at England. Then talk about England. Then you say, but it did have its flaws.
>
> *Sara James*: So are we supposed to say, this may seem a little shaky in this area, but blah, blah, blah?
>
> *Pete Lane*: Don't say it like that. Not that terminology.
>
> *Sara James*: I know, but that train of thought? . . . .
>
> *Pete Lane*: It's like this, Sara. Talk about England and how great it was, a mixed government with its parliament, and its king. Well then why did Cromwell step in? That's the question someone might ask you. [In deep, hokey voice of the antagonistic someone:] "Well, if England was so great, why did Cromwell step in?" And then you have to talk about [preventing anarchy]. But then you look at France—no anarchy. But then why the French Revolution? You got to keep asking questions. Just like, be sceptical about what you're saying.
>
> *Sara James*: I was going to ask you if I should . . . just present the whole thing without any possibility of there being counterarguments, but firstly that's, like, almost impossible, and secondly that's not what he's looking for. You're probably right.

Lane tried to help James with the sceptical, dialogic frame of mind necessary to frame counterarguments, and with the linguistic framework in which counterarguments are couched. It is no surprise that in writing his in-class Essay 2 the next day, he incorporated counterarguments and answers to counterarguments. James was less successful because her essay lacked both effective organization and sufficient specific information from the readings, but the pre-draft notes she had made during or after the study session contained specific passages marked "argument" and "counterargument."

In this section, then, we have explored some teaching methods that seemed to help students achieve the arguer/debater role by raising and answering counterarguments. The methods included Breihan's choice of textbooks, the language of the assignment sheets and the checksheet, his response to drafts, the in-class discussions, and the seven in-class debates. But again, more than the number and type of teaching methods was Breihan's intense, careful guidance of students' thinking and writing processes, his frequent feedback, and his consistent, strong focus, with all his teaching methods pointing students toward developing their ability to raise and to answer counterarguments. Breihan wanted his students to adopt the arguer/debater role, and in many ways the whole class became a debate, with both oral and written language used dialogically at many levels.

DIFFICULTIES WITH USING DISCIPLINE-BASED METHODS TO ARRIVE AT (AND SUPPORT) A POSITION

In this section, we take up a third area of difficulty—using discipline-based methods to arrive at the position and to support it with evidence. Again, as in the first two sections, we discuss the nature of the difficulties, students' development, and how Breihan's teaching methods affected students' learning.

In addition, we have two other points to make in this section: (1) there were some significant differences in the models for good/better/best reasoning used in Sherman's and Breihan's classes. Exploring these models can contribute to an understanding of what constitutes "good" thinking and writing in various academic disciplines or classes; and (2) our study revealed some areas in which Breihan wanted to change his teaching methods.

We make all these points by telling the story of how Bonnie Kraft learned to use discipline-based methods to arrive at a position and to defend it with evidence. Accordingly, this section is organized differently from the rest, though it addresses similar issues.

Bonnie Kraft was the student who realized on the first day of class that her previous notion about the text-processor role that would be required for the class had been "WRONG!" We've seen how she used dialogic thinking as she planned arguments and counterarguments about constitutional monarchy, and how she cut up and taped her notes to create an outline for her Loyoliana essay. During the first six weeks of the course, however, as she was learning the techniques of counterargument in preparation for her Loyoliana essay, Kraft struggled hard to learn how to use discipline-based methods to arrive at a position and to support it with evidence—a struggle that other students experienced as well. The story of her struggle comes from her log, think-aloud tapes, notes, and drafts for the daily writings and debates that preceded the Loyoliana essay, and from interviews conducted by a freshman composition student during the course (p. 27) and by Walvoord three years later.

Kraft entered the course with several strengths that helped her in her struggle: she was well motivated, she had good learning skills, she set goals and worked deliberately toward them, and she could take detailed notes about her reading. At 530, however, her verbal SAT score was 12 points below the mean for the class and about 100 points below the mean for the other students who received "A" as a final course grade. Interviewed by Walvoord three years after the course, she remembered it as "THE hardest course I ever had," but also one of the most useful because "there was a lot of writing involved and that was something that I hadn't come into so far" and as a result "my writing improved so much."

TEACHING THE HISTORICAL METHOD: FOUR STAGES

Breihan's teaching worked in many ways to help Kraft. One of the things he did was to structure in four stages the use of discipline-based methods to arrive at a position and to support it with evidence. Figure 4.6 shows selected exercises and debates that formed the four stages.

Stage 1: Showing How a Single Reading Can Be Used as Evidence

Kraft achieved:
Detailed summary of sources

Exercises	Skills

STAGE 1: SHOWING HOW A SINGLE READING CAN BE USED AS EVIDENCE

Author's Purpose and Summary: Week 1

What do you know about the textbook author?	Recognize that history is written by people who reflect their cultural biases.
What can you guess? When was the text written? published?	Pay attention to author's subheads.
List its subheadings and summarize a chapter.	Summarize.

Narrative of the English Civil War

Write a one-paragraph narrative incorporating eight terms provided by Breihan.	Summarize events accurately.

Analysis of Anarchic Episodes: Week 2

From eyewitness accounts of 17th-century riots, find evidence of the following factors: economic, political, social, religious, etc.	Become familiar with various analytical categories, and use them to categorize evidence.

Primary Sources on Louis XIV: Week 3

What is the issue at stake in this collection of documents?	Understand how "primary source" material can be used as evidence by stating connections between eyewitness material and opinions on the historical issue.
Who was the author of each document? When did he/she live?	
How can his/her material be used as evidence on this issue?	
[Questions repeated for each source]	

Secondary Sources on Louis XIV: Week 4

What is the issue at stake?	Understand what a "secondary source" is.
Who is the author and when did he/she write?	Use secondary sources as models for shaping historical arguments.
What is his/her position on the issue?	Understand how arguments are backed by evidence.
How does she/he back it up?	

continued

Figure 4.6. The four stages of learning to use discipline-based methods to arrive at a position and to support it with evidence

Figure 4.6 (cont.)

STAGE 2: CONTRIBUTING TO AN ARGUMENT ON AN ASSIGNED HISTORICAL OPINION

Louis XIV Debate Worksheet

Prepare notes in support of your assigned position on whether or not Louis was a "good king" plus counterarguments against the opposing opinion.

Understand that history is argument about the past.
Collect evidence for a position.
Take notes that allow easy access to evidence during debate.

Second Chance on Louis XIV Debate

Write two points that were not discussed in the class debate.
For extra credit say why you did not say them in the debate.

Learn skills and points not used in the debate.

STAGE 3: CHOOSING ONE'S OWN POSITION ON A HISTORICAL ISSUE AND BRIEFLY DEFENDING IT WITH EVIDENCE

Best Solution to Anarchy Essay: Week 5

In a one-paragraph essay, state which solution to the problem of 17th-century anarchy—French or English—you personally find more realistic and attractive. Try to explain why you feel the way you do and to back your feelings with evidence.

Choose one's own position.
Address the relevant issue.
Support the position with evidence.

STAGE 4: CHOOSING ONE'S OWN POSITION AND DEFENDING IT IN A FULL ESSAY, INCLUDING COUNTERARGUMENTS AND ANSWERS TO COUNTERARGUMENTS

Essay 1: Week 7

Select from among 3 essay questions:
1. The Loyoliana question.
2. Whose theories about the French Revolution—Burke's or Paine's—were more "valid"?
3. From class readings by Burke and Paine, infer their views, pro and con, of Louis XIV's reign.

Use several techniques for historical argument: analyzing problem, stating position, supporting it with evidence, answering counterarguments.

Kraft had difficulty:
   Recognizing bias in sources
   Stating the specific arguments the source could support
   Assessing a source's value as evidence

Bonnie Kraft struggled during the first weeks of the course to move from the text-processor to the arguer/debater role and to learn how to construct arguments as Breihan expected. In the third week her difficulty showed up clearly in the exercise analyzing primary source documents on Louis XIV (see Figure 4.6).

The assignment sheet asked students first, "What is the issue at stake in this chapter?" Like most students, Kraft correctly wrote, "The issue at stake is whether Louis XIV was a good king." The next questions asked for each of the primary source readings, "How can [this reading] be used as evidence on the issue at stake?" After completing the exercise, Kraft remarked in her log,

> I really am not sure I did this assignment in the way the Professor planned it to be done. I took specific examples to back up what I thought the point of [the reading assignment] is.

For the finished exercise she had merely summarized the textbook, focusing on specific information and on "examples" as her way of expanding her writing. (In Sherman's class, "example" was a common mode for text-processing students to relate the assignment's issue or problem to their textbooks. See p. 72.) Here is Kraft's exercise:

> Saint-Simon felt Louis XIV, as an absolute monarch was a bad thing because he had little education; he had spies everywhere that could tell him everything and when Courtenvaux made this known to the public, Courtenvaux position was taken from him; members of the Church sometimes acted as he wanted. For example, Abbe de Vatteville, ordained a priest, committed crimes yet made a deal with the government to be pardoned and live as abbey of Baume; in 1706, France lost wars and sustained losses on account of the cost of war. When Chamillart, the head of both finance and war department, could not carry on affairs due to lack of money, he asked to be relieved of his position; however, the king refused; finally, there was a tax put on baptisms and marriages because the need for money was so great. Poor people began to perform marriages themselves and their children were considered illegitimate. Peasants revolted against this tax, and it eventually had to be lifted. Louis was hurting the poor when he claimed he was trying to help them.

Kraft's shortcomings are evident when we see how a more successful student, Tom Siegel, after summarizing the reading, went on to assess it as evidence:

This all presents Louis as a bad king; however we must not forget that this was written after Louis' death and by a member of the social class which had the least to gain from Absolutism and who were viewed by Louis as the biggest threat to his person and his rule. But the material itself could be used to support the ideas that Louis' vanity made him a bad king; or that he was merciless in his demand for money to squander; or that he acted only on his own best interest rather than the best interest of the country by spying on his subjects and appointing ignorant people to positions of authority.

Siegel did several things that Kraft did not do:

- recognized bias in the source
- stated the specific arguments the source could support
- assessed the source's value as evidence

Breihan's written comments on Kraft's exercise called for her to transcend summary and to evaluate the evidence. For example, next to Kraft's summary of Bishop Bossuet's rationale for absolute monarchy (not reproduced here), Breihan wrote "true?" a version of another common question he wrote on many papers, "Yes, but is he [she] right?"

Another way that Breihan helped Kraft and other students transcend mere summary was through in-class discussion. Earlier in the chapter we analyzed the discussion that Breihan led on the day the Primary Sources exercise was handed in (pp. 105–107). After that discussion, Kraft, like several other students, wrote in her log, "I have a better understanding of the types of answers Professor Breihan expects because of the lecture on Primary Resources [*sic*]."

In Stage 1, then, Kraft was still merely summarizing readings, not fully treating them as evidence within the discipline-based method for arriving at a position and supporting it. Breihan gave specific feedback to her and other similar students by comments on their exercises and by in-class discussions of the exercises. Kraft came to some realization that she had not done what her teacher expected, but felt that she was coming to a "better understanding." She was switching from the text-processor role to the arguer/debater role, which was Breihan's version of the professional-in-training role that all four teachers expected from their students. However, as her experiences in Stage 2 will further demonstrate, Kraft still lacked a basic understanding of *how to construct* the arguments she had begun to realize Breihan wanted her to make.

Stage 2: Contributing to an Argument
on an Assigned Historical Opinion

Kraft achieved:
Stating *why* something was good
Trying to find evidence
Constructing subtheses to organize source material
Using the teacher's linguistic formulas (e.g. "X is good because") but
  in a limited way
Trying, through revision, to bring herself closer to Breihan's expec-
  tations
Kraft had difficulty:
Transcending a limited "find good things" strategy
Forming an explicit definition of "good"
Recognizing evidence when she had it
Envisioning how to construct an argument to support a thesis
Understanding her teacher's previous written comments

Students entered the second stage of learning the historical method
when, in the third and fourth weeks, they had to collect evidence to
help their team support the position it had been assigned to defend
in the debate on whether Louis XIV was a "good king" (see Figure
4.6).

Good/Better/Best Reasoning in Breihan's Class

An analysis of Breihan's model for good/better/best reasoning as
opposed to Sherman's will clarify the problems that arose for Kraft at
this stage (see Figure 4.7).

Sherman's define/analyze/prescribe model emphasized definition
very heavily and reflected his explicit instruction for students to begin
with definition. Virtually all students in his class did so, but two major
problems materialized: (1) Some students did not relate the definition
to the analysis and prescription and (2) some students spent all their
time on definition and/or analysis (often paraphrased and summarized
from the textbook) and never got to a position or prescription at all.

Breihan, on the other hand, emphasized to students the need to

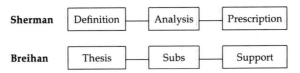

Figure 4.7. Sherman's and Breihan's models for good/better/best reasoning.

open with a statement of their position or "thesis" (Sherman's prescription), with the result, as we have seen, that virtually all of them learned to state a position. The hard part for Breihan's students, however, was stating a clear definition of "good." In his model, the definition was worked out through the subtheses or "subs." We can see the difference in Sherman's and Breihan's models by how each would critique this weak argument:

> Louis was a good king. Louis controlled the nobles and improved the military.

In Sherman's terms, what is missing is an opening definition of what a "good" king was for 17th-century France, and Sherman would encourage students to begin their decision-making process and their papers with that definition. But Breihan did not talk explicitly about definition at all. In Breihan's terms, the argument appropriately begins with a thesis (Louis was a good king), but is faulty because it does not "connect" the "thesis" to the "facts" (Louis controlled the nobles and improved the military).

Breihan's model for good/better/best reasoning is similar to that of Toulmin, Rieke and Janik (1984) in that the warrant and backing (which would contain a definition of "good") are in the middle, connecting the grounds (or historical information) to the claim (or thesis). See Figure 4.8. Our exploration of the models of good/better/best reasoning in Sherman's and Breihan's classrooms indicates that teachers or researchers who use the Toulmin model should be aware that the language and the placement of elements in relation to one another may vary by classroom or discipline, and that these differences may shape the students' difficulties.

Breihan had four ways of talking to his students about how to make the connection between thesis and facts:

1. He urged them to tell why something (e.g., controlling the nobles) was "good."

2. He told them they must "use as evidence" the historical facts and material from their readings.

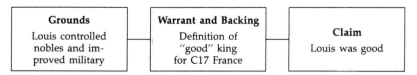

Grounds	Warrant and Backing	Claim
Louis controlled nobles and improved military	Definition of "good" king for C17 France	Louis was good

Figure 4.8. Breihan's model in the framework of Toulmin Logic.

3. He urged them to construct "subtheses" or "subs" to "connect the facts to the thesis."

4. He gave them a linguistic formula to develop the thesis: "Louis was good because. . . ."

Breihan's models for reasoning and his four ways of making connections shaped Kraft's and other students' learning in the second stage.

Bonnie Kraft's Second-Chance Exercise

In the in-class debate on Louis XIV, Kraft remained silent, leaving her teammates to carry the argument. She was still tied to textbook summary and unsure of herself in the role of debater. Three years later, she remembered that, in the first weeks of the course, "I was *so* intimidated."

The day after the debate, the Second Chance exercise asked students to write two points that no one had mentioned during the debate. On Kraft's think-aloud tape as she plans the exercise, she tries to use all four of the ways Breihan has suggested for connecting thesis and facts: telling why something was good, using facts as evidence, constructing subtheses, and using the linguistic formula "X is good because" (italics are ours):

> *I think that Louis was a good king because* that was what the people needed at the time. They needed someone to take control and to get their lives back in order, but I don't have any *evidence* to back that up, so I think I should just leave that out [13 sec. silence]. *I think Louis was a good king because* when he did come to rule, there was a lot of disorder. Finances were exhausted, the administration of justice was filled by money instead of selection, people were poverty-stricken, and Louis did what he felt was best to reform these things. You know, he [Louis] was the one to know about everything going on in France through reports, and people were allowed to petition him, and he developed new whole industries which stimulated the economy. That wasn't in the debate. But on my evaluation of primary resources [*sic*], Professor Breihan wrote, "Does this mean he was a good king?" So I don't know, I guess that's wrong. [She abandons the point.]

Kraft uses Breihan's formula "X is good because" to generate her two subtheses, each of which states one reason why Louis was "good." Kraft is also concerned about evidence to back her points. However, she does not understand what counts as evidence or how she could structure an argument about Louis. She makes a promising start at a definition of "good" as "what the people needed at the time," and she refers to the facts she has about the chaos in France. But she does not recognize those facts as "evidence" (defined by Breihan as "facts linked to argument"), which would show that France needed order more than anything else. So she uses Breihan's formula: "Louis was a good king because . . ." in a very limited way, merely generating things that Louis did and calling them good, without explaining why they were good in terms of the needs of 17th-century France. This find-good-things strategy is akin to the find-reasons strategy we saw in Sherman's class (p. 80). In both classes, the thesis/subthesis model made it easy for students to fall into that trap.

Kraft's difficulties in her think-aloud planning are compounded by her misunderstanding of Breihan's response to one of her earlier exercises—a response in which Breihan had again sought to alert her to the need for evaluating Louis XIV's rule. Breihan had written next to her summary of what Louis did: "Yes, but is this good?" In her planning for the Second Chance exercise, she remembers that earlier comment, misunderstands it, and abandons the whole point as "wrong" because she does not yet see how to integrate the issue of what was "good" in Louis' time. Kraft's decision to abandon the point altogether was a rather common strategy, especially for low-success students.[5]

Figure 4.9 shows Kraft's Second Chance exercise with her revisions marked. It is weak because, following her find-good-things strategy, she merely picked two points from her notes, made them into her subtheses, and then tried to justify at the end of each point why these things were good, without formulating an explicit definition of "good king."

Despite the difficulties we have discussed in her planning and in the exercise itself, Kraft's Second Chance exercise exhibits her progress in Stage 2. Although each paragraph of her exercise is essentially a summary of one reading, it takes a step beyond her reading-by-reading debate notes, which had opened each section with the name of the author ("Mousnier says. . . ."). In the Second Chance exercise, she opens each paragraph with a statement of the subthesis: "Louis was good because. . . ." The names of the writers being summarized under each subthesis are subordinated as a phrase ("according to Mousnier") or as the second sentence in the paragraph ("Voltaire writes. . . ."). She has begun to use subtheses to organize her information.

To state her subtheses, Kraft uses Breihan's formula, "Louis was good because." In her explanation for her silence in the debate, she also employs Breihan's language of specific evidence, thesis, and subtheses—words she had written several times in her class notes and her planning notes for Stage 2.

A third sign of Kraft's progress is that virtually all her revisions

[Single brackets are Kraft's. The underlined words were written later in the margins. We have indicated words that Kraft scratched out.]

1. Louis was a good king because, according to Mousnier, he tried to make opposing classes, the Bourgeouisie versus the Nobility, more equal in social standing. ~~This wa~~ In order to make the Bourgeoisie rise in the social scale, Louis chose ministers, counselors, and intendants from among the bourgeois officers. ~~By opposing the Nobility~~ At the same time, Louis opposed the Nobility. He kept them busy by ~~filling~~ having them fill most grades of the army and by creating the artificial society at Versailles. ~~In Louis' Letters to His Heirs, Louis says he feels the Nobility~~ This was good because Louis, by establishing an equilibrium ~~on the stu~~ between the bourgeoisie and the nobility, he also was able to establish ~~more unity and~~ more order ~~to the state. He also~~ in France.

2. Louis was a good king because he introduced discipline into the armies and developed new military ideas. Voltaire writes

"It was he [Louis] [brackets around Louis are Kraft's] who instituted the use of the bayonet affixed to the end of the musket" p. 44

"The manner in which artillery is used today is due entirely to him. He founded artillery schools." p. 45

"In 1688 [Louis] established thirty regiments of militia, ~~where were prove...These militia ha~~ which were provided and equipped by the communes. These militia trained for war but without abandoning the cultivation of their fields." p.45

[Next sentence was written in later] Inspector Generals and directors were used to report on the state of troops to Louis.

The strong armies could ensure more control within France ~~and could be used to expand France's borders. More control was exercised within France by. The armies could control more exercise control within France.~~ This was good because France now had military resources to fall back on whenever necessary. ~~Also, armies were not no longer uncontrollable within France. There were inspector generals and directors who reported on the state of the troops.~~ Armies ~~coul~~ also helped trade?...

[Two arrows also mark the above paragraph: one moves the first sentence to the very end; the other moves the "Also, armies" passage to the beginning of the paragraph.]

Extra. Credit. I thought, at the time of the debate, that these arguments ~~ideas~~ were not as important as the economic ideas. I also was not prepared to back up my thesis with specific evidence tied together with subtheses.

Figure 4.9. Bonnie Kraft's Second Chance exercise.

forswear further summary of her sources and insert sentences that attempt to answer Breihan's questions on her earlier exercise, "Was this good?" and "Why was this good?"

For extra credit students might tell why they had not originally made those points. Berkenkotter, Huckin, and Ackerman (1988) note how a new rhetoric graduate student, faced with a demanding new kind of discourse he must learn, went through a stage in which he communicated with his professors by personal notes—a forum which seemed, for a time, to help him deal with his insecurity in writing formal papers. Breihan's Second Chance exercise served much the same function for Kraft. She spent two hours on the page-long exercise and wrote in her log:

> This activity was worthwhile because it gave me the opportunity to explain my ideas in writing. [During the debate I had been] nervous about speaking and explaining myself in class.

In Stage 2, we have seen that Breihan asked students to contribute evidence to a team argument on an assigned historical position. Kraft was still basically organizing material reading by reading. She was still confused about the nature of evidence, about how to construct an argument to support her thesis, and about the role of a definition of "good" king for 17th-century France. She used merely a find-good-things strategy. Her confusion was compounded by a misunderstanding of one of Breihan's comments on a previous exercise. However, she made progress: she tried to state why Louis' actions were good, she tried to find evidence, she organized her Second Chance exercise around subtheses, she tried to use the linguistic formulas Breihan had modeled, and she revised to bring herself closer to Breihan's expectations. Her explanation about why she had not made her points during the debate reveals her insecurity in assuming the role of debater, but reveals, too, her eagerness to learn and her desire for Breihan's good opinion.

Stage 3: Choosing One's Own Position on a Historical Issue and Briefly Defending It with Evidence

Kraft achieved:
Stating a thesis
Using the teacher's linguistic formulas (e.g. "X is good because"),
but in a limited way
Testing her position against counterarguments

Kraft had difficulty:
Transcending a limited, "find good things" strategy
Formulating an explicit definition of "good" that addressed the "issues" Breihan had defined in the assignment
Distinguishing between "evidence" and "feelings"
Envisioning how to construct an argument to support a thesis

After the Louis debate, Breihan pushed students to a third stage: choosing and briefly defending their own positions. His wording on the single-paragraph exercise is important because it helps explain some of Kraft's difficulties:

> In a one-paragraph essay, state which solution to the problem of 17th-century anarchy—French or English—*you* personally find more realistic and attractive. Try to explain why you feel the way you do, and to back your feelings with some evidence.

Kraft's "Best Solution to Anarchy" paragraph was a disappointment, both to Breihan and to Kraft herself (she received points equivalent to a "C+"). Her paragraph begins nicely with a thesis statement: "I find the English solution to 17th Century anarchy to be more realistic and attractive than the French solution." Following that, however, she merely uses a "find good things" strategy to list three things about the English solution: it established a Bill of Rights, it built a system of checks and balances, it lasted a long time. Only once in her paragraph does she even refer to how a feature of the English system was a "solution to anarchy," and she never explains why any of the features were more "realistic" or more "attractive" to her, as Breihan's assignment had requested. Responding to her paragraph, Breihan wrote:

> You need to *link* your facts to your argument. *Why* do these things make the English solution "more realistic and attractive"? You only mention those 2 words once.

Three aspects proved difficult in Kraft's "Best Solution to Anarchy" paragraph:

1. Transcending a limited "find good things" strategy
2. Formulating an explicit definition of "good" that addressed the "issues" of the question—solving anarchy and being "realistic" and "attractive" to her
3. Distinguishing between "evidence" and "feelings."

Breihan's model for good/better/best reasoning and his phrasing on the assignment sheet helped to shape these difficulties.

"Find Good Things" Strategy

In her planning session for her paragraph, Kraft, as she had done in Stage 2, merely flipped through her notes, using the "X is good because" formula to generate "good things" about the English system, but without a controlling definition of "good." She begins her planning (italics are ours):

> Okay, I obviously feel the English solution was better. [4 seconds silence] First of all, I think it was, I would say that it was less traumatic for the English people *because* [3 seconds silence] their individual rights were guaranteed, they were given rights by the Bill of Rights, they weren't taken advantage of. I think in Louis XIV's reign, in France, he didn't really c- I don't know, the common people weren't his main concern. He wanted to accomplish a lot of things, like, like let's say, um, taxes. He would tax the people, even though he knew they were poor. He just thought that taxing people was a way for him to get a lot of money to do things he wanted. This leads to another reason I think the English solution was better *because um, because um,* there were checks and balances, like the king, and the House of Commons, and the House of Lords, all had checks and balances on each other, so they could, um, regulate what, what was going on, like the king's decision vs. the Parliament's decision.

Formulating an Explicit Definition of "Good"
That Addresses the "Issue" of the Question

In merely flipping through her notes to find "good things" about the English system, Kraft failed to define "good" so as to address what we call the "issue" of the question: that is, Breihan expected her to explain how her favored type of government was a "solution to anarchy" and was "realistic" and "attractive" to her. In a sense, these phrases in the assignment sheet laid a foundation for defining "good," but, after stating them in her thesis sentence, Kraft ignored them.

Kraft's shortcoming is clearer when we examine how Joe Walker saw the issues in the question. He explicitly stated how each feature of the system he favored solved the problem of anarchy or was "realistic" or "attractive" to him. In this excerpt from his exercise, Walker has been citing reasons why the French solution was superior to the English in preventing anarchy (italics are ours):

> In addition, I feel the French solution to anarchy (Louis absolutism) is also superior to that of the English because of the efficient flow of information which it provided. Louis had established clear and well defined lines of authority and communication. In this absolute system all information flows in an orderly path up through the

chain of command to the king. This, I believe, is another major reason why *this is such a good system for stopping anarchy.* This information system allows the king to stay abrest of problems in his country and his government, which *allowed Louis to maintain order and diffuse potential problems before the[y] arrose into major disruptive problems.* Some people may argue that the issuing of power and authority to a single absolute ruler is [a] radical move and may be a mistake. However, if we view this problem in relation to the time, it becomes apparent that *radical action was required to end the anarchy of the 17th century* and reintroduce order. In this regard I think *absolutism is the more efficient form of government for halting anarchy.* This doesn't mean I feel this is the best form of government . . . [he goes on to explain why the English system is more attractive to him personally.]

Distinguishing Evidence from Feelings

The assignment sheet's language about "feelings" and "evidence" was confusing for many students. Walker handled it about as well as any, by stating "I feel" to open many of his points, and then presenting evidence to back his feelings, but distinguishing evidence about preventing anarchy from his personal preferences for a type of government. Kraft had more difficulty. She began her planning session, as we saw, with the phrase "I feel." The planning that followed contained evidence. But at the end of that long planning session, she said, "So I think I have a good idea of the way I feel. Now I need evidence." She defined her long planning session as "feelings" and did not recognize that it contained evidence. She marked off the composing process in her mind into the two sections of Breihan's instructions: choose topic by how you feel, then gather evidence to support it.

In Sherman's class, also, teachers' instructions, labels, and categories were literally interpreted by the students in ways the teacher did not intend. Here, too, as in Sherman's class, written instructions about how to perform a decision-making and argument-building process were very hard for students to follow on their own. Finally, we see in Breihan's and in Sherman's classes the difficulty for students of the fourth good/better/best reasoning task we mentioned—the task of integrating feelings and evidence in the decision-making process.

Testing the Thesis Against Counterarguments

Throughout the planning session for her one-paragraph exercise, Kraft's insecurity was evident. However, she met her fears by a strong strategy—testing her position against counterarguments. After she had generated some good things about the English system, she said,

I think I, I've, um, got good ideas here and I think I can write
them in a coherent way, but that doesn't necessarily mean I, Dr.
Breihan's going to like what I'm going to write and how I'm going
to present it, because in other assignments I've thought I've done
really well and I haven't gotten the grades I thought I should
have. [5 sec. silence] But obviously I need practice or help in my,
in the way I write. [7 sec. silence] Let me see if there's anything
else I wanted to say [7 sec. silence] The English solution didn't
go without any problems [resumes consideration of the question
by raising and answering counterarguments to her support of the
English].

In the rest of her planning session, Kraft addressed her fears about
the adequacy of her evidence by raising and answering counterarguments. Throughout this long process, she kept trying to gain closure
on her planning, saying things like "I think I'll just leave it at that,"
only to come back again to raise more counterarguments. Her careful
consideration of counterarguments, though not much of it appeared
in her finished exercise, presaged her later achievement of both written
and oral arguments that raised and answered counterarguments as
Breihan expected.

In sum, then, in Stage 3, where students had to choose a position and
defend it in a paragraph with "some evidence," Kraft firmly stated a
thesis at the beginning of her paragraph. She used Breihan's "X is
good because" formula, though in a limited way, as part of a find-
good-things strategy. In planning her paper, she tested her position
repeatedly against counterarguments, seeking to strengthen it. She did
not form an explicit definition of "good king" for Louis' time, nor
address the issues that Breihan had posed and that should have helped
to shape her definition of "good." Further, she did not recognize what
was "evidence" and what was "feelings." More broadly, she still could
not clearly envision how to construct the argument that would best
support her thesis.

Breihan's Teaching Methods

An analysis of Kraft's and other students' difficulties led us to see the
potential pitfalls for students in Breihan's model of good/better/best
reasoning, his presentation of thesis and subtheses, and his "X is good
because" formula. These insights caused Breihan, in succeeding semesters, to focus earlier and more heavily on the need to define
"good" so as to address the "issue" of the question. He added that
item to the checksheet, and he emphasized it more clearly in the

exercise instructions, in the class discussions, and in his responses to exercises and essay drafts.

Stage 4: Choosing a Position and Defending It in a Full Essay

Kraft achieved:
  Recognizing evidence when she had it
  Constructing an argument to support her position
  Transcending the limited "find good things" strategy
  Forming an explicit definition of "good"
  Addressing the issue Breihan had defined in the assignment
  Revising effectively to bring herself closer to Breihan's expectations

In writing the full essay that comprised Stage 4, Bonnie Kraft made a great leap to success. One factor that helped her was the Loyoliana question, which stated up front what General Perez wanted: to avoid anarchy and bloody revolution. There was no confusing language about "what you personally feel," or about a solution that was "realistic and attractive to you," as in the one-paragraph Best Solution to Anarchy exercise. General Perez's goals could become the definition of "good."

Breihan's past advice also appears to have helped her. In his written comment about Kraft's one-paragraph exercise, Breihan had concentrated on helping her address the issue of 17th-century government by asking, "Why do these things make the English solution more 'realistic and attractive'?" and he advised her to mention those two words throughout. Repeatedly on her and others' exercises, he had written "*Why* is this good?"

For the Loyoliana topic (see p. 101), she adopted Breihan's advice in the sense that throughout the essay she referred again and again to General Perez by name, and specifically to his goals of avoiding anarchy and bloody revolution. Several times, in the margins of the notes she was making for the essay, she added revisions that clarified how aspects of English government she was summarizing prevented anarchy and bloody revolution, the issue defined in the assignment. She also wrote, in large capital letters down the side of her notes for the Loyoliana essay, "KEEP IN MIND PROVING THIS GOOD." After the in-class draft, Breihan advised her to tighten her "connections" still more, and in the revision she did so by inserting additional explicit statements about how the English government prevented anarchy and bloody revolution. Her breakthrough was to transcend a mere find-good-things strategy by linking all her subtheses to a clear definition of what was "good" in that situation.

Another factor that helped her and other students is that Breihan, throughout the course, continually referred not to the English or French "form of government" or some other general term, but to the English [or French] *solution to anarchy*. That tag phrase appears throughout students' notes, think-aloud planning, and drafts. In the one-paragraph exercise, Kraft had ignored the part of the question that asked "which solution to anarchy" do you prefer. On Essay 1, however, Kraft made explicit, from the beginning of her planning, that the English system was a solution to anarchy. For example, in her earliest outline for the essay, after jotting down some notes about French absolutism, she wrote, "It is advisable to follow the English Solution to C17 Anarchy" and then went on to draw a number of parallels between Loyoliana and England before the English Civil War—both were threatened by anarchy and bloody revolution. At another place in her notes, she wrote, "One reason Parliament established the Bill of Rights was to ensure protection against anarchy." This is a significant step beyond her single paragraph in Stage 3, where she merely described the Bill of Rights as good, without linking it to the issues of the assignment or to an explicit definition of "good." Breihan's constant emphasis on the French and English systems as different responses to the threat of anarchy had sunk in. His specific statement that Perez wanted to avoid anarchy and his advice to Kraft on her earlier exercises helped her make the connection.

Once she had the structure of the argument—that Perez wanted to avoid anarchy and bloody revolution and that the English system had to be proven good *because* it would help him do that—then she could integrate into that structure the "X is good because" formula. She could also integrate her feelings, already expressed in the one-paragraph exercise, about the value of meeting people's demands and granting individual rights. She argued to General Perez that he could best avoid anarchy and bloody revolution by meeting the people's needs and demands, as the English system had done, rather than by repressing them and inviting their rebellion, as in France.

Kraft's in-class draft for Essay 1 received points equivalent to a "B+"; her revision after Breihan's comments not only received an "A" but was submitted, at Breihan's suggestion, as a candidate for a departmental prize awarded each semester for the most successful student essay from all sections of the Modern Civilization course taught by Breihan and others. (She did not win the prize.)

Here is a condensed version of her revised Loyoliana essay. We have italicized the points where she links her arguments explicitly to the issue of how Perez could prevent anarchy and bloody revolution by meeting the needs of the people and respecting their demands. Notice, too, the many echoes of her earlier exercises and debate notes: her information about Louis XIV, her feeling that no one was there to regulate what he did, her early summary of how Louis hurt the poor, and (slipped quietly in at the very end) her point that the English solution was good because it lasted a long time. The exercises and debates thus served in important ways as preparation for her essay.

> General Perez, you have stated that you would like to leave your office as dictator of Loyoliana to be replaced by a constitutional government. After examining European politics from 1500 to 1800, I am confident there exists a way for you to transform Loyoliana's government peacefully, *avoiding both a recurrence of anarchy and violent revolution.* The constitutional government to be established in Loyoliana *must conform to the needs of the people while maintaining political order within the state.* These goals can be obtained in Loyoliana if you follow the example of the English and their solution to seventeenth-century anarchy by establishing a mixed government.
>
> Because the positions of the relatively small landowning elite and the majority of the impoverished inhabitants of Loyoliana are similar to those in France in 1789, I am forced to draw my conclusions from the occurrences in France at that time. I find it necessary to prove to you that the French example of revolution must be avoided because revolution is drastic and harmful to the citizens. [historical information on effect of revolution in France, used as evidence to support the previous sentence]
>
> General Perez, it is necessary for you to take action to *meet the demands of the bourgeoisie and the peasantry before revolution.* Revolution may only lead to the oppression of the people by a military despot. This would not be a final solution to political unrest; military despotism would only contribute to unrest. I believe *the French example of violent revolution in 1789 can be avoided by following the constitutional government of England in order to provide for the demands of the people.*
>
> The position of your government is similar to that of England during the seventeenth century. The civil war that Loyoliana experienced 40 years ago is synonomous to the English Civil War of 1640–60. General Perez is similar to Oliver Cromwell, who emerged from the English Civil War as a military dictator. Just as citizens of England swung steadily in favor of a formation of a constitutional government instead of despotism, it is advisable for you to do the same.

The rest of the essay makes a number of points about the constitutional government of England, each time showing *how England avoided anarchy and bloody revolution by providing for the demands of its people before they resorted to revolution.* Here is her paragraph developing one of those points—that Perez should adopt something like the English Bill of Rights.

> The Revolution Settlement occurred peacefully and the Bill of Rights, passed in 1689 by Parliament, created a legal government with defined rights of the people and rules by which to govern. The Bill of Rights declared parliamentary supremacy over the crown. The landowning elite now had a say in government as a governing aristocracy was established. The Bill of Rights also enlarged the exercise of individual freedoms. As a result, the peasantry now had basic inalienable rights, and the taxes imposed by the king needed the approval of Parliament. These improvements *were good for the bourgeoisie and the peasantry because their demands were being met before resorting to revolution.* This shows the French example of revolution is unnecessary when solving political problems. The Bill of Rights was also peacefully abolishing absolutism by setting up a mixed government constitutionally. When establishing the Bill of Rights, the government demonstrated an interest in the liberty and freedom of the people. Whereas, in France, the absolute monarch had the ability to do what he wanted, which was not always for the good of the most people. For example, Louis XIV wanted to accomplish much in the culture of France. He had the Louvre constructed, a town at Versailles created, the Observatory built, and an Academy of Sciences founded. However, the peasants bore the costs of Louis' cultural accomplishments in the form of taxes. I realize it has been said that the aristocracy of England, in the Bill of Rights, made laws to suit themselves, such as the game law against the poor. Nevertheless, the benefits of the Bill of Rights greatly outweighed the harm of such game laws. The Bill of Rights protected farmers by guaranteeing rights such as freedom to bear arms, to petition Parliament, to be free from excessive bail or punishment, and to a trial by jury. Also, because taxes could be more evenly distributed, less of the burden now fell on the farmers. The benefits of these laws, only to name a few, significantly offset the harm caused by hunters and their dogs running through fields and ruining some crops of the farmers.

Kraft makes additional points like the one above, each supported with information used as evidence, and each explicitly linked to the definition of "good" provided by General Perez's need to *avoid anarchy and revolution by meeting the people's needs.* Each point also includes relevant counterarguments raised and answered. Her reference to game laws is a response to a suggestion by Breihan written in the margin of her earlier one-paragraph exercise. Again, she *uses* his advice. Below is her final paragraph:

> General Perez, from the conclusions and arguments I have drawn in favor of the English example of mixed government, I hope you

can understand the benefits of this kind of government. *The demands of the landowning elites and of the impoverished inhabitants can be met peacefully and successfully, making revolution unnecessary.* By establishing a Bill of Rights, you can ensure inalienable rights of the people of Loyoliana and a system of government in which Parliament and the king will balance the powers of each other most effectively for the betterment of the country and its citizens. The successfulness of the English may be measured by the fact that the ideas and laws established in 1689 still exist today. I hope you will be able to learn from history and realize the *English solution to seventeenth century anarchy would be most productive* for you to implement in Loyoliana.

Kraft's Final Victory: Fully Assuming the Role of Debater

The Loyoliana essay represented a major step in Kraft's struggle to learn how to use discipline-based methods to arrive at a position and to support it with evidence. But it was not the end of Kraft's struggle to learn in Breihan's course. After the success of her essay, she soon set a further goal for herself.

We continue to follow her story because it illustrates the importance of the roles that students adopt. This final piece of Kraft's story can serve as a conclusion to our discussion of all three areas of difficulty—stating a position, raising and answering counter evidence/argument, and using discipline-based methods to arrive at a position and to support it with evidence. In her Loyoliana essay, Kraft had achieved those aspects privately, in the writing seen only by her teacher.

Kraft's next goal was to assume publicly the role of arguer/debater by participating in debates and discussions. No longer was she content merely to write to Breihan as in her Second Chance exercise, telling what she might have said; now she wanted to say it herself in public, though she knew that to do so would expose her to what she feared—attack by counterarguers—a fear that had been evident in her think-aloud planning for the one-paragraph exercise. But that planning, where she anxiously tested her position over and over against imagined counterarguments, was also a dress rehearsal for an actual debate. A week after she got back her successful in-class Essay 1, there was another in-class debate. After it, she wrote in her log:

> The in-class debate went well over-all. But I need to develop more confidence in my ideas and to speak up in class. I find other people have similar ideas; these people have the nerve to present their ideas. I am afraid of being wrong or misinterpreting a written passage. I want to be right 100% of the time. I am afraid of being

criticized or not having enough evidence to back up my ideas. I am disappointed with myself today; I must learn to speak up.

Two weeks later, after a class session that (like several others in the course), Breihan had billed in the syllabus as a "class discussion," rather than simply listing a topic for lecture, Kraft was again disappointed with herself, but still trying:

> I again did not contribute much to the class discussion. I did partially answer someone's question on the White Man's Burden. I have my own questions but I just [sic] so afraid of appearing stupid. I really have to get over this feelings [sic] because I'm only hurting myself.

Two days later, on November 14 in the in-class debate on an aspect of the Industrial Revolution, she achieved the breakthrough, and wrote ecstatically in her log,

> I finally did it! My group as a whole was not very outgoing, but if I had an opinion I stated it out loud and not just to myself. I actually got into practically a one-on-one debate with another member of the class. I feel much better about myself. After all, no one stood up and said "you are absolutely wrong."

Kraft's achievement points, among other things, to the importance of students' roles. Her ability to meet Breihan's expectations that she would state a position, answer counterarguments, and use discipline-based methods to arrive at her position and to support it with evidence was intimately connected to her growing ability to assume the role of arguer/debater. She, herself, did not feel she had fully succeeded in the course until she had publicly assumed that role, both in writing and in oral discourse.

BREIHAN'S AND WALVOORD'S CONCLUSIONS

Our conclusion from all this is that Breihan's careful, consistent teaching methods helped his students in many ways. Wanting students to be arguers and debaters, Breihan succeeded in using language in ways that encouraged that role. His daily focused writing exercises, his essay assignments, his in-class discussions, his responses to students' exercises and drafts, and the seven debates all offered guidance and feedback throughout students' thinking and writing processes. We saw how Breihan's teaching methods shaped students' ways of reading, of defining their tasks, of approaching texts, of arriving at and defending positions, of using models learned in other settings—all factors that were important in all four classes we studied.

The study also revealed some differences between Breihan's and Sherman's classes in the models for good/better/best reasoning. Sherman's business decision-maker model features the manager's careful decision-making process, which begins by defining "good," uses factor rating, considers alternatives and counterarguments, and arrives at a responsible decision for implementation. Breihan's debater model, on the other hand, features the prominent statement of a thesis followed by the generation of subtheses, as the arguer supports the thesis and defends it against counterarguers. The definition of "good" is incorporated in the subs, but is not as visible or primary as in Sherman's model. Each model significantly influenced students' thinking processes and the difficulties that arose in each class. Writing teachers and researchers who use Toulmin's model for instruction or for data analysis need to keep in mind that the model's implied relationship among parts, and particularly the role of the definition of "good" in evaluative reasoning, may differ by classroom and discipline and that these differences may affect students' thinking and the difficulties that arise as students try to meet their teachers' expectations.

Our study focused on how difficulties were affected by students' strategies and teachers' methods, not on the influence of other factors such as gender, past education, learning style, or socioeconomic class. Nevertheless, we were very aware that, for example, Kraft's socialization as a woman must have affected her difficulty in publicly entering a dialogue where one stated a position boldly and defended it against counterarguers—in our culture a more typically male way of operating (Belenky et al. 1986; Chodorow 1978; Gilligan 1982). Breihan, we knew, faced a class of students with many differences which made it easier or harder for a given student to learn and adopt the role that Breihan expected. In the face of these factors, Breihan's response was to try to explain his expectations ever more clearly and guide his students' learning processes ever more effectively.

Breihan's primary goal for entering our research project was to find out how well his methods were working and to improve them. This study showed some difficulties that Breihan addressed in succeeding semesters—particularly the need to forefront the importance of defining "good," to make explicit his expectation that students would address the "issue" he outlined in an essay question, and to reshape the instructions for the paragraph exercise on the best solution to anarchy. More broadly, our study gave him an appreciation for how hard his students worked to understand and meet his expectations and how important his guidance was to them.

Particularly, we stand amazed at Bonnie Kraft. Entering the course expecting to be merely a text processor, she struggled through what she remembered, three years later, as "THE hardest course I ever had," a course in which "I was SO intimidated." Her persistence, her keen desire to learn, her determination to use her teacher's guidance, her pluck and courage won our respect and admiration. It was no surprise that she graduated from Loyola College *summa cum laude* and planned to enter law school—the ultimate forum of public argument and counterargument.

Notes

1. To conduct this analysis, we used the primary trait scale (p. 35). We each independently rated a random sample of 11 essays to identify those that reached the stated standard, which was equivalent to a score of 4 or above. We achieved 91 percent agreement. Walvoord then completed the analysis for the rest of the in-class Essays 1 and 3 written by the focus group.

2. This count was based on 25 drafts by ten focus group students, some high success and some low success (p. 36).

3. Sample of 12 essay drafts written by eight students—four who received "A" in the course and four who received "C."

4. Our sample was a random selection of one high-success and one low-success in-class essay draft for each of five essay questions, including essays for all three units across the semester—a total of ten essays.

5. Among our focus group who earned course grade "C," 30 percent of the marginal comments resulted in the student deleting the passage, resulting in no improvement of the paper (in Breihan's judgment; see p. 36). Among "A" students, 7 percent resulted in deletion with no improvement. At times, abandoning a passage that the teacher had marked with marginal comments may have been a low-effort way out, but, as this example of Kraft shows, at times it might also have been the student's way of dealing with an issue not yet understood.

5 Using Social Science to Help Oneself and Others: Robison's Human Sexuality Course

Barbara E. Walvoord
Loyola College in Maryland

Susan Miller Robison
College of Notre Dame of Maryland

This chapter explores Susan Miller Robison's Human Sexuality class at the College of Notre Dame of Maryland, a small Catholic college whose undergraduate day program contained about 600 students, all women. We explore how the roles of teacher and students differed from those in Sherman's and Breihan's classes at the much larger, more selective, coeducational Loyola College, and how those roles affected thinking and writing in Robison's class. Here we concentrate on four areas of difficulty:

1. Constructing the audience and the self
2. Stating a position
3. Managing complexity
4. Using discipline-based methods to arrive at and support a position

At the end of the chapter, we examine the effects of Robison's and peers' responses to student drafts. Our theoretical framework and our methods of data collection and data analysis are described in Chapter 2. The characteristics of the class and of the focus group of students we used for some of our analyses are described on p. 18 and in Appendix B.

ROLES IN ROBISON'S COURSE

The professional-in-training role (pp. 8–9), which all four teachers expected students to adopt, took a somewhat different form in each

144

class. In Sherman's class, there was an underlying assumption of power embedded in the business decision-maker role—the assumption that the decision maker was a manager in charge of a firm's production and, though she or he was obligated to listen to others' opinions, gather information, and consider alternatives and counterarguments, the final decision was in the hands of the manager who had the power to see that it was carried out. In Breihan's class, the role was arguer/ debater who selected a position and defended it against counterarguments. The dominant image was one of dialogue, but dialogue in which each person defended his or her own position. The debates, for example, ended with a tally of each side's score, not with the two sides amicably working out a middle position (though individuals might do that privately after they had heard the debates). In contrast to both these roles, Robison modeled, and expected from her students, several interrelated roles, including

- social scientist
- counselor
- mentor/friend
- the self who used professional knowledge for personal decision making

We explore the meaning of these complex, interrelated roles in two ways: through Robison's own description of her background and goals, and through Walvoord's observation of Robison's class. Robison tells her background here in her own voice:

Robison: Background and Goals

I [Robison] am by training a cognitive psychologist. I was a full-time faculty member at the College of Notre Dame from 1972 to 1982, but when we collected our data in spring, 1986, I was dividing my time between teaching and my private practice as a counseling and consulting psychologist.

In 1979, my dean supported with released time my participation in a semester-long writing-across-the-curriculum workshop where I met Walvoord, who was leader of the workshop, Breihan, who was coleader, and Anderson, the biologist whose chapter follows next. The workshop made the writing process so enjoyable and understandable that I got excited about writing and writing research, and I began using writing more effectively in my classes.

The 1986 Human Sexuality course we studied was a freshman

general studies course. It could be used by non-psychology majors to fulfill their social science requirement. During the year of our research the class had an unusual number of upper-level students because the course had not been offered the previous year while I was on leave of absence to participate in a post-doctoral program in counseling. Although the class composition changed the tone of many class discussions, I made the choice to teach the course as it had been designed—a 100-level, social science course for freshmen/sophomores.

In keeping with the college's philosophy for general education requirements, the Human Sexuality course attempted to teach students how to "think" in the discipline of the requirement—in this case, social science. Therefore, students were expected to learn something about research methodology in the social sciences while at the same time they were studying the content—human sexuality. Outcomes I valued were that students should find out how social scientists collect data and draw conclusions, and that students should learn to reason from evidence and apply principles to practical situations. Also, many of the students had both a paraprofessional interest and a personal interest in the course. That is, they might be future nurses, counselors, teachers, parents who would want to understand human sexuality for their life's work and for their own decision making.

In addition, the course number had a "6" in the middle, which was the psychology department's code for an "experiential course." All jokes aside about labs on sexuality, an experiential course meant using learning activities that involved more than lecture. I used films, small-group discussions, value clarification exercises, and so forth. In addition to the variety of activities, the course also involved writing assignments designed to provoke application of material to "real life" situations such as sexual decision making. The various experiential learning activities tended to promote a community of learners where students helped one another.

Oftentimes people remark on the curiosity of a Catholic college having a sexuality course and wonder what restrictions might be placed on content. Actually in respect to academic freedom, none were. The course was seen as a course in the psychology department that happened to study human sexual behavior. For my part, being a practicing Catholic, I tried to attend to Catholic values in the selection and presentation of topics. Not all the college's students were Catholic, but most were. I pointed out to the students that often religious groups, parents, counselors, and other well-meaning advice givers are so concerned about youth making poor sexual decisions that they are antisexual in attitude—seeing sex as an evil force that can ruin one's life. Without being preachy, I tried to show students that it is possible to make prudent sexual decisions while still holding a positive attitude about sexuality and sex as God-given gifts to be used for good purposes. I brought in a theologian to discuss Scriptural traditions on sexuality and a physician who discussed all methods of family planning including both "natural" and "artificial" methods. Also in class I tried to take a counselor's nonjudgmental stance toward the variations and plurality of human sexuality and suggested that the students do also as they learned to model the counselor's role for the future professions in which they might use the course material.

Walvoord: A Class Discussion Illuminates Teacher and Student Roles

The interconnected roles we have mentioned—social science researcher, counselor, mentor/friend, and person who uses her professional knowledge for her own life—are evident in an excerpt from a class session that I (Walvoord) observed on March 18, about two-thirds of the way through the course.

Nearly 30 students, all women, were gathered in Knott Science Hall at the College of Notre Dame. The class opened with a review of the past week's session, when the class had been addressed by a theologian. Robison reminded them of his name, admitted he went fast and used lots of technical terminology, and answered a question about what would be on the test. As a review, she gave a quick, oral sequence of true-false questions, to which students volunteered answers. Then she picked up the major topic for that day: the stages of love.

Robison was down-to-earth, lively, and witty. At one point, discussing the early stages, she reminded her students, "Remember, St. Augustine played around a lot before he became St. Augustine." At another point, she humorously emphasized the link between in-class discussions and outside behavior: "Any questions on what we covered last time? Any of you try any outside labs?" (laughter). When she discussed the infatuation stage in which people believe they were made for each other, she did a funny little imitation of two infatuated lovers: "Golly, gee, we both wear sneakers! We're made for each other!" (more laughter).

In her use of everyday language, Robison was modeling the friend or counselor who can interpret technical material in terms that ordinary people can understand. Students picked up on this language: for example, later, in a dormitory room discussion between two students who taped their discussion for us, the students remembered the sneakers scene and had another chuckle over it. Informal language to translate or illustrate social scientific concepts also appeared in students' writing, as we will see.

During the class session, Robison also acted as social scientist. For example, she asked, "What are the symptoms of infatuation?" (Students were to have read this section in their textbook.) One student volunteered, "You feel high." Robison built on the answer by explaining, in a more technical way, the "neurologic changes" that accompany infatuation. When students no longer volunteered, Robison turned to a more directed mode that still involved student response: she began a series of "do you" questions with "Do you think that the two of you were made for each other?" It became a kind of game, with the class laughing in self-recognition and murmuring assent.

She mentioned the aspects of infatuation and referred students to "B on your chart," a handout Robison had given the students, presenting the five stages of love. An older student leaned forward to give a copy of the handout to an oriental student who had missed some class sessions, as I later learned, because the death of her father had necessitated a return to Korea. A group of three Spanish-speaking students sitting together occasionally whispered among themselves, evidently helping one another to interpret class material.

There seemed to me to be more such personal helping in Robison's classroom than in Breihan's or Sherman's, a function perhaps of the class lab sessions with their collaborative activities, as Robison has suggested earlier, but perhaps also a function of Robison's modeling of the helpful role of friend and counselor, the service orientation of many of the students who planned to go into nursing or social service, the small size of the college, and the all-woman constitution of the college day program and of the class. The College of Notre Dame has a reputation in Baltimore for its nurturing, caring atmosphere.

In her social scientist role, Robison explained the physiological aspects of infatuation, presenting the results of research. A student asked, "Why does this [the release of endorphins/endomorphins] happen when you're infatuated?" Robison replied, "Yes" and grinned, stonewalling to illustrate the lack of knowledge about that issue among experts (laughter). Later, another student asked a scientific question: "Is it, like, egg first or chicken first?" In other words, do you fall in love because you're secreting endorphins or do you secrete the hormones because you're falling in love? Robison replied in scientific terms: "I think, from the way I read the literature, that [summarizes the literature] . . . but that's only a nice little hypothesis." Now Robison invited students to become social science researchers: "How would you design such a study?" [i.e., to determine whether hormonal secretion comes first or infatuation comes first]. Students volunteered their ideas.

In addition to the social scientist role in this discussion, Robison adopted a mentor role: "You'll fall in love often throughout your life, while you're single and while you're married—maybe with your husband, maybe with others."

So far in this discussion, she had made four references to clients; her role as counseling psychologist was highly visible.

By occasional references to her own personal experience, Robison reflected herself as a person who used social science knowledge to understand and shape her own life. By sharing such experience with her students, she assumed the role of an older or more experienced mentor or friend. At one point, discussing how people approach commitment warily, she said, " 'I'm almost ready to say I love you'— that was my husband's phrase after we'd been going together for awhile."

Robison invited students to test theory, hypothesis, or Robison's views against *their* experience. They were to be skeptical, as research-scientists-in-training, and also they were to expect social science to impact directly on their personal lives. The class was discussing what Robison called the "wildcard approach" that occurs during infatuation, where the newly beloved is merely a wild card who is created in the mind of the lover according to the lover's fantasy.

An African American woman challenged her: "Women, not men, use the wildcard approach?"

Robison replied, "That's one view—is your experience different?"

It was, and the student said so, drawing on her four years in the army and her experience with "those guys."

Robison offered a different explanation for the soldiers' behavior.

Another student disagreed.

Still another student entered the fray.

We might compare this exchange among upper-level students to the multistudent exchanges that Breihan orchestrated among his freshmen, which were much more carefully controlled, with a single role being modeled: the historian showing students how to argue and present evidence in the ways that historians do. In Robison's class, however, the discussion was much looser: students entered and exited from it more freely, there was more private whispering among them as they voiced their own reactions to neighbors in the classroom, personal

experience seemed more highly privileged, and both the teacher and
the students played a wider variety of roles in the discussion.

The value that Robison placed on personal and social goals is
revealed in her pleasure over the following incident: A client in her
private practice was having difficulties that affected the client's job
performance, so the client talked with her colleagues, explaining that
she was working with "Dr. Robison" and was improving. Her colleagues
were supportive. One of them came to the client after the group
conversation and said, "I graduated from the College of Notre Dame
and I had Dr. Robison for Human Sexuality class. When you see her,
tell her I said 'Hi,' and tell her I've used what she taught us in my
own marriage, and I'm very happy." Robison was pleased both that
the former student had used the course for her own life and also that
she had been a sympathetic coworker to someone in emotional
difficulty.

Sensing this goal of personal application, which they shared with
their teacher, students commented in their final evaluations of the
course about the fulfillment of that goal with statements such as:

> Now I have much more information and am able to make more
> sound choices.

> I have more info that I previously did not have. And, I have
> thought about my beliefs and values a great deal. I am more
> comfortable with my own sexuality. Negative thoughts have been
> dispelled. This course has had a very positive effect on my personal
> and professional life. It was GREAT!

In contrast, then, to Sherman's and Breihan's classes at Loyola
College, Robison's Human Sexuality class at the College of Notre
Dame modeled and encouraged four interrelated roles: social scientist,
counselor, mentor/friend, and self who uses professional knowledge
for personal decision making. Robison, as we will see, encouraged her
students to adopt these roles in their written assignments.

ROBISON'S EXPECTATIONS

Unlike Breihan's and Sherman's classes, where Walvoord and the
teacher collected data over the entire semester, in Robison's class we
chose only one assignment for data collection: the students' last writing
assignment before their exam—a letter to a friend who is about to
marry, advising him or her "how to have a good marital sex life."

To describe her expectations to the students, Robison gave them an assignment sheet (Figure 5.1) that followed the CRAFT formula (Criteria, Role, Audience, Form, Theme). She had devised this formula as a guide for teachers in constructing assignments (Robison, 1983).

The criteria spelled out on the assignment sheet were repeated both in the peer review sheet (Figure 5.2) that guided both students' in-class peer response to one another's handwritten drafts, and in the teacher response sheet Robison used for her comments on students' typed drafts and final papers. She awarded points under each category of the criteria listed on the teacher response sheet, and also wrote comments.

In addition to the expectations listed on the sheets, other expectations,

Criteria	Points
Organizational structure	10
Outside reference	3
Selection of relevant material	7
Accurate information	10
Mechanics—spelling, punctuation, grammar, clarity	5

Role: A friend has written you about her up-and-coming wedding. She knows that you have taken a human sexuality course and has asked you for any advice you might give for her and her husband to have a good sex life in their marriage.

Audience: Imagine someone that is a friend similar to you. You might even imagine writing to a real friend. Assume the friend has any characteristics that you want in the way of educational background, religion, etc. as long as these assumptions are clear to a reader (e.g., "Now, Mary, I know that since you and Fred are both Catholic. . . ."). The tone of the letter can be casual like you would use to a friend but should still include academic technical material.

Form: A letter, obviously, but may have sections with headings for easier reading. This assignment can probably be done in 3–4 pages.

Theme: You may select any topics from the course, both from the book or lectures or classroom exercises. Please include one outside source (magazine, journal, or book). Be sure to reference it properly at the end of the assignment. Use whatever referencing form you have used in your major (APA, MLA, etc.). Organize the material any way you wish but try to have an organizational scheme that is obvious and logical to a reader.

Due

April 15	Peer review in class
April 22	Draft due in class (5 points off for not being handed in during class)
April 29	Returned to you
May 6	Rewrites due in class

Figure 5.1. Robison's letter assignment.

---

1. Is the paper well organized? Outline a few of the main points. What would you suggest?
2. Is the material selected accurate and relevant? How could it be more so?
3. Did the author use an outside reference?
4. Are mechanics OK? Any suggestions?

Figure 5.2. Robison's Peer Review Sheet.

which had been tacit, emerged after the course was over, as we constructed the primary trait scale (p. 35), analyzed Robison's comments on the papers, and conducted other forms of analysis described in Chapter 2. We then added the following expectations to the ones Robison had stated on her assignment sheet:

> When presenting research results, the student:
>
> (a) describes characteristics of the research (method, population, etc.)
> (b) presents data in precise terms (i.e., 38% not "some")
> (c) gives operational definitions
>
> The student articulates at least three counterarguments or views of opponents
>
> The student uses social science terminology and is careful to define and translate for the lay reader.

Our post-course analysis of Robison's additional expectations would lead, in a future semester, to an amplification and revision of the criteria on the assignment sheet, peer review sheet, and teacher response sheet.

Our analysis of Robison's explicit and tacit expectations showed us that her letter assignment cast students into a combination of the four interrelated roles we saw reflected in the in-class discussion: social-scientist-in-training, counselor-in-training, mentor/friend, and self who applies course knowledge to personal decisions. Students were expected to report social science research accurately and in a scholarly way. As counselors they were to choose and translate research for the needs of the client, while also maintaining the tone and closeness of a friendship. Because the assignment suggested that students choose a friend "similar to you," there was also a hint of the role of the self who uses social science for personal decisions.

The rest of this chapter is an exploration of the difficulties that students encountered in the letter assignment and our insights about how students' strategies and the teacher's methods affected the difficulties. Particularly, we explore those areas of difficulty that were most influenced by the varied and complex roles that Robison modeled and expected of her students:

1. Constructing the audience and the self
2. Stating a position
3. Managing complexity
4. Using appropriate discipline-based methods to arrive at and support a position

DIFFICULTIES WITH CONSTRUCTING
THE AUDIENCE AND THE SELF

THE NATURE OF THE DIFFICULTIES

In three of the four classrooms the team studied, teachers asked students to address a peer audience; Robison's letter to a friend was one. Sherman and Walvoord maintained that assigning a peer audience for students is not an "act of hostility" as Bartholomae (1985) suggests (p. 70), but rather a potentially good idea that can easily cause many difficulties for students if it is not handled well. Robison and Walvoord, in this chapter, concur. Robison's goal in asking students to write to a friend was to place her students in a social-scientist/counselor/mentor-friend relationship that she considered excellent training for the roles they would assume once they graduated. But as in Sherman's class, the peer audience could cause difficulties. Robison's students fell short of her expectations when they:

1. ignored the peer audience and adopted the role of text processor addressing teacher checking textbook knowledge
2. adopted a layperson role rather than the appropriate professional-in-training role.

The first difficulty is illustrated by Sharon Enders's letter, which fails to meet Robison's expectations because it delineates the recipient only minimally, and it primarily adopts the text-processor role:

Sharon Enders: Brief, minimal delineation of letter recipient

Dear Jane,
 You expressed to me that you are concerned about a good sex life in your marriage. I would like to tell you some of the information that I have received in my sexuality course because we have just completed a section on marriage and sex.

[The rest of the letter presents information from the course but does not further delineate any of Jane's characteristics and makes no mention of her except occasionally to insert "Jane" as direct address ("Jane, we have learned in our sexuality class that communication is very important.")]

Contrast Enders's letter with the more successful self and audience in the next two letters where the writer delineates the reader more fully and establishes a relationship between herself and her friend. The relationships retain some of the equality of a friendship but yet give to the writers some basis for an expert stance from which to meet Robison's expectations for transmission of course-related learning.

Danielle Voorhees: Full delineation of letter recipient

Dear Kelly,

I can't believe that you are getting married in only three months! I can remember when we were kids talking about our "future" husbands, and now Its really true for both of us. Your letter sure expresses your happinesses and not to mention a hint of "cold feet." Marriage is a big step and commitment in one's life. I know that you and Dwayne want a good marriage, who doesn't? The last time I talked to you I got the impression that you feel that your marriage will be as exciting as your engagement. I know, there is nothing like sneaking around to make love without either of your parents catching you. But I got some information about marriage that might interest you.

[The next section is angled toward helping the letter recipient overcome her misguided notion that the marriage will be as exciting as the engagement. The rest of the letter integrates more details about the letter recipient and chooses course material to address those characteristics.]

Lei Kung: Full delineation of letter recipient

Reyna:

Hi! How are you? Gathering from your latest news, you're probably riding on cloud nine. Tell me, how did you make him propose to you, after all these years? Anyhow, congratulations!! Mike is a good man and I know you'll be happy together. Did you set the date, yet? We'll have a blast picking out wedding gowns, flowers, and all that good stuff! I know this gown shop called the Buckener's, they design beautiful gowns and they're really reasonable with their prices or we could head to N. Y. and visit the bride gown shows during June. I can't wait.

Yes, I agree with you hundred percent; marriage is a big step and I do sympathize with you for being nervous and unsure. I felt that way when Keith asked me to marry him. At first, I was so excited, all I could think was I finally have him; he's all mine and I realized I wasn't thinking sensibly. After a while, however, I knew I really didn't love him enough to jump into bed with him for life, so I told him I wasn't ready, yet and he's still being very patient.

Just look at me, at the time when you most need me, here I am blabbing on about nothing but nonsense. Well, I did read the letter you mailed me, very carefully and I think you're kind of scared of marrying Mike, are you? Is that why you asked me about my experiences with Keith and my Human Sexuality course? I knew the course would come in handy some day!

To be honest with you, this course is really helpful. It's a lot different than the health courses we took in high school (Remember Ms. Lamb, the old horny lass?) This course goes more in depth and because I'm a little more experienced, I understand it clearly and can discuss sex objectively. So, what I'll be telling you isn't biased opinions, but facts and my true experiences in breathless details!!!

[The next section helps the letter recipient in working through her questions about whether Mike is the right person to marry, and then allaying her fears about marriage.]

Voorhees and Kung avoided the text-processor role and fully delineated a letter recipient. Students who did so sometimes disappointed Robison's expectations because they delineated the "self" merely as layperson and friend, not as social scientist/counselor-in-training.

TEACHERS' METHODS AND STUDENTS' STRATEGIES

Idea-Generating Strategies

Idea Generating and Students' Roles

Students who delineated the letter recipient only minimally and who adopted the text-processor role typically copied the letter formula from the "role" section of the assignment sheet, as Enders did in the first letter opening above. They swiftly gave the recipient a name, and then launched quickly into the body of the paper, perhaps giving a nod to the letter format by sprinkling the person's name in direct address throughout the letter ("Celia, there are four basic positions for intercourse. . . ."). The letter format served as a minimal device to frame the course material taken, often with considerable care, from the textbook and class notes. One such student said on her think-aloud tape, "God, this sounds like a term paper, not a letter," but didn't do anything about that problem.

Students who delineated the letter recipient more fully generated their ideas very differently. Their first concern in beginning the papers was to delineate the letter recipient. They typically spent a good deal of time thinking about who the letter recipient would be, pondering, rejecting, and choosing characteristics, then spent considerable time drafting the first few paragraphs, in which the letter recipient's characteristics and the relationship between the letter recipient and the writer were established. As in Voorhees's and Kung's letter openings reprinted earlier, these writers tended to integrate throughout the letter specific information about the letter recipient and to angle their advice toward the letter recipient's situation. Such letters also typically included shared remembrances that further defined the letter recipient and the writer's relationship to him or her (all students were women, and all but one delineated the letter recipient as a woman). One said in exasperation, "This sounds stupid," and she scrapped the draft and began again.

The Webbing Technique: Strengths and Weaknesses

Robison's early in-class exercise, designed to help students with idea generation, sent a mixed message to students about the two kinds of idea-generating processes we have described. She began the class session by explaining the "web," an early planning device shaped like a spider's web, which the writer can use to generate ideas and to begin organizing them. Then she wrote "marital sexuality" in a circle in the middle of the board and asked students to call out topics for the branches of the web. To do this, students worked from their class notes, textbooks, and memories of class discussions and readings. Once the blackboard web was developed, Robison asked students to construct webs of their own at their desks. The in-class blackboard web is shown in Figure 5.3.

A web is often recommended in textbooks on writing and in writing-across-the-curriculum workshops. Discussions of webs usually point out that they are not so rigidly linear as an outline, and thus are easier and more flexible for early planning. In the context of Robison's class, however, other characteristics and functions of the web, as she used it, became apparent. First, by its emphasis upon generating large amounts of material from course readings and lecture notes, the web reflected the high value that Robison, as reader of the students' papers, placed on using course material. Second, the web also demonstrated the teacher's interest in students' planning and composing procedures, and it forced an early start on thinking about what to include in the paper.

The webbing technique was new to almost all the students. Two mentioned in their logs or tapes that they found the webbing technique

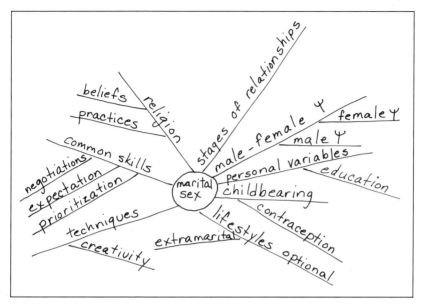

Figure 5.3. In-class web constructed by Robison from student input.

a useful new idea, which they would use in other settings. Several others made their own second, or revised, webs for their letters. Many students worked from their webs, often writing numbers beside the various points to indicate a position in the planned letter, thus making the web into a kind of outline.

However, our analysis showed us that the web actually modeled the idea-generating process of a text-processing student, and not that of a student who more fully delineated the letter recipient. The in-class web worked directly from class and lecture notes without reference to a letter recipient.

Our insight into the function of the web exercise is parallel to our insight into the structure of the in-class discussions in Sherman's class (p. 83). Both encouraged a writing process that the teacher did not want, or omitted a part of the writing and thinking process that the teacher considered important. The web exercise was useful in emphasizing both the composing process itself and Robison's expectation that students would use a range of course material in their papers. In another semester, however, she might also include an early exercise for delineating a letter recipient and some discussion of how to choose course material for the letter recipient's needs. She might model two webs—each for a different type of letter recipient.

For the remainder of this section on constructing the audience and the self, we focus on the students who fully delineated the letter recipient, and in so doing met the challenge of also adopting the social-scientist/counselor/friend role by constructing a self who was appropriately expert vis-à-vis the letter recipient. This made it possible to include the social science course material that Robison expected them to learn and use. To create the expert self, students drew upon familiar models from their own experiences of passing information to peers, but they also had to go beyond that to construct in the letter a self who was more consistently the expert than their peer experience normally allowed.

Students' Use of Models from Other Settings

We saw one model for passing information to peers that was useful but not sufficient for students' letters.

Connie Hatch composes her letter in the dorm with her roommate, who is not in the Human Sexuality class, sitting nearby. On the tape, they get into several conversations as Hatch works on the paper. In one conversation about birth control, they discuss a mutual friend who is using withdrawal, and then discuss the roommate's mother, who has used the rhythm method and talked to her about it. Hatch, adopting the information-giving role, now mentions the other methods covered in their text. The roommate has never heard of a diaphragm, so Hatch shows her the picture of one in her textbook, to which the roommate exclaims, "That big thing? How do you get it in?" leading Hatch to explain that it folds up and that you put lubricating jelly on it.

In this conversation, a level of information-giving takes place that is useful—but not sufficient—as a model for the letter assignment. Between Hatch and her roommate, no direct advice is given. Further, despite the fact that Hatch has had the Human Sexuality course, the role of "expert" shifts back and forth between her and her roommate on the basis of two elements: personal experience and contact with others who rank as "experts" in some way. For example, when the subject of the Pill is raised, the roommate recounts her own experience of having forgotten to take her birth control pill, taken two the next day, and then asking a doctor whether that had been a good idea. At this point, because of her personal experience with a problem and the answer she learned from an expert, the roommate is the expert.

The assignment sheet's suggestion, then, that the student writer offer the letter recipient "technical information" seems consonant with a common, relatively easy mode of interaction between peers. What is perhaps not so common is for the letter writer *consistently* to maintain the information- and advice-giving role of the expert. How students did that is the subject of the next sections.

Robison's Language on the Assignment Sheet

The assignment sheet, reproduced earlier in this chapter, did several things that appeared to help students create the "expert" self:

1. It mentioned "role" and "audience" specifically.
2. It conveyed that one might "imagine" a "real" friend, thus indicating the mixture of the real and the created that we found was necessary for success in the letter.
3. It gave explicit instruction and a sample of the language that would be needed to make the characteristics of the friend clear to Robison. Because of Robison as the other reader, students could not merely write as they would in a letter to a peer, but would have to use some techniques of the epistolary novel.
4. It suggested a basis for the writer to create herself as "expert"— the friend is embarking on a new path; the friend has written to ask advice; the writer has taken the Human Sexuality course.

We saw many students directly using Robison's language on the assignment sheet. They thought about real friends but combined real and imaginary traits; they used language that revealed the letter recipient's traits to Robison; they referred to the friend's earlier letter asking for advice.

Strategies for Strengthening the Expert Stance of the Writer

The high-success students (p. 36) went beyond the assignment sheet's formula and beyond their own familiar experience to strengthen their expert status vis-à-vis the letter recipient, so that they could assume the counselor role and could meet Robison's expectations for presentation of course-related learning. They created the expert self in three ways: (1) by citing personal experience, (2) by creating an approximation of the counselor's role, and (3) by delineating a letter recipient who needed their help.

One way students added strength to their expert roles was by citing their own personal experience—a factor that helped establish the expert role in their normal peer relationships, as illustrated by the Hatch-roommate dormitory discussion. For example, Kung, the writer of the letter opening reprinted earlier, cites her own experiences on the path toward marriage that her friend is now traveling, and promises "facts and my true experiences in breathless details!!!"

Other students enhanced their expert status by adopting approximations of the psychologist's counseling role. Kung jokes later in her letter (in a part not reprinted in this chapter) that her friend should pay her for her expertise. On her think-aloud tape, she voices, "Who gives free counseling?" but says she can't spell "counseling," so decides to write, "who gives free adivise? [sic]" Another version of the clinical psychologist's role occurs in another student's paper as the student establishes herself as a protégée of Dr. Ruth, a popular media psychologist. This student writes in her letter that if the friend has questions beyond what the writer can answer, the writer can arrange for the friend to talk directly to Dr. Ruth. The student adopts the role of counselor-in-training with privileged access to the certified counselor.

In addition to these two ways of creating the self to enhance expert status, high-success students created the letter recipient so as to enhance their own expert status. The typical opening strategy of students who delineated the letter recipient fully was mentally to run through their real friends. One student wrote in her log, "I went through all my friends who are about to get married." Another student rejected a friend because the friend was too knowledgeable, remarking wryly on her think-aloud tape, "She should be telling me!" The letter recipient, then, had to be needy in some way, so as to justify the expert stance of the writer.

One strategy for establishing the reader's need for advice and the writer's consistent expert stance was to posit a misguided (rather than merely ignorant) reader, as does Danielle Voorhees in the letter opening reprinted earlier, who addressed someone who expects marriage to be as exciting as engagement.

Danger may be a friend or counselor's basis for a more authoritarian stance than normal. One student achieves such a stance in part of her paper by positing a reader who is using the Pill, despite the fact that she is a smoker. The letter writer, assuming a strong advice-giving stance, earnestly warns about the dangers, advises her friend to go off the Pill, and recommends several other possible contraceptive methods, elaborating on the pros and cons of each. This strategy allows the writer nicely to meet Robison's expectations for discussion of alternatives and counterarguments.

Some students posited a reader who had heard wrong or bad advice, or had been given inappropriate models by others—again allowing a strong counselor stance and the incorporation of counterarguments. One student writes about the inappropriate models presented by friends and the inappropriate advice from mothers that she and the letter recipient have experienced:

> You and I both know the success rate of our friends and their marriages—you know—the success rate that is non-existent. Funny how all of their marriages fell apart or ended due to outside lovers. Actually, it's not funny at all—so let's get down to some serious business, girlfriend.
> [and later in the letter:]
> You and I both had mothers who did not let the word sex come out of their mouths, except to tell us that all men were after only one thing . . .

Though the writer above establishes the recipient's misinformation as the basis of her expert stance, she also maintains a peer relationship by characterizing herself as also formerly misinformed. Such strategies for maintaining the "friend" relationships despite the expert stance are common in the letters.

Students occasionally posited a reader who might in the future make a wrong move. One writer warns her friend against extramarital affairs, discussing the kind of damage that affairs can do, and invoking the church's teaching. The danger of an affair provides the basis for a strong stance on the letter writer's part.

Another type of recipient is the one who has a difficult decision or path ahead. For example, the note of doubt introduced in Lei Kung's letter opener is followed by a long passage in which Kung urges her friend to ask, "Are you really in love?" and takes her friend through some of the moves necessary to decide whether or not to marry (despite the fact that the assignment sheet suggests a friend who has already made that decision). One Spanish-speaking student posits a reader who has gotten pregnant unintentionally and has decided to marry the father of the baby rather than have an abortion (adoption is not mentioned). Her letter assumes that the couple is not necessarily well suited or in love, and may have difficulty establishing a healthy relationship after a less than ideal start. Another Hispanic student posits a reader who is about to marry a middle-Eastern Muslim and will face significant cross-cultural adjustment between his assumptions and her own Hispanic Catholic upbringing.

The one Asian and the four Hispanic students in the class were the ones who most frequently posited some sort of difficult decision or path, perhaps because they found the whole issue of entering marriage difficult, due to cross-cultural conflicts. Robison notes that Hispanic and African American students typically enrolled in her class in disproportionate numbers. Her contacts with them as they sought her out after class or in her office, and the information they revealed through their writing and in-class contributions, led her to believe that a large part of their motivation for enrolling in the class was to get a handle on the problems of courtship and marriage as people whose cultural background was different from the mainstream. It may be that assignments that raise issues of cross-cultural differences, even obliquely, will be treated in a significantly different fashion by students who are dealing in their own lives with cultural differences.

In summary, then, successful students in Robison's class had to build a consistent role of "expert" that was in some ways like their familiar roles, but in some ways different. Robison's suggestion in the assignment sheet that they posit themselves as someone who had taken the course and whose friend had asked for advice seemed genuinely helpful, and virtually all students used it to help them construct the self as expert. Some students, however, used additional strategies to further strengthen their expert status. They:

- used personal experience as a further basis for expertise
- added a counselor-like role for themselves
- posited a reader who was needy because she:

  was misguided

  was in danger

  had had wrong information or model

  might make a wrong move in the future

  faced a difficult decision or path

These strategies were strong because they retained the peer-to-peer "friend" situation the assignment specified, yet helped the writer develop a strong, consistent "expert" voice that allowed the student more naturally to incorporate the amount and complexity of social scientific information and the counselor-like stance that Robison expected. Once we saw these strategies that high-success students used, Robison could, in later semesters, deliberately suggest them to all her students.

Strategies for Achieving an Appropriate Tone

Rightly predicting that students would have difficulties with tone, Robison addressed the issue in her assignment sheet by suggesting that "The tone of the letter can be casual like you would use to a friend but should still include academic technical material."

In doing the primary trait analysis, we realized that one of Robison's ways of recognizing the academic course material was through vocabulary. Successful students combined technical information and vocabulary on, say, the stages of sexual arousal, but translated the information for the lay recipient of the letter and also set the technical material within a context of casual, informal address. Thus Robison's suggestion that a casual tone be combined with technical material gives a hint in the right direction, and some students did it very successfully. Here is a letter that, in Robison's judgment, successfully combines material from class notes and textbook with direct address, a conversational tone, translation of technical terms, and reference to both the writer's and the reader's experience. The writer, Danielle Voorhees, has already established a misguided letter recipient who thinks marriage will be as exciting as courtship (p. 154). The excerpt here begins soon after that opening paragraph:

> Now back to all that love making that you are expecting. According to Blumstein and Schwartz (1983), the average American couple makes love about two or three times per week when they are in their twenties. Statistics show that 45% of married couples who have been together for 2 years or less engage in intercourse 3 times a week or more. At 2 to 10 years together, only 27% engaged in intercourse 3 times or more a week but, the majority of couples in this range engaged in coitus 1 to 3 times per week. Well, Kel, it looks like there is a possibility that sex during marriage is not going to happen every night like you and Dwayne have planned. Although, it could happen often if your make sex one of your priorities and not just something that is done late at night once you have come home from work, cooked, cleaned, and put the kids to bed. During a lecture, my instructor mentioned that couples tend to get into a "rut" with their sex lives because they don't make sex important, they just "do it" at a set time, same place, and use the same techniques.

Voorhees refers to Robison's in-class language. In fact, her own language in this letter is in some ways similar to the combination of scientific and conversational language that Robison used in class.

Though Voorhees achieved a successful tone, many students struggled to do so. Lei Kung, after rereading a draft of her opening paragraphs, told herself:

> Unh unh, that's stupid. I should start all over again. Stop thinking
> that this is an assignment and just write to Reyna like I'm writing
> to a friend—like I always write to her.

Other students also remarked that a letter draft sounded "stupid,"
or "like a term paper, not like a letter." In their peer reviews, the issue
of whether the paper "sounds like a letter" also came up frequently,
even though it was not included on the Peer Review sheet. For example,
one student praised another: "It sounds like something I would pick
up and read from you."

Students often did not know how to revise a paper that seemed to
have the wrong tone. After her sentence about the letter sounding
"stupid," and the resolution to write to Reyna as always, Kung
abandoned her draft and began again with a different tone: "Dear
Reyna, Hey, what's up? Long time no see."

But her new draft lacked the content and substance the teacher
would expect: forgetting that the letter was an assignment placed her
in an inappropriate layperson role. She abandoned the new "Hey,
what's up?" draft and returned to the "stupid" one, which she changed
very little (pp. 154–155). In Robison's judgment Kung's letter achieved
a successful tone, but clearly students could not simply use the tone
they normally used in letter-writing to their friends, but had to construct
a tone for the assignment—a tone that often seemed "stupid" or
difficult to achieve.

One student who achieved a successful tone that was among the
most informal in the class, yet still had the substance Robison expected,
talked her letter onto the tape as though talking to a friend and then
typed from the tape with only surface changes. She thus used our
research device directly as a composing tool to help her solve the
problem of tone. Nonetheless, she, too, struggled with issues of tone,
remarking at one point about her draft, "This is stupid." She made
some changes, too, in honor of the teacher-reader and the letter's
status as an assignment: for example, the letter as talked on the tape
is free of four-letter words, though this African American student
sometimes used such words in class discussions and presumably would
also use them in a letter to a friend. She formalized the tone still more
as she wrote from her spoken, taped draft, for example changing
"whore" on the tape to "prostitute" in the written final copy.

Tone was thus a significant difficulty for Robison's students. In a
future semester, Robison decided, she could give examples of the tone
she considered appropriate for the letter, analysis of how successful
writers achieved that tone, and some process suggestions such as
talking the letter aloud onto a tape.

Thus the letter format, which seemed, on the face of it, an easy format in which to ask students to write, in fact imposed some difficulties because it was actually a hybrid form that had to sound something like a letter to a friend yet adopt the counselor-in-training role and meet the academic expectations of the teacher. Students' difficulties lay in combining the characteristics of each, particularly in transcending a textbook-processor approach in order to fully delineate and address the letter recipient, maintaining a consistent "expert" self in the letter, and achieving an appropriate tone that fit the letter recipient yet also served the expectations of the teacher for technical information and vocabulary. Yet Robison viewed these as tasks both necessary to the future roles her students would have to play and akin to the roles she herself played as she translated and shaped social science information for clients and students, addressing them in friendly, helpful ways with an informal tone, yet offering them substantive social scientific information and a counselor's help. Through our study, she learned more about her students' difficulties and about how her teaching methods were working or might be improved.

THREE INTERRELATED DIFFICULTIES: STATING A POSITION; USING DISCIPLINE-BASED METHODS TO ARRIVE AT (AND SUPPORT) A POSITION; MANAGING COMPLEXITY

Three other interconnected areas of difficulty were heavily influenced by the different roles that Robison modeled and expected from her students: stating a position, using discipline-based methods to arrive at and support a position, and managing complexity. As a basis for our discussion, we first explore the nature of good/better/best reasoning in Robison's class as compared to Sherman's and Breihan's classes.

We have noted that in all four classes we studied, students had to perform the five tasks of good/better/best reasoning (p. 12). However, the classes differed in emphasis. In Sherman's and Breihan's classes, the student decision maker or arguer performed all five tasks. In Robison's assignment, however, the student as social scientist/counselor/friend concentrated on Task 2, choosing information and analysis according to the needs of the client, leaving the definition of "good" (Task 1) and the decision making (Tasks 3–5) in the hands of the client. In response to the friend's request for advice, when following the roles Robison modeled in the classroom, the writer might:

1. Describe the central issues or points of concern that ought to be considered in shaping a good marital sex life.

2. State general principles that have been shown to be helpful (e.g., when conflict arises, share thoughts with your partner in a negotiating mode).

3. Under each issue, present alternatives (e.g., there are several modes of contraception).

4. Discuss consequences and outcomes of various alternatives.

5. Provide technical information or research results needed for good decision making (e.g., the failure rates of each form of contraception).

6. Discuss the decision-making process.

7. Give direct "you should" advice only in cases of danger.

In Sherman's class, decision makers managed complexity by considering alternatives and counterarguments before making a decision; in Breihan's class by defending their positions against counterarguers. In Robison's class, the counselor was expected to manage complexity by choosing and interpreting social scientific information germane to the client's needs, and by sensitively facilitating the client's decision making.

Figure 5.4 shows Sherman's, Breihan's, and Robison's models for good/better/best reasoning.

Robison's model is a version of Sherman's define/analyze/prescribe, but with the writer playing a counseling, not a decision-making, role. To "take a position" in Robison's class, then, meant to define one's client and one's relationship to the client, offering *appropriate* help to the client's decision-making process. It follows, then, that the text-processor students who delineated a letter recipient only minimally could not arrive at a position, in Robison's sense, because they had

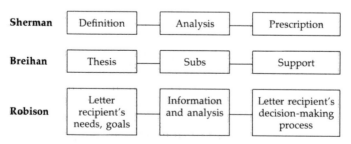

Figure 5.4. Sherman's, Breihan's, and Robison's models for good/better/best reasoning.

no reader characteristics, needs, and goals to determine what information and analysis should be offered. But other students who *did* fully delineate a letter recipient nonetheless had difficulties defining their own positions, supporting them, and managing complexity as Robison had expected. These students sometimes failed to meet Robison's expectations in two ways:

1. Abdicating their responsibility to guide and counsel the client/friend.
2. Not including enough specific, course-related, social science information to meet Robison's expectations.

We will explore these more fully as we discuss how students' strategies and Robison's methods influenced them.

TEACHER'S METHODS AND STUDENTS' STRATEGIES

Strategies That Circumvented Complexity

Students used three strategies that prevented them from establishing an appropriate counselor position, using the methods of the discipline, and managing complexity as Robison expected.

1. *Positing the letter recipient who has already made a decision.* One student writes, "Since you and Jim are interested in having children you would want to know when is the best time to have intercourse to increase your chances of conception." She then presents the basal temperature method as a way of increasing chances for conception, not mentioning its contraceptive function or allowing the possibility that the letter recipient would even face the question of contraception. By so doing, she limits her ability to represent the complexity of the issues and the alternatives the class has studied.

2. *Making the decision for the reader.* One student, instead of presenting options, writes, "Since you and Francis don't want children right away, I think you should know something about the birth control pill." She follows this with a discussion of how the Pill works, its failure rate, and its side effects, but she does not present alternative methods of birth control. Rather, she limits herself to the reasons why her friend may safely use the Pill: "for healthy women like you, it is [an] extremely effective, safe means of contraception."

3. *Shifting responsibility inappropriately to another expert.* In the same letter quoted above, consideration of other birth control methods is

shifted to an expert, as the student writer advises the letter recipient to see a doctor for further questions.

In contrast to these three strategies, more successful students constructed a reader whose needs led the writer to present the pros and cons of a number of birth control methods, discussing their moral and religious as well as medical implications, using material taken from class notes, and *then* suggesting that the friend consult a doctor for specific medical examination and advice before making a final decision. Sometimes such high-success students would also add advice about the decision-making process. After a condensed but informative review of contraception, one student advises her reader:

> This is just a briefing more or less about certain contraceptives. I encourage you to check other forms. Shop around for what you think is best for the two of you. You wouldn't buy the first car you test drive until you've had some chance to browse. The same goes with a contraceptive. Some forms have more risks than others. Weigh them out before making a final decision.

Though the assignment sheet gave some good advice about how to adopt the counselor position vis-à-vis the letter recipient, clearly the task was complex, and students might have benefited from some examples and instruction regarding the ways in which they could define their positions and their readers so as to take an appropriate counselor role and to include the course-related learning that Robison expected.

PRE-DRAFT WRITING

In Sherman's and Breihan's classes, students' ability to use the methods of the discipline to arrive at and support their positions seemed related to their pre-draft writing (i.e., any writing that precedes the first draft of two-thirds of what the student intends to be the paper). For example, we noted that students who achieved success on Sherman's McDonald's-Popeye's paper took notes *at* the fast-food restaurants rather than later or not at all. Likewise, we noted the functions of pre-draft writing for Breihan's students, as they learned to create dialogue between argument and counterargument. Similarly, in Robison's class, students' ability to use the findings of social science seemed related to their pre-draft writing.

In Robison's class one aspect was whether or not the student took full class notes. Consider this very minimal paragraph on the stages of love from a low-success letter by Sharon Enders:

> It is also important to remember that there are stages in a marriage. You and Bob will not always be as happy with each other as you are right now and that this is normal in a relationship. There will be periods of disillusionment all through your marriage but they will pass and soon you and Bob will be getting along again.

We do not have Enders's notes on the stages of love, but we do have some of her other class notes. Here is a sample:

4/8
Unit IV
how mind/psyche interacts w/ body?
4 main emotional disturbances
depression
anxiety
anger
guilt

1. Intellectual insight
2. Practice
3. Cognitive/emotional dissonance   head and gut split
4. Emotional Insight
5. Personality change

Premarital Sex
sexual rev.—in females having pre-marital sex

	'48 53	'74
	Kinsey	Hunt
[male sign]	71%	97%
[female sign]	33%	70%

increase use of contraception
age of marr. up—puberty age down
women's movement

A student with such minimal notes in a course that the teacher described in an interview as "80 percent notes, 20 percent textbook" is in trouble. She has no way to easily access information, to classify information, to get details about her topics, or to see the organizational headings for material. She's left with fragmentary, undifferentiated notes that are too thin to be the basis for a letter that presents specific, detailed information to the recipient.

Using Notes While Composing

In addition to creating appropriate pre-draft writing, successful students used their textbooks and class notes directly as they composed. Less successful students did not use their sources; rather, they relied on a composing process that was like the normal friendly letter—composed without direct reference to sources (Figure 5.5).

An example of a successful student is Connie Hatch, whom we have seen in dialogue with her roommate as Hatch planned and composed her letter. To plan the letter, Hatch began by fully and carefully delineating her letter recipient. Then she flipped through all her textbook chapters and class notes for the semester, considering each topic, including or rejecting it on the basis of whether it fit the letter recipient. This strategy helped her do what was difficult for Sherman's and Breihan's students as well as Robison's—bring information about the options into disciplined relationship with the definition of "good" (here, with the characteristics of the letter recipient) so that a single decision could be made—reasoning Task 3. Further, her strategy helped Hatch include specific social scientific information because, when she decided to include a topic, she had her textbook and notes right there.

In contrast, a less successful student did not begin by delineating a reader, but rather by deciding to use only a certain section of her textbook; she did not look over or consider other sections; her letter disappointed Robison's expectations for selection of a breadth of information related to the letter recipient's needs. Still other students, as we have said, did not have specific notes or did not consult them while composing the letter.

High-Success Students   Low-Success Students

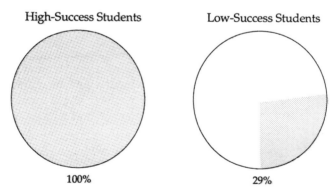

100%   29%

Figure 5.5. Percentage of high-success and low-success students who composed directly from class notes. N = the 7 lowest-success and 6 highest-success students. "Success" refers to paper grade during the course and score on the post-course primary trait analysis (p. 35). Evidence is based on think-aloud tapes or, in the case of three low-success students who did not tape their drafting or mention in the log that they used class notes, on evidence from the drafts.

RESPONSES TO DRAFTS

One teaching method Robison had instituted after the writing-across-the-curriculum workshop was draft response, both by peers and by herself. These responses required class time for peer review and Robison's time, outside of class, to write comments on the drafts. Like Sherman and Breihan, Robison also asked during our study, "Was draft response worth it?"

Successful Peer Response and Revision

The student Alice Smith illustrates peer response that worked well. During the in-class, think-aloud training session (p. 28) before beginning the letter assignment, Smith described her "usual" composing process: "When I begin the initial writing I usually start and finish (including typing) in the same night." Peer response changed that pattern and helped Smith substantially improve her paper. In class, Smith's peer suggested both a reorganization of the letter draft to bring two similar points together into the same part of the paper, and further development of her topics by "providing more examples." Smith followed this advice and conducted a major revision, which improved her paper.

Low Rate of Student Revision in Response to Teacher and Peer Comments

Despite the success of peer response for some students, however, peer and teacher response did not result in high rates of revision by the class as a whole (Table 5.1). Sherman's and Breihan's students revised in response to more than 90 percent of the meaning-changing comments. Robison's students, however, revised in response to only 50 percent of their peers' meaning-changing comments, and to none of Robison's. Why?

Robison's Methods for Mandating Revision

We believe one reason is the teacher's methods for mandating revision. Breihan required revision from his students after Essay 1; revision was optional after Essay 2. Sherman required revision after his response

Table 5.1 Student Revisions After Peer and Teacher Suggestions

Suggestion	Peer Suggestions		Teacher Suggestions	
	Low Success[a] Papers	High Success Papers	Low Success Papers	High Success Papers
Meaning-Changing[b] Suggestions				
Select relevant materials[c]	3 (2)[d]	3 (0)	5 (0)	0
Paper is vague	0	0	1 (0)	0
Improve organization	2 (1)	0	1 (0)	0
Add topic sentences	2 (2)	0	0	0
Answer the question asked	0	0	1 (0)	0
Correct inaccuracy	0	0	1 (0)	0
Surface Suggestions				
Type the paper	n.a.	n.a.	2 (2)	2 (2)
Revise paragraphing	1 (1)	1 (0)	0	0
Clarify sentence meaning	0	1 (0)	0	0
Add/correct citations	0	4 (3)	4 (2)	4 (3)
Correct mechanics	14 (13)	16 (16)	6	0

[a] "Success" refers to grade given to paper both during the course and on the post-course primary trait analysis (p. 36).

[b] See p. 40 for definition of "meaning changing."

[c] Material refers to sufficient specific information relevant to the recipient.

[d] Parentheses contain the number of suggestions that resulted in revisions by the writer.

N = The six lowest-success and six highest-success students who attended peer response sessions (a seventh lowest-success student in our sample did not attend).

to drafts, except for the few drafts that were already at an "A" level. Robison did not require revision. Also, both Breihan and Sherman mandated changes in the revised version separate from the teacher's specific comments. Breihan mandated that the introductory or thesis paragraph be changed in the revision. Sherman mandated that the final paper be reduced to a maximum of five pages. Robison did not mandate particular changes in phrasing or length.

Sequence of Peer and Teacher Responses

Second, we believe that the sequence of peer and teacher responses and their position within the total writing process played a role. In Sherman's and Breihan's classes, the teachers responded to mainly handwritten drafts and there had been no peer response. In Robison's class, students first brought handwritten drafts for peer response, then revised their papers and submitted a typed draft for Robison's comments, after which they could revise once more for the final grade.

Several dynamics may be at work here. By the time the drafts reached Robison, students had already invested a great deal of time and effort. The act of typing may have locked in the copy, making students unwilling to retype them after Robison's suggestions. Timing may also have been a factor. Students received their drafts back with Robison's suggestions in the class period after having submitted them. But it was late April, lovely weather, and only two weeks from the end of the school year. Half the class were seniors. Further, with Robison's ongoing point system, students knew exactly where they were (except for the final exam) in terms of a final grade for the course, and the number of points they would have received for revising their papers was relatively low (see the assignment sheet earlier in this chapter). Finally, revision for some aspects such as "selection of relevant material," Robison's most frequent suggestion, would have required a fundamental reshaping of the paper and a return to textbook or notes in order to meet Robison's expectation that students would include specific course material over a range of topics angled to the needs of a fully delineated letter recipient. Some students did not have the detailed class notes needed to provide specific course material, as we have seen, but others did not have the time, energy, or motivation to undertake such a major task.

Differences between Peer and Teacher Response

Peer response took place in class and was guided by the Peer Review sheet (p. 152). Students revised after peer response and then, finally, presented a draft to Robison for her comments, after which they could revise again for the final grade. We noted several difficulties in this pattern.

First, peers' evaluations of "selection of relevant material" did not correspond to Robison's judgments (Table 5.1). On four low-success papers, peers did not comment on selection of relevant material, but Robison later did. On three high-success papers, peers suggested changes, the writer ignored the suggestions, and Robison thought the papers were fine.

Peers seemed to do best on aspects for which there were clear rules or conventions—mechanics, presence of topic sentences, handling of the outside reference, and organization of the paper (a fairly simple affair in the letters, meaning basically that topics were treated one at a time and only one topic was treated in a section). We speculate that if the requirements for vaguer areas such as "selection of relevant material" were made more specific, using insights we gained through the primary trait analysis, peer responses might more nearly match Robison's. For example, for "selection of relevant material," peers might be asked to check whether the writer had covered at least 4 topics of the 14 that had been covered so far in class; whether each topic was developed by citing specific information from the course material; how each topic was justified by the situation or need of the letter recipient; whether the vocabulary of the course was used, yet translated for the letter recipient; and so on.

Sequencing the Writer's Attention

In addition to the difficulties caused by peers' and teachers' varying responses, there were also difficulties in sequencing the writer's attention to various aspects. The Peer Review sheet (Figure 5.2) begins with substantive issues (such as organization and selection of relevant material) and works down to mechanics. Our tape recordings of the peer responses show that students followed that order. However, Table 5.1 shows that mechanics was the most frequent subject of comment among peers and resulted in the highest rate of revision. Thus, despite Robison's attempt to establish a hierarchy of response that postponed mechanics, the actual effect of the peer response was to provoke students to revise their papers for mechanics before they had received their teacher's response on more substantive issues.

For these reasons, we question the common pattern of having peers respond first, before teacher response. The metaphor seems to be that peers serve as a kind of "frontline troops," addressing the most significant or visible problems, and then the teacher responds to the finer points. Data from Robison's class suggest that this may be a problematic model for the relationship between peer and teacher response. It may be that the teacher should comment first, addressing the substantive issues that peers are not well able to evaluate. The weight of the teacher's authority early in the process might provoke the substantial reworking or return to information gathering that some students need. Peer comments might then address issues that are guided by more specific conventions.

Importance of Early Guidance

Another implication from our analysis is the importance of *early* teacher guidance before drafts are produced. The six high-success students and the four middle-success students from our focus group were the ones who had appropriately planned the paper, relying on the early web exercise, on their counselor roles, and on their use of class notes and textbook as they composed. These successful students received very few substantive suggestions from peers, ignored some of those suggestions, and received no substantive suggestions from Robison (Table 5.1). On the other hand, students who had ignored the early web or missed class, who either adopted a textbook-processor role or did not invest energy in delineating a reader (or both), and who had minimal class notes or did not use their notes and textbooks in composing, did not generally correct all those problems through revision.

ROBISON'S AND WALVOORD'S CONCLUSIONS

In this chapter, we have "read" Robison's class in terms of the complex roles of both teacher and students, showing how the roles influenced the nature of good/better/best reasoning and the nature of students' difficulties. The professional-in-training role was expected by teachers in all four classrooms, but the specific nature of that role was quite different in each. Similarly, the five tasks of good/better/best reasoning were necessary in each classroom, but the different roles expected of students meant that the reasoning was different in Robison's class, where the writer did not make the final decision but rather facilitated the decision making of the client.

Though students' roles created some differences, nonetheless, we also said in this chapter that the same six areas of difficulties existed and that those difficulties appeared to be influenced by some of the same students' strategies and teacher's methods we constructed in Sherman's and Breihan's classes—for example, the teacher's language on the assignment sheet and students' ways of using the assignment sheet; students' use of models from other settings and the teacher's guidance of that use; students' idea-generating strategies and the teacher's guidance (especially the web); students' and the teacher's different approaches to the textbooks; students' pre-draft writing and teacher's guidance.

Finally, in this chapter, we explored how Robison's method of peer and teacher draft response worked. We compared the relatively low rate of student revision in Robison's class to the higher rates of revision after teacher response in Sherman's and Breihan's classes. We concluded that contextual factors can significantly affect how, and whether, students respond to peer and teacher comments. We questioned the metaphor that represents peers as "frontline troops" offering the first, broad-level response.

In each of the three classrooms under study, our data analysis spurred changes in the teacher's methods. The next chapter reports what Walvoord and Anderson discovered, not only in Anderson's initial class, but in the same class three years later, after Anderson had implemented changes based on the initial study.

6 Conducting and Reporting Original Scientific Research: Anderson's Biology Class

Virginia Johnson Anderson
Towson State University

Barbara E. Walvoord
Loyola College in Maryland

As in the other chapters, here we present and analyze students' difficulties, but more importantly we describe and document what happened when a teacher-researcher, after identifying these difficulties through systematic observation of her classroom, changed her teaching methods.

Like the other classroom chapters, this one begins by describing the teacher's expectations. We note particularly the similarities and differences between Anderson's and the other three teachers' expectations for the professional-in-training role and for good/better/best reasoning. Then we describe Anderson's teaching methods for 1983—the first of the two sections of her class that we studied. Next, we discuss the difficulties that arose, how Anderson changed her teaching methods to address those difficulties, and the improvement we found in the research and the papers of students in 1986—the second section we studied.

Though we used outside raters to establish that the papers of the second class had improved, this chapter is not a report of a scientific experiment to prove the efficacy of Anderson's procedures. It is, like our others, a naturalistic study of events in a particular classroom, and it takes place within the theoretical framework and research approaches outlined in Chapter 2. This chapter is a story, actually—the story of how a biology teacher and a collaborating colleague observed her class, identified what she took to be the difficulties that had arisen, and then shaped teaching methods to address those difficulties. Particularly Anderson tried to provide *concrete experiences* through which her students could learn to use the scientific method—in other words, to teach procedural knowledge procedurally. It is the story of Ander-

son's attempt to see whether the improvement she thought had resulted
from her changes could be recognized by others.

Anderson: Background

For Virginia Johnson Anderson, the process of change began in the
fall of 1981 in a writing-across-the-curriculum workshop for college
teachers. She recalls in her own words:

I would love to tell you that it was great insight on my part or great
recruitment by the writing-across-the-curriculum (WAC) movement
that brought me to study how students write in science, but it wasn't.
I was pregnant. Not just pregnant, but over 40, with two years left to
finish my doctoral dissertation on scanning electron microscopy, jug-
gling a full-time, tenured, biology assistant professorship and two
children 12 and 15, thrilled to death—pregnant! My motive for taking
the WAC workshop was to get the "release time and/or other recognition" that my university was offering to lure faculty into the
workshop.

Well, my darling son was born in February and bundled off to WAC
workshops once a week from March through May. Also, he slept,
almost unnoticed, in a carrier on my back as I delivered the last ten
Biology 101 lectures for Spring 1982. Although I never got the released
time and never figured out what the "other recognition" was, I knew
that what I had learned about the writing process had profoundly
changed my professional life.

Before the WAC workshop, I had told myself that students wrote
poorly in their biology courses because they didn't spend enough time
doing it and/or they had not been adequately trained to write in
English 101. Once the WAC workshop had dispelled these myths, I
wanted to know more about how students wrote in science. I shared
this interest with Barbara Walvoord, one of the coleaders of the
workshop. We decided to collaborate.

ANDERSON'S EXPECTATIONS

THE SCIENTIST-IN-TRAINING ROLE

We (Anderson and Walvoord) selected one assignment in Biological
Literature as the focal point of our research. Since the 1983 class had
only 13 students enrolled, we used the entire class for all analyses,

rather than choosing a focus group as in Sherman's, Breihan's, and Robison's classes.

Biological Literature was a one-semester, three-credit course offered by the biology department at Towson State University (TSU). It enrolled juniors and seniors. Although it did not count for credit for the biology major or minor, Biological Literature did fulfill the university requirement for an advanced writing course, usually taken in the student's major discipline. To enroll in Biological Literature, students had to have earned a grade of "C" or better in the freshman composition course and completed ten or more semester hours in biology. Characteristics of the class are on p. 18.

The professional-in-training role (pp. 8–9) that Anderson expected of her students was the scientist. Biological Literature was designed to include many types of writing that scientists do (see Pechenik, 1987, for a survey). Thus Anderson's assignments in both 1983 and 1986 included:

- Paragraphs and short papers summarizing laboratory results, procedures and equipment descriptions; defining and/or describing specimens; comparing and/or contrasting taxonomic groups

- Short written exercises on *BioAbstracts*, *Science Citation Index*, ERIC, and/or *Index Medicus*, all of which are indexes to science literature

- Informative abstracts of scientific journal articles

- Written text to accompany graphs, illustrations, micrographs, etc.

- Short evaluations of biology seminars, lectures, or texts to simulate short position papers by scientists

- Letter to the Editor for a scientific journal

- A short library research paper designed to give the student experience in researching scientific literature, specifically *BioAbstracts* and *Science Citation Index*, or a student grant proposal (1986 innovation)

- An original scientific research report designed to give the student an opportunity to conduct and report original scientific research

Our data are related to a single assignment—the last one listed above. The longest and most demanding of them all, this assignment spanned ten weeks.

In constructing the original research assignment, Anderson was influenced by her perception of what her students would need if they were to succeed in routine research and development laboratories

(R&D labs in scientific jargon). This is the type of job that many biology graduates experience during their first years of employment. In the Baltimore area, TSU biology graduates are often employed by Noxell (manufacturers of Noxzema facial cream), Doxsee Food Corporation, and McCormick (spices). As entry-level scientists, TSU graduates might work on research questions such as which purple eye makeup pigment is easiest to remove, which milk product is most stable, or which grind consistency of pepper is most aromatic.

Similarly, Anderson's assignment required students to conduct original scientific research in which they compared two commercially available products to discover which was "better." Students were expected to prepare five pages of text in the scientific report format and to include a minimum of three appropriately labeled graphics. They were to address an audience of their classmates, to whom they were also to give oral reports of their findings.

We have noted in the other three classes how the language of the classroom helped to shape roles and students' reasoning. Strikingly characteristic of Anderson's classroom, as Walvoord observed it, were collaboration and scientific problem solving. The class of 13 students met in a small science laboratory. Seated around the lab tables in groups of four, they easily formed small working groups, and Anderson frequently broke them into groups for interactive work during the class period. They resembled scientific teams working in a scientific environment. The tasks Anderson gave them were to solve scientific problems and/or to question one another's scientific methods or ideas, not in the spirit of confrontation so much as in the spirit of helping one another. We will see some of these interactive, small-group activities later in this chapter, and we will see how, after our analysis of the 1983 data, Anderson changed the nature of some of these small-group activities to make them more effective.

Anderson parked her purse and auxiliary bags and boxes of equipment up front at the instructor's lab table, where she conducted demonstrations if she needed the equipment. Otherwise, her style was to move fluidly among the groups in the manner of a project director or senior scientist directing scientific teams. Her participation in the groups struck Walvoord as quite different from what she herself might experience in a composition class, where students are revealing their own perceptions and stories about which they are the only experts, and into which the teacher may hesitate to intrude. Anderson dipped into one group after the other with energy and direction. These were groups whose procedures were open to public scrutiny and accountable to the scientific community. Often a group would motion Anderson to their table to consult with her about a procedure or problem. Anderson's expectations and the dynamics of her classroom, then, were oriented toward helping students to become scientists—Anderson's version of the professional-in-training role.

ANDERSON'S EXPECTATIONS FOR GOOD/BETTER/BEST REASONING

The good/better/best question that Anderson's assignment addressed was "Which of two consumer products is 'better'?" As in the other disciplines, Anderson's students had to perform the five tasks of good/better/best reasoning (p. 12) in order to answer it. Figure 6.1 shows how the models for good/better/best reasoning differed in each class.

Anderson saw herself as enforcing the expectations for scientific experimentation and scientific writing that were common to the scientific community. We discuss her expectations here under two headings: Expectations for using the scientific method and expectations for organizing the research within the scientific format.

Anderson's Expectations for Using the Scientific Method

To arrive at their conclusion about which product was better, students had to use the scientific method; i.e., they had to formulate a hypothesis,

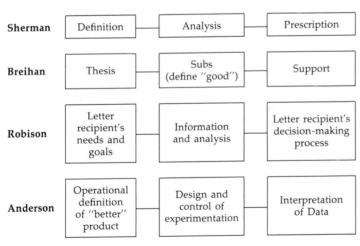

Figure 6.1. Models for good/better/best reasoning.

construct operational definitions, design an experiment, control the variables, and interpret the data.

Formulating a Hypothesis

Students could not test a statement like "Jumpy tennis balls are wonderful." As novice scientists, they had to learn to structure ideas into testable statements such as, "Tennis players will express a preference for Jumpy tennis balls over Bumpy tennis balls," or "Jumpy tennis balls will bounce higher than Bumpy tennis balls." Students were further encouraged to construct a null hypothesis: "There is no difference between Jumpy and Bumpy tennis balls." Anderson considered null hypotheses easier to accept, reject and/or interpret than directional hypotheses such as "Jumpy tennis balls are better than Bumpy tennis balls."

Defining "Better" Operationally

Anderson required the definition of "better product" to include at least four experimental factors plus cost (cost is not an experimental factor because one does not need to conduct an experiment to find it—just read the price tag). In other words, students could not decide that pickle *A* was better than pickle *B* merely because it tasted better at room temperature. They had to consider three other factors, such as taste under refrigeration, shrinkage, and pH (a measure of acidity) over time. This information had to be integrated with the nonexperimental factor of cost, as well as with any other nonexperimental factors the student chose. Further, the assignment called for students to weigh the factors, using values they chose, much as in factor rating in Sherman's class (pp. 74–76). Would shrinkage, for example, count as heavily as taste under refrigeration in defining "better pickle?" As in the other classes, the choice of factors in the definition of *good* or *better* implied that the product might be better for some people or situations than for others. Students therefore had to target the various subgroups for the product's users. By defining "better" product in this way, the student performed good/better/best reasoning Task 1 (defining "good") and also Task 4 (integrating values with evidence).

The student also had to operationally define each of the factors that comprised the definition of "better." For example, if a student was comparing Utz's[1] with Herr's potato chips, what does "better chip" mean, and if one factor in "better chip" is crunchiness, how is "crunchier chip" defined? One experimenter might define crunchier chip as the chip that 75 percent or more of persons sampling the potato chips rank higher on a 1–4 test scale. Another experimenter might define crunchier chip as the chip that breaks into the greatest number of pieces when hit with a mallet. Either definition is satisfactory, but to achieve what Anderson considered the cardinal rule of scientific inquiry—that one's research can be replicated—the researcher had to state that definition.

Designing an Experiment

Having constructed a hypothesis and defined terms operationally, students then had to determine how to answer the question, "Which is the better product?" by designing an experiment. An appropriate experimental design included operational definitions for "better" and for each factor to be tested. Then the student had to determine how to test the factors. If the student were testing shampoo, for example, what factors (bounce, cleanliness, odor, durability, sheen, growth of new hair in three months, number of split ends) were important to identify? How could quantifiable information on these factors be obtained? If some factors were to be judged by people, how many people should be included? How many times should hair be checked for "shampoo durability"—once a day? once a week? Designing an experiment, then, was Anderson's form of Task 2—analysis of the various qualities of the product—and Task 3—bringing the information about the product's traits into disciplined relationship with the definition of "good" so that a single judgment can result.

Controlling Variables

The students had to restrict the variability that entered into the experiment in order to attribute results to the proper cause. Variables in science, Anderson taught, could be controlled in three ways: manipulation, randomization, or writing the variable out of the design.

Manipulation: If the student were examining the frying ability of Crisco and Wesson Oil, the material being fried had to be the same; students could not fry chicken in one oil and potatoes in the other.

Randomization: If a student were testing the size of cereal flakes, he or she would randomly choose, say, 20 flakes, measure these, and get the average. A random selection insured that the researcher did not pick out large flakes in one cereal and small ones in another.

Writing variables out of the design: In testing for shampoo durability, the student could simply state that for this experiment the environment of the shampoo evaluators was assumed to be comparable and that the effects of relative humidity were not considered.

Interpreting Data

After the experiment was complete, conclusions and implications had to be drawn within the framework of scientific logic constructed by the researcher. Students had to use the information as evidence to support their positions, and the conclusions had to be limited by the nature of the designs. If a student designed soap comparisons and found that 40 male soap users wash with Dial for 3.2 minutes and Ivory for 4.1 minutes, the student could not conclude that *people* use Ivory soap longer than Dial soap, but would have to make the conclusion gender specific.

In interpreting the data, the student had to address the question of "better for whom?" by designating various subgroups of users. For example, a more absorbent paper towel costing twice as much might be better *for those who could afford the extra cost.*

Within Task 5 (balancing rationale-building with solution-searching), Anderson placed heavier emphasis on solution-searching than any of the other teachers. Once the definition of "good" was determined, feelings and values should not enter the process of decision making; rather, the student was expected to adopt the scientific stance, attempting to reach results through objective, quantifiable experimentation.

Anderson's Expectations for Organizing the Research Report with a Scientific Format

As research scientists, students had to report their findings in the traditional research report. Format in Anderson's class was therefore more convention-driven and more specific than in the other disciplines, where students were told to "write a letter" or "write an essay," with specific sections left to choice.

Anderson expected the students to use the standard scientific journal article format and taught them to organize their papers according to the following sections: Title, Abstract, Introduction, Review of the Literature, Methods and Materials, Results, Discussion, and Literature Cited. As we describe Anderson's format expectations, we will give excerpts from the paper of Jim Wilkerson, a high-success student from the 1983 class who wrote what Anderson considered a good report on his experiment to compare two types of erasable pens. ("Success" is defined on p. 36.)

Title

The title of an original science research paper should be explicit because the major science reference sources such as *BioAbstracts, ChemAbstracts,* and *Science Citation Index* use the title's key words (descriptors) to index the article. Anderson explained that titles were restricted to 25 words or less and expected students to adopt the tone of the many research article titles they had read earlier in the course. Wilkerson's title, "Comparable Research on Papermate Erasermate$_{TM}$ and the Scripto Erasable$_{TM}$ Pen," was appropriate in length and tone, but it lacked any descriptors of the qualities for which the pens were being tested. The title, "A Comparison of the Writing Ability, Erasability, and Ease of Use of Papermate Erasermate$_{TM}$ and Scripto Erasable$_{TM}$ Pen" would have been more effective in Anderson's judgment.

Abstract

Anderson expected an informative abstract in which the first sentence explained what the researcher did. Subsequent sentences were to describe how the researcher did it, what he or she found, and what implications could be drawn from the study. Never to exceed 5 percent of the original work, most abstracts, Anderson taught, are limited to about 250 words (Biddle and Bean, 1987, 41–46). Here is Wilkerson's abstract:

> The Papermate Erasermate$_{TM}$ and the Scripto Erasable$_{TM}$ Pens were evaluated on the basis of smoothness of writing, tendency not to skip, tendency not to smear, erasability, overall appearance and writing comfort. The Erasable$_{TM}$ Pen was found to be better. Seven volunteers (four males and three females) from ages 16 to 58 made up the study group. Three of the seven volunteers were left-handed. The length of time required before the erasable inks became permanent was studied inconclusively. Both pens photocopy about the same.

Introduction

Anderson told her students in class that the Introduction "attracts the reader's attention and states the purpose of the research." It was therefore important to set up a framework for the research and to identify interested audiences. In addition to this, some recent texts on scientific writing such as Day's (1979) *How to Write and Publish a*

Scientific Paper (23–25) advocate including a brief statement of findings in the Introduction. In *Writing Papers in the Biological Sciences*, McMillan (1988) explains, "Other writers, along with some journal editors, criticize this practice, arguing that results are already covered in their own section and in the Discussion and Abstract. Ask your instructor what he or she prefers" (15). Anderson preferred the more traditional form and did not instruct or expect the students to include results. Wilkerson's Introduction met Anderson's expectations:

> If you are a perfect writer who never makes mistakes, you will probably not be interested in this paper. But if you have to spell a word three different times before you get it right, you may benefit from this research. Erasable pens can make your notes or even your final drafts look much better. Instead of crossing out mistakes, you can simply erase and correct them. The frustration of ruining a birthday card by misspelling your best friend's name can be cured with an erasable pen. The embarrassment of asking for two job applications because you know you will mess up one can be forgotten. Erasable pens can give the writer freedom from mistakes and the power to write neatly with ink.
>
> In this paper the Papermate Erasermate$_{TM}$ and the Scripto Erasable$_{TM}$ Pen are evaluated. The aim of the paper is to demonstrate that one pen is better than the other or that both pens are of similar quality. Various aspects of the performance of both pens will be used in the evaluation.

Review of the Literature

Scientific writers ordinarily prepare a review of the literature to draw in previous information and techniques or to associate their research with that of others. In this assignment the review of the literature was omitted because the emphasis was on demonstrating the scientific process skills.

Methods and Materials

This section reveals how the scientific experiment was conducted. Anderson taught that it must be thorough, once again to insure replicability. The organization of the Methods and Materials section hinges on the nature of the tasks involved; it is not merely a chronological narrative. In *The Craft of Scientific Writing*, Alley (1987) states, "In scientific writing, logical sequences may be based on time, space, or any number of variables. The variable that you choose depends on your research and your audience" (156). Wilkerson's Methods and Materials section begins with the heading "Evaluation of Six Aspects of the Erasermate_TM and the Erasable Pen_TM." Here is his explanation of how one of those tests was conducted:

> Seven volunteers were asked to write the first three paragraphs of the Declaration of Independence two times in order to evaluate the performance of each pen, the first time using the Erasermate_TM and the second time using the Erasable_TM Pen. The volunteers included four males and three females. They ranged from 16 to 58 years of age. Three of the volunteers (two male and one female) were left-handed. The volunteers wrote in a spiral notebook at their leisure. They were instructed to correct immediately any mistakes they made. In case they did not make any mistakes, they were told to erase four words at random and rewrite them.
>
> The volunteers were asked to rate the pens on six criteria. The rating scale ranged from one (very poor) to five (very good). The six criteria are defined as:
>
> 1. Smoothness: Smooth writing pens have minimum drag on the paper. A smooth writing pen glides easily across the paper.
> 2. Tendency not to skip: The ink flows evenly and regularly.
> [continues with the other criteria]

Results

The Results, Anderson taught, should include both written text and graphic information. Quantitative data should be introduced by appropriate text. Further, as McMillan (1988) explains, "The Results section should be a straightforward report of the data. Do not compare your findings with those of other researchers, and do not discuss why your results were or were not consistent with your predictions. Avoid speculating about the causes of particular findings or about their significance. Save such comments for the Discussion" (21).

Anderson was pleased that Wilkerson did just as McMillan advocated, and that he presented the results to his readers in both text and graphics. Here is an excerpt from the text of his Results section:

> Evaluation of six aspects of the Erasermate_TM and the Erasable_TM Pen by volunteers (see tables 1, 2 and 3)
>
> Smoothness: The Erasable_TM Pen was found to be a much smoother writing instrument than the Erasermate_TM for the left-handers. The right-handers rated the Erasermate_TM as the smoother pen. By including both groups together, the Erasable_TM Pen is rated smoother.
>
> Tendency not to skip: The left-handers rated the Erasable_TM Pen as better by two points on the rating scale while the right-handers preferred the Erasermate_TM. Summing both groups gives the Erasable_TM Pen a clear advantage in this category.
> [continues with rest of results]

The organization of Wilkerson's results followed the same sequence of topics in his Methods and Materials section. (See Table 6.1).

Discussion

The Discussion section is also called "Conclusions" or "Implications." In this section, students should summarize major findings, support or reject the hypothesis, and provide explanations of the significance of the data and relevant nonexperimental information. The statements in this section are interpretive. McMillan (1988) suggests that the prose in this section, unlike the Introduction which moves from the general to the specific, should move from the specific to the general and "convey confidence and authority" (26–27). Here is the first part of Wilkerson's Discussion:

> Left-handed writers clearly preferred the Erasable_{TM} Pen. The tendency not to smear was an important category. Left-handed writers tend to drag their hands through their writing as they move across the paper. This causes smearing with both pens, but the Erasable_{TM} Pen smeared less.

Literature Cited

This section was necessary only if outside sources were used. In Anderson's research assignment, library sources were not required; however, many students did cite advertising claims or commercial publications.

Table 6.1   *Jim Wilkerson's table with his title:*
Averaged Responses of Right- and Left-Handed Volunteers to the Six Criteria Rated.*

Volunteers were asked to rate each pen on six different criteria and their responses were averaged. The scale is from one (very poor) to five (very good). Overall averages are also included.

Criterion	Erasermate$_{TM}$	Erasable$_{TM}$ Pen
Smoothness	3.29	3.43
Tendency not to Skip	3.00	3.71
Tendency not to Smear	2.43	2.86
Erasability	3.29	2.86
Overall Appearance	2.57	3.14
Comfort	3.71	3.28
Overall Average	3.05	3.21

*$\underline{n}$ = 7

Graphics

Anderson required that each student include at least three appropriately labeled graphics in the report. Wilkerson constructed three data tables (one of which is reproduced as Table 6.1) as well as a bar graph that visually illustrated the discrepancies between preferences of right-handers and left-handers.

ANDERSON'S 1983 TEACHING METHODS

When we studied her class in 1983, Anderson had already instituted some of the teaching methods she had been led to consider through the writing-across-the-curriculum workshop. Particularly, she depended heavily on peer response. Further, she had begun to work out the philosophy of teaching that would guide her throughout our study: she believed that she was a "facilitator" of learning. But she realized after our study that she was not using many concrete experiences to guide the students in using the scientific method. That was the main ingredient she added after our analysis of her class in 1983, as will become clear in later sections. In 1983, however, she used three types of teaching methods: lecture/demonstration/response to questions, peer and teacher response, and auxiliary activities. We discuss each in turn.

Lecture/Demonstration/Response to Questions

To help her students meet her expectations, Anderson introduced the original research paper early in the semester. She identified it in the class syllabus and, after Walvoord visited to explain data collection procedures, she explained the assignment more fully in class. Classroom activities that related to the assignment included:

1. A 50-minute lecture and discussion on the scientific method using a comparison of Crisco and Wesson oils as a model.

2. A 50-minute lecture on the do's and don't's of the scientific format.

3. Two 15-minute "warning and review" sessions, where Anderson reminded students to decide on their two commercial products by the date she had set for that decision.

4. A 30-minute session in class when students announced their topic decisions.

5. Occasional class time answering questions students asked about the assignment.

Peer and Teacher Response

Anderson also used several techniques she had learned in the writing-across-the-curriculum workshop, particularly peer and teacher response:

1. A 50-minute planning and focusing activity where students, in groups of four, discussed "How I am going to test _____."

2. A 50-minute class session during which students responded to one another's drafts of the Introduction and Methods and Materials sections.

3. Individual 15-minute conferences with each student to return previous writing assignments and answer questions about experimental design.

4. An interactive 45-minute class session to review the scientific method, encourage revision, advocate peer review, and urge students to edit their papers meticulously.

5. A 50-minute session just before the final papers were due, in which students worked in pairs interviewing their peers and asking such teacher-supplied questions as "I had trouble writing the _____. What part of the paper did you find hardest?"

6. Class sessions after the reports were completed, in which students gave 7- to 10-minute speeches to their classmates, reporting their research.

Auxiliary Activities

Three other activities conducted at various times throughout the semester were also important. Anderson assumed (wrongly, it turned out) that the students would recognize the relevance of these activities to their original science research. These activities were:

• Two periods (150 minutes) in the library learning how to retrieve scientific journal articles from *BioAbstracts* and *Science Citation Index*. In separate practice assignments for each resource, the students used a generic topic descriptor (i.e., *Felix rex* for the lion or *Drosophila melanagaster* for the fruit fly) to locate a title and an author of a relevant work. After the students located, read, and cited an appropriate abstract, they used a computerized locator system to determine whether the journal article was in the TSU library.

- Five reading assignments for students to read and abstract a minimum of five original research reports taken from scientific journals. All the reports followed the format that students were to use for their own reports.

- Two class periods (150 minutes) learning how to select, construct, and label graphics.

OUR METHODS OF DATA COLLECTION AND ANALYSIS

EARLY DATA COLLECTION AND ANALYSIS

We collected our first set of data in the spring 1983 semester. The data and our analytical procedures were those described in Chapter 2. Later, we expanded those procedures, as we explain.

We had promised Anderson's students that Anderson would not look at any of their process data until after course grades had been turned in. That was optimistic. Anderson was busy (remember the 12-year-old, the 15-year-old, the new baby, the full-time teaching position, and the doctoral dissertation). Anderson completed her dissertation in May, 1984, and that summer we began to examine the data. As we listened to the students' tapes and studied their notes and drafts, Anderson kept saying, "Oh, if only I'd known they were doing that, I would have . . ." Anderson knew *that* the students had fallen short of her expectations when she graded the papers in 1983, but now she was constructing explanations for *how* and *why* some of their difficulties had occurred.

We were intrigued with the difficulties. Although we were still "knee deep in data" as the spring 1985 semester started, we wanted to know more. We collected similar data—logs, tapes, rough drafts, and so forth, to help broaden our understanding of the difficulties. Although our basic analysis of student difficulties was formulated solely from the 1983 students, in this chapter we have occasionally augmented the descriptions of those difficulties with some particularly cogent examples from 1985 students.

COMPARISON OF THE 1983 AND 1986 CLASSES

By the following year, 1986, Anderson had made significant changes in her teaching methods, and we wondered whether students' thinking and writing would appear different as a result. Thus we studied the 1986 class and collected the same kinds of data, then used outside raters to compare the quality of the final products of the 1983 and 1986 classes.

Comparing the quality of the final products of two classes and using outside raters may appear outside the naturalistic paradigm and the theoretical assumptions we explain in Chapter 2, so we want to clarify what we think the comparison study portion of our research does and does not do.

First, we do *not* view the two classes as control and treatment groups. Although the classes were remarkably similar in some ways (Table 2.1, p. 18), we could not meaningfully compare SAT scores because so many of the students were transfers for whom none were recorded by the university. Further, the classes were small (each 13 students, with 11 students submitting data). More broadly, students' performance, in our theoretical paradigm, is viewed as socially constructed, shaped by multiple interacting factors within each classroom, many of which we did not investigate or try to measure. Thus we do not claim that the improvement the raters found in the 1986 class is due to Anderson's changes in teaching. Rather, that part of our investigation was simply another tool we used to get a handle on some of the ways in which teaching, thinking, and writing might be interacting in Anderson's classroom. We *do* consider Anderson's changed teaching methods as likely candidates to have influenced the improvements in 1986, and we look at the process data for explanations of how that influence worked.

The Primary Trait Analysis

Following the principle that we would keep evaluation as close to the classroom context as possible, we tied the scoring of the paper by outside raters as closely as possible to the expectations that Anderson had held during the course. In 1983 we had drafted a crude primary trait scoring scale primarily to help us articulate Anderson's expectations and to serve as a check on in-class grades to determine students' success, as we explain on pp. 35–36. In the fall of 1986, Anderson refined the primary trait analysis and constructed a primary performance scale of 1 to 5 to serve as an instrument for evaluating students' papers. (See Appendix A for the complete instrument.) Anderson then trained Walvoord, after which the scale was refined and tested again with McCarthy. We eliminated the abstract from the rating because we had found, in developing and validating the primary trait scale, that the abstract had a "halo effect" on the raters' marking of the paper.

In January 1987, Anderson trained the two outside raters. Both were experienced, tenured, college biology teachers who had not previously been involved in the project. In a one-hour training session, Anderson answered questions about the scoring scale as the biologists evaluated components and examples from the 1985 research papers. Next, the biologists read and scored two papers from the 22 papers of the 1983 and 1986 classes. Then they were asked to compare their marks in each category and to resolve discrepancies of more than 1 point by consensus; no such discrepancies occurred. Subsequently, they evaluated the remaining 20 papers independently in the order of their choice. They believed that they were ranking a single set of 22 papers; they were not told that the purpose of the research was to compare 1983 and 1986 achievement.

In compiling the data, we gave each student a score for each primary trait from each evaluator; we averaged the scores. The highest score for each primary trait was 5. We will present pertinent data excerpts from these primary trait analyses as we discuss each student difficulty; the complete set of ratings are in Appendix A.

In the following pages, we discuss all six areas of difficulty. Under each area of difficulty, our discussion is organized under two headings:

1. The nature of the difficulties
2. Teacher's methods, student performance, and implications

DIFFICULTIES WITH CONSTRUCTING
THE AUDIENCE AND THE SELF

THE NATURE OF THE DIFFICULTIES

Anderson, like Sherman and Breihan, expected her students to address their audience both as classmates and as fellow professionals-in-training. For example, Jim Wilkerson achieved an appropriate role and tone in his Introduction by appealing to his classmates' everyday experiences with pens while stressing that they, as scientists, would also be interested in the results of his experimentation.

A Variety of Roles

In contrast, some students constructed themselves and their readers in roles taken from other settings. In her research on paper towels, for example, Susan Bell concludes:

> Since people usually tear more than one off the roll no matter what the job is, it is wiser and economical to buy the A&P brand. It is *silly* to pay for Bounty's quality if they will not use it *properly*. [Italics ours]

Bell appropriately wants to address the issue "best for whom?" but "silly" and "properly" reflect the voice of a moralizing parent. Doug Cipes's title, "A Quality Comparison Between Two Commercial Electrophoresis Units: The BioRad DNA Sub Cell Versus the BioRad DNA Mini Cell Unit" was incongruous. "Versus" is fine for sports fans, but inappropriate, in Anderson's judgment, for the scientific reader. Kitty Cahn seemed to be writing to the Speech 101 class throughout her paper entitled "Would You Eat Machine-Made or Homemade Cookies?" Sometimes students constructed the reader as the "generic teacher": perhaps the author of "Research to Determine the Better Paper Towel" recalled succeeding with "Book Report on *Silas Marner.*"

Occasionally, low-success students addressed the audience with an exaggerated or stereotyped view of scientists. On her think-aloud tape, Amy Olds read aloud from her notes Anderson's instruction that "The Introduction should get the audience's interest and state the purpose." She immediately looked at the container and wrote this dullest of first sentences: "Ivory Liquid Detergent and Lemon Fresh Joy are both manufactured and distributed by Proctor and Gamble."

Olds's difficulty—reading the instructions and then immediately taking a step that contradicts them—is another example of how hard it can be for students to use procedural instructions that they merely read or hear. We saw this same difficulty in Sherman's class, as Carla Stokes read the steps for making a location decision, and then began her task by skipping the first two steps (p. 79).

A possible influence behind Olds's opening with Proctor and Gamble is students' common way of writing a paper in school: reading first, then taking the paper from written sources. We have noted the ubiquity of the text-processor role students adopted in all the classes. Olds's final paper was still haunted by the ghosts of that early dependence on reading the labels: she never separated her own findings about the products from the claims that the manufacturers made on the labels and in TV ads.

Students had difficulty constructing not only the reader but also the self. Penny Reno, who compared two men's fragrances—Polo$_{TM}$ and Timberline$_{TM}$—began her introduction with a beautiful quotation—fine, Anderson thought, for the literary essay, but not for the scientific report. Further, Reno adopted the role of persuader in a way that violated Anderson's expectations for the balanced, objective voice of the scientist. Reno's log says: "I first convinced myself that this was a good thing to write about and then I convinced my reader in my introduction."

Scientists do "convince" their readers in certain senses, but Anderson did not consider it appropriate for a scientific research report to exhibit the persuasive tone that Reno adopted on the basis of her notion of "convince." Anderson believed that "an objective tone," similar to Wilkerson's, was "convincing" to the scientific community.

Another inappropriate model for the writer's ethos was a chatty, "stream of consciousness" voice that violated Anderson's expectations for objectivity and conciseness. Compare this excerpt from Mike Siliato's low-success final paper to Jim Wilkerson's earlier statement of the purpose of his research. Siliato's paper says:

> At the start of the original research I have no evidence of which cleaning product is superior. Comet and 409 are just two names for household cleaning products. As far as I am concerned, there exists absolutely no difference between the products. The research carried out was to identify any superiority between the products. Both products are considered to be the same at the start of the research, but when I am true [sic] I will pick one as better. The null hypothesis prevails in this study.

The vocabulary of the passage, particularly the last sentence, shows how Siliato attempts to see himself and the readers as scientists, but his ethos is also partly that of the storyteller.

Sharon Tissinger, who grappled with many aspects of doing science, also had a hard time writing about it. She selected a personal narrative approach for the Results section:

> When I first began to prepare homemade french fries, I found the most difficult part to be cutting the potatoes into exact sizes and shapes of the frozen french fries. After measuring 10 frozen french fries, the sizes were recorded on a table. (Table 1) As I began to prepare the potatoes using the various instruments, I observed that more pieces of equipment were needed for the homemade

french fries. In this respect the frozen french fries were more accessible than the homemade french fries. The basis for this conclusion is based on the fact that it took four instruments to prepare homemade french fries and only two instruments to prepare the frozen french fries (these include the drying spoon).

Tissinger's strategy seemed doubly inappropriate to Anderson as a biologist: results should not be presented in narrative form and results should not ring with the personal voice.

TEACHER'S METHODS, STUDENT PERFORMANCE, AND IMPLICATIONS

Titles

Difficulties in constructing the audience and the self showed up in many sections of the report format; they were most easily apparent in the report's title. In Anderson's 1983 lecture, she instructed students to "choose a title of less than 25 words with appropriate descriptors." Descriptors had been clearly defined in the library sessions, and earlier in the course the students had read and abstracted a minimum of five research articles. Anderson had assumed they would use these as models.

The 1983 class did not very well meet Anderson's expectations for titles: on the outside raters' primary trait scoring, the group mean was below 3.0 (Figure 6.2). As a matter of fact, the only title receiving a perfect (5.0) primary trait score—"Comparison of the Stain-Removing Qualities of Shout$_{TM}$ and Spray and Wash$_{TM}$"—was written by Ben Blount, who told us on his think-aloud tape that he had made up the research the night before. (He really trusted our promise that Anderson would not look at the data until after the final grades were in—or perhaps he half-wanted to be found out. When students are going to invent titles for bogus papers, they probably model very carefully.) Despite his good start in deception, Blount received a "D" on his two-page paper because it failed to meet so many other requirements

												$\bar{x}$	$\underline{P}$ Value
1983	1.5	1.5	2	2.5	2.5	3	3	3.5	4	4	5	2.95	.24
1986	2	3	3	3	3	3	3	3	3.5	4.5	4.5	3.22	

Figure 6.2. Comparison of 1983 and 1986 students' primary trait scores for "Title." Shaded areas show students receiving scores of 3.0 ("adequate") or better. $\bar{x}$ = mean score. $\underline{P}$ = the probability under the null hypothesis that improvement is due to chance is 24 in 100.

(1200–1500 words, 3 graphics, etc.). Later he retook the course from Anderson and compared two car waxes, bringing to class for his oral report an actual waxed car fender to bolster his credibility.

The 1983 logs and tapes did not produce a single other piece of evidence that suggested that students made any connection between composing their own titles and the titles of the research reports they had read a few weeks previously. Students' lecture notes about the project indicated that Anderson had not made that connection explicit for students, either.

In 1986, however, Anderson supplied a concrete, teacher-directed experience designed both to help students to notice the ethos implied by titles in the articles they read and to apply that lesson to composing their own titles. The 1986 students participated in the same library tour, prepared the same number of abstracts, and received the same instructions in class as in 1983, but after they had abstracted a scientific journal article, "Relative Climbing Tendencies of Gray (*Elaphe obsoleta soiloides*) and Black Rat Snakes (*E. o. obsoleta*)" by Jerome Jackson (*Herpetologica* Vol. 32–4), Anderson asked the students how they would have felt about the author if the article were entitled "Do Snakes Get High?" In a five-minute discussion, the students were encouraged to see how what they had learned about "audience" in English was relevant to scientific writing. The discussion also reviewed the importance of adequate descriptors and communicated to students that the articles they abstracted had titles that could be modeled.

In contrast to the 1983 class, 10 of the 11 students in the 1986 class composed adequate (3.0 or above) titles (see Figure 6.2). Although not many students constructed superior (4.0 or above) titles, they were able to avoid titles that were modeled inappropriately from other disciplines and settings.

Introductions

Students' Introductions also reflected their difficulties in constructing the reader and the self. In a 1983 lecture, as we have said, Anderson told them that the Introduction section in scientific writing "gets the audience's interest and states the purpose of the paper," and she gave them several opportunities to discuss their Introductions with classmates. During one class session, pairs of students talked for about 15 minutes about their Introduction and their Methods and Materials sections. In a later session, pairs responded to each others' drafts of the Introduction. In addition, some students used parts of "open" peer conferences to discuss their Introductions.

Despite all of this activity, many students still wrote inadequate Introductions. Apparently, peers did not effectively help each other write as scientists-in-training to other scientists-in-training.

The data reveal two strategies used by the successful students in 1983:

1. Drafting or revising their Introductions *after* beginning their data collection.

2. Consulting people they considered "experts" for help with their drafts.

But these successful strategies were not common. Logs, tapes, and rough drafts document that 8 of the 11 students had conducted no research at all before writing their Introductions. Three successful students who had tried to write theirs before any experimentation with their products, succeeded only after three or more revisions. Kay Price wrote her Introduction four times before designing the experiment. Hilary Nearing ended up with a one-half page, typed paragraph Introduction, but her rough draft contains ten handwritten pages from her first effort; this includes a tedious chart in which she copied the ingredients listed on each soap powder box before using the soaps (the text-processor role again?). It seemed that when students had not *acted* as researchers, they had difficulty adopting the *ethos* of researchers. Again, as in our other classes, the creation of ethos seemed closely connected to the roles that students adopted for other aspects of the thinking and writing process. Kathy Carr seemed to have found the key: she did not draft the Introduction until two days *after* she conducted her first tests and then needed to make only surface revisions.

The second possible reason why Carr wrote a high-success Introduction is that she asked for reader response not only from peers, but from others whom she saw as experts. For her project—comparing diet colas—Carr documents in her log that she talked with both a Coca-Cola spokesperson and an avid diet cola drinker. Likewise, in the 1985 class, Doug Cipes sought help from someone he felt could give expert advice.

Early in the semester, Cipes, a senior who worked in a genetics lab, jokingly(?) remarked that he thought the assignment was "dumb." Anderson countered by suggesting that he compare some product he used in the genetics lab where he worked. He decided to compare two brands of electrophoresis units. In the first peer conference, he discovered that his classmates knew nothing about these units. After one unsuccessful draft, Cipes asked a biology graduate student for help. On a tape that Cipes marked "4-20-85, A friend gives some comments on paper," we hear the graduate student make some candid comments about constructing the audience and the self:

> I hate the way you introduced this because somebody could read this and have never seen your hypothesis. Proven, never say proven. Nothing is ever proven. [Instead, say] this can be demonstrated. Then I get to down into this other thing which I hate. You are writing it almost as if you are explaining it to a graduate student who already has a good idea about it and you don't expect him to remember much of what you're saying. It's just like a general tour. It's like: This is the Empire State Building, it weighs 30 billion tons and took three million people—anyway nobody expects anybody to remember, and that's bad news in a written paper. Your written explanation has to be perfectly clear.

After his friend's response, Cipes significantly improved his Introduction. Evidently, students' strategies of conducting some experimentation before they wrote the Introduction and consulting experts for draft response appeared to help them succeed in creating an appropriate audience and self in that section of the report.

To capitalize on the insights about how successful students had worked, Anderson made two changes in her 1986 teaching methods. Using a principle that often guided her teaching changes, she guided *all* students through the processes she found had worked for successful students. In 1986, Anderson said the same things about the Introduction as in 1983, but she required all students to bring to class a pilot report first—"two or three paragraphs on what you have learned in experiments with your two products so far." By placing initial pilot experimentation *before* they began their reports, she hoped to engage the students as scientific investigators before they drafted their Introductions. Anderson also reduced the amount of peer conference time focused on the Introduction. She retained one 15-minute session on the Introduction, but scheduled it *after* the pilot report, so that students were responding to one another as fellow scientists who had each conducted some experimentation. The second change Anderson made was to encourage 1986 students to ask "fellow scientists" in other classes to critique their Introductions.

In 1986, 10 of the 11 students wrote an adequate Introduction (3.0 or above). Over half the class performed at or above the 4.0 level (Figure 6.3).

											$\bar{x}$	$\underline{P}$ Value
1983	1.5	2	2.5	2.5	2.5	3.5	3.5	4	4	4	5	3.18	.14
1986	2	3	3	3	3.5	4	4	4	4.5	4.5	4.5	3.64	

Figure 6.3. Comparison of 1983 and 1986 students' primary trait scores for "Introduction." Shaded areas show students receiving scores of 3.0 ("adequate") or better. $\bar{x}$ = mean score. $\underline{P}$ = the probability under the null hypothesis that improvement is due to chance is 14 in 100.

FOUR INTERRELATED DIFFICULTIES: STATING A POSITION; USING DISCIPLINE-BASED METHODS TO ARRIVE AT (AND SUPPORT) A POSITION; MANAGING COMPLEXITY; GATHERING SUFFICIENT SPECIFIC INFORMATION

In Anderson's class, stating a position meant stating which product was "better." The discipline-based method was the scientific method. The scientific method manages complexity through experimental design, operational definitions, and control of variables. It also defines ways of gathering sufficient specific information.

Anderson expected students to design an experiment, construct operational definitions, control variables, gather sufficient specific data, present data in graphic form, and interpret their data in the Results section of the report. We take up these aspects one at a time in this section; however, we do not treat presenting data in graphic form. As in earlier sections of this chapter, under each aspect we first discuss the nature of the difficulties, then Anderson's teaching methods of 1983 and 1986, the student performance for each year as measured by the raters, and the implications of those findings.

DESIGNING AN EXPERIMENT

The Nature of the Difficulties

Designing an experiment was the most difficult task the students faced. It seemed difficult partly because it precluded the text-processing role we have found so common in the other classes (though, as we have seen, some of Anderson's students began with the only print available—the product container). As one student put it, "It's your baby all the way. You have to do the research and you have to write it. You can't go to a library and read about it and summarize."

Three 1983 students—Mike Siliato, Jeremy Lucas, and Sharon Tissinger—had poorly designed experiments. We will use their data to illustrate six ways in which some students had trouble in this area:

1. *Students considered few topics seriously.* The logs and transcripts revealed that most 1983 students considered and/or expanded very few topics. Siliato, for example, revealed on his think-aloud tape on February 5 that he thought of one food product "but since I'm not much on cooking myself, it is out of the question. I do feel I would perhaps start my research comparing 409 and Comet." He never considered another topic. Jeremy Lucas, an international student, began on Feb. 25 with the think-aloud statement, "There is so many house products flashed in my mind that it does make me choice (unintelligible two words) is comparing between Palmolive and Joy dish-washing liquids." These were the only products he recorded having examined on a trip to the store on February 27, although he did not purchase his Joy and Palmolive bottles until March 3.

Sharon Tissinger, on the other hand, appeared to think about possible products because she listed several words in her log, but she did not expand these ideas. When her father suggested french fries on the evening of March 14, Tissinger, like Lucas, seriously considered various factors in experimental design for only one topic. She said on the tape:

> Now for some reason I really like this idea. It seems to me differences could include the cooking time, the storage, you know, even a taste test, you know . . . even the stipulation that there is, are, different instruments. . . . This idea has definitely topped my list because I feel like it is something that could easily be compared whereas something like soap or shampoo—it's very hard to tell the difference of clean, you know, you have to define clean. . . .

Tissinger did not work out the details of experimental design for any other products.

2. *Students concentrated on peripheral issues rather than on the critical task of designing the experiment.* Mike Siliato's data suggest he was preoccupied with making a good grade. For example, on his tape dated 2/26/83, he notes that "I just hope that this will be a success." Jeremy Lucas recorded on his March 4 tape:

> How am I going to start this paper? It is surely difficult to start the paper. Yet once I start it everything will be easy. I am thinking of a thesis statement, of all of them. I hope I come up with something good. [Long pause] Yes, I've got what I wanted—a good thesis statement.

Throughout his log it is evident that the actual writing was Lucas's main concern. On March 29, he gave the paper to a friend, as he says in his log, to "proofread," not to ask for feedback on the experimental design or content. Lucas was focused on writing the paper correctly; designing the experiment was a side issue for him.

To write the paper, Lucas, like a number of the students in Sherman's class, tried to use the "thesis" model, but interpreted forming a thesis as the writer's first act, rather than the position a scientist would reach after experimentation.

Siliato, Lucas, and Tissinger all demonstrated a third possible reason for poorly designed experiments:

3. *Students did not conduct preliminary investigations (pilots) to aid them in planning the experiment.* Only 2 students out of the 11 in the 1983 group conducted a pilot. Since this seemed so counterproductive and naive for science majors who had taken at least ten semester hours of college science, Anderson wondered whether the students had conducted pilots without recording them. However, analysis of students' experimental procedures as recorded in their logs and tapes made it clear that there had been no pilots. For example, Tissinger exposed the spontaneity of her investigation as she recorded, while conducting her experiment,

> It seems the frozen french fries are exceeding the fresh cut french fries in cooking time amazingly, immensely! In fact they are almost done and it has only been two minutes. It is now—the total cooking time is 2 minutes and 20 seconds! The frozen french fries are definitely done—brown, very crispy. I have now turned off the flame. I am immediately taking them out and putting them on a towel (pause, laughter from assistant)—there seems to be a problem with the towel.

Siliato's tapes reveal that he did not conduct a pilot project either. He records on the tape:

> Right now I am starting the project. I'll clean one half of the bathroom, rather the bathtub, with 409 and the other half with Comet. . . . What I plan to do is, one day I'll clean the toilet with Comet, the next day I'll clean it with 409 or better yet how about if I do it this way—the first 15 days of March I'll clean it with Comet and the last with 409. . . . As time goes on, I will probably think of new ways to test both products.

Thinking of new ways to test the product as one goes along is good strategy for a pilot, but a disaster for conducting the actual experiment.

As we examined the students' experimental designs in their final papers, we found three more reasons that students had poorly designed experiments. These reasons were very closely related to difficulties in gathering sufficient specific information.

4. *Students failed to locate* sufficient *information because they designed experiments that had inappropriate sample sizes.* For example, Jeremy Lucas recorded in his Methods and Materials section:

> I measured 2 mls of cooking oil in one plate and 2 mls in another. 5 drops of Joy were placed in one of the plates and 5 drops of Palmolive in the other plate. The effects were noted.

In this case, Lucas selected a sample size of N = 1 for the plates. He did not collect sufficient data. If he had tried this procedure with five plates and taken an average, his data would have been more credible. Sharon Tissinger asked evaluators to compare homemade and prepared frozen french fries. Sample size didn't seem to worry her as she recorded her results in a table—two people for homemade and two for frozen french fries.

5. *Students failed to locate sufficient* specific *information because they failed to design ways to quantify information.* In contrast to Lucas and Tissinger, Mike Siliato collected a lot of data. In his Methods and Materials section, he describes how five evaluators compared the two cleansers on five different occasions:

> When I began my research on Comet and 409 I spent 10 different days just cleaning the bathtub and toilet. On five different days I washed out the toilet with Comet and on the other 5 days likewise with the 409. The purpose of this was to see among members of my family if there was any opinion in regard to odor or looks. . . .

Table 6.2 shows Siliato's chart.

Notice that Siliato designed an experiment that records no *specific* information on "the odor or looks," the two factors he said he wanted to examine. Siliato had a sufficient amount of data for Anderson's expectations in this project, but data were not specific enough to be useful.

Compare Siliato's chart to Wilkerson's chart on page 188. Wilkerson, like Siliato, asked judges to compare two products, but he clearly defined the criteria for comparing the two brands of pens and constructed a rating scale of 1 through 5, thus allowing him to collect specific data.

In his chart (Table 6.2), Siliato reveals that he did not know what to do with his own opinion, and so he simply listed it with the opinions of his other rankers. Siliato's difficulties arose because he failed to distinguish himself as scientific researcher from himself as observer. His difficulty may be related to the difficulties of students in Breihan's class who could not distinguish between "feelings" and

Table 6.2   *Mike Siliato's Chart Comparing Comet*$_{TM}$ *and 409*$_{TM}$
Chart #1. ("X" marks superior, "O" same)

	Date	Rankers	#1	#2	#3	#4	#5	my view
1st	3/1/83	Comet	X	X	X	X	X	X
comparison	3/2/83	409						
2nd	3/3/83	comet	O	X	X	X	X	X
comparison	3/4/83	409						
3rd	3/5/83	Comet	O	X	X	X	X	X
comparison	3/6/83	409						
4th	3/8/83	Comet	X	X	X	X	X	X
comparison	3/11/83	409						
5th	3/12/83	Comet	X	X	X	X	X	X
comparison	3/15/83	409						

10 days set aside, 5 comparisons made. Of my view 100% of the time I saw Comet as a superior cleaner and 0% of the time for 409. Of the 5 Rankers, 92% of the time they saw comet superior, 0% for 409 and 8% no difference.

"evidence" (p. 134). Clearly, issues of roles and of the construction of the self are also involved in Siliato's difficulty with his chart.

6. *Students failed to include four experimental criteria, and they did not know what to do with nonexperimental data.* The "Factors Tested" column of Table 6.3 shows the criteria that each 1983 student chose as experimental criteria, to be reported in the Results section. The I as a factor type identifies nonexperimental criteria inappropriate for Results. Siliato, for example, selected price. Price is a nonexperimental factor that should be handled in the Discussion section, because to find it one merely reads the price tag. Tissinger counted the utensils needed for homemade and frozen french fries—useful but not experimental information; Kathy Carr surveyed can color.

Table 6.3   Experimental Designs, 1983 Students

Name	Product	Factor Type	Factors Tested	Subgroups for Interpretations
Jim Wilkerson	erasable pens	J J J J	erasability xeroxability tendency to skip smudgeability	Righthanders & lefthanders
Hilary Nearing	laundry soap	J M	7 stains suds durability	Users at 3 temperatures; ecologists
Kay Price	diet sodas	M M M J	flat time (cup) flat time (bottle) flat time (ice) taste	Servers of diet drinks; heavy users & novices
Mike Siliato	tile cleaners	J J J I	on tubs on tiles on stains price	— —
Susan Bell	paper towels	M J M J	total absorbency window cleaning absorbency rate hand drying ability	Users of 1 or more paper towels
Kitty Cahn	chocolate chip cookies	J M J	visual appeal stretch of chip combined tastes	—
Sharon Tissinger	french fries	J J J I	taste/appearance greasiness crispness no. of utensils	—
Ben Blount	pre-washes	J	4 stains	—
Amy Olds	dish soaps	M M M J	spots on glass suds life baked-on foods hand preference	—
Kathy Carr	diet sodas	J J J I	blind taste test known taste test can preference can color	—
Jeremy Lucas	dish soaps	J J J	spot removal grease removal combined preferences	—

J = judged factor   M = measured factor   I = nonexperimental factor inappropriate to design

N = 11 students

Teacher's Methods, Student Performance, and Implications

Aware of these indications about how and why the 1983 students were having difficulty designing experiments, Anderson reexamined her teaching techniques. Her first assignment in 1983 had asked students to submit a topic to her by a certain date. She had done this to help the students start early in the semester, but our data revealed that since the students thought seriously about very few topics, Anderson's assignment caused many to close prematurely on a poor topic. The next exercise was for students, in groups of four, to discuss "How am I going to test [my product]?" In 1983 they were not, at that point, able to help each other with experimental design. We saw in Robisons' class, also, how peer response could fail when students did not know enough, or did not have sufficiently specific guidelines, to appropriately evaluate others.

On February 14, 1985, Anderson experimented with a new set of beginning assignments designed to encourage students to consider more topics in greater depth, and to help them to help each other with experimental design. She asked the students to bring in ten topics that might be used for the original research paper. She put students in groups of four and they shared their lists for about 10 minutes. Their next assignment was "Do *not* decide on a topic; decide on at least four possible topics. Write a paragraph about how you would design an experiment to test each of these." The next assignment was to list four criteria each for two kinds of products. This was followed by a pilot report.

The logs and tapes of the 1985 class convinced Anderson she was on the right track. For example, Matt Brady, raised on Maryland's Eastern Shore renowned for duck hunting, recorded his quest for a topic in his log:

Feb. 15.   Thought about testing two brands of Beer. Heniken vs Molsen, or Molsen vs Moosehead.

Feb. 16.   Talked to my girlfriend's father who is a surgeon hoping to gain some insights. He suggested testing trash bags. Considered trash bags, remembered that someone in class suggested them so I did not want to do it.

Feb. 23.   Talked to my dad—he suggested shot gun shells.

March 17.   Called my old high school Science Teacher talked to him about research paper he suggested that I talk to a pharmacist he knows because the pharmacist had said that brand name drugs were a rip-off compared to generics. I did not feel qualified to test drugs on people.

March 23.   Talked to my dad and decided to test the difference between steel and lead shot in shotguns—lead shot is supposed to be hazardous to diving ducks who eat the shot and die of lead poisoning.

Unlike the 1983 students, Brady took his time, considered a number of different topics in a serious way, talked to other people, and worked through each possible topic far enough to decide specifically why he rejected it.

In 1986, Anderson again used these new activities. In addition, on the day the students brought their rough drafts of the pilot reports, she asked them to share these reports in groups of three or four and to focus on helping each other develop a list of "4 to 6 testable, quantifiable" criteria by which they would judge which product was "better." Immediately after that 30-minute, in-class session, Anderson lectured for about 10 minutes on the importance of sample size and the difference between experimental and nonexperimental information. Table 6.4 describes the 1986 experiments. By comparing it with the 1983 experiments (Table 6.3) in terms of experimental design, we identified several telling differences between the two classes (Table 6.5).

These differences between the 1983 and the 1986 classes were reflected in the judgment of the raters (Figure 6.4).

We concluded that in 1983 Anderson used peer conferences prematurely to accomplish a task too complex for students to handle at that time. The new activities helped students focus on the many aspects of designing an experiment before limiting their options. In the other three disciplines, as well, teachers came to the same conclusion—put more time into guiding the *beginning* of the thinking/planning/writing process. In Anderson's class, as in Robison's, peer-group success seemed to depend on giving the groups specific, structured tasks and enough teacher guidance so that they knew what to look for and how to help each other.

CONSTRUCTING OPERATIONAL DEFINITIONS

The Nature of the Difficulties

Once students had designed experiments, they were expected to demonstrate two less complex but essential scientific skills: to define operationally and to control variables. Each skill was independent but integral to the student's success on the final paper. We will discuss each separately.

208

Table 6.4   Experimental Designs, 1986 Students

Name	Products	Factor Type	Factors Tested	Subgroups for Interpretations
Betty Farr	beer	J	taste	Drinkers of
		M	bitterness	cold or warm-
		M	foam (amount)	ing beer
		M	foam (duration)	
Tia Stoffer	pickles	J	flavor	Smokers and
		M	texture	nonsmokers;
		J	appearance	those who do
		J	aroma	and do not refrigerate
Ken Johnson	trashbags	M	puncturability	—
		M	dragability	
		M	stretchability	
		M	tie performance	
Valery Hobbs	laundry soaps	J	5 stains	—
		J	softness	
		M	static cling	
Duncan Solski	paper towels	M	strength	Users of wet &
		M	absorption rate	dry paper towels
		M	pull test	
		M	total absorption	
		J	scrubability	
		J	softness	
Donna Conner	raisin brans	M	crumbliness	Vitamin users;
		M	crispness in milk	fiber users
		M	no. of raisins	
		J	taste	
Gary Galvez	typing papers	M	durability	—
		M	strength (wet/dry)	
		M	ink retainability	
		J	photocopiability	
Molly Sutton	peanut butters	M	texture/oiliness	—
		M	spreadability	
		J	combined tests	
Roy Dodd	popcorns	M	volume	Users hot/cold;
		M	percent waste	smokers & non-
		J	combined tastes	smokers
Kara Pettit	breakfast beverages	J	taste	Adults &
		J	shelf life	children; dorm
		M	dissolvability	students
		I	storage	
Mary Hart	horsehair polishes	J	shine	Routine users;
		J	durability	horse show
		M	mane/tail tangles	users
		M	preparation time	

J = judged factor   M = measured factor   I = nonexperimental factor inappropriate to design
N = 11 students

Table 6.5   Experimental Design Strategies (1983 and 1986 Classes)

Strategy	1983	1986
Students seriously considering four or more topics	4	11
Students choosing four or more appropriate experimental criteria	4	7
Students adequately distinguishing/using nonexperimental data	6	9
Students designing superior experiments (4.0 or above on primary trait score)	1	6
Number of quantified, measured criteria included by all students	10	26

N = 11 students (1983); N = 11 students (1986)

Difficulties in constructing operational definitions cut across all levels of achievement in designing an experiment: Mike Siliato designed a poor experiment, Susan Bell designed an average one, and Karen Price designed an above-average experiment for the 1983 group, but they all had difficulties in defining operationally. We use their data to illustrate three aspects of these difficulties: (1) Constructing no operational definition, (2) confusing operational with vocabulary definition, and (3) including no operational definition for a "better" product.

Constructing No Operational Definition

Some students did not make any operational definitions. Choosing the simplest approach, Siliato makes a heading "Operational Definitions" and writes, "When I compared the Comet and the 409 I looked for such qualities like abrasiveness, smoothness of certain areas cleaned, cost ratio and scent." Later, he writes, "Several variables were employed during the course of the research project. One was a test removing bacon grease, bathtub rings, dirt (common ground dirt) and some food stains. The same number of sponge strokes were used in the removal of the filthy substances."

If Siliato had understood operational definition, he could have defined "better grease cutting agent" as, for example, "the cleanser that required the fewest strokes with a sponge to be returned to clean in the judges' opinion after equal quantities of bacon grease, bathtub rings, and dirt have been applied."

											$\bar{x}$	P Value
1983	1	1.5	1.5	2.5	3	3	3	3	3.5	3.5	4	2.68	.07
1986	1.5	1.5	3	3	3.5	4	4	4	4	4	4	3.32	

Figure 6.4. Comparison of 1983 and 1986 students' primary trait scores for "Designing the Experiment." Shaded areas show students receiving scores of 3.0 ("adequate") or better. $\bar{x}$ = mean score. P = probability that improvement is due to chance is 7 in 100.

Confusing Operational with Vocabulary Definitions

Some students confused constructing operational definitions with locating or composing vocabulary definitions. Susan Bell records in her log on 3/24/83, "Towel—an absorbent cloth or paper for wiping or drying." Next she copies the definition of "paper" from the *Concord Desk Encyclopedia*. Bell is trying to operationally define, but she doesn't know what to do. She is only describing the words. She is not constructing an operational definition of "paper towel" for this experiment (e.g., one perforated section from a 2-ply roll made by Bounty or A&P). We noted in Sherman's chapter, also, the students' tendency to use dictionary definitions instead of constructing definitions for the purpose of their arguments (pp. 88–89).

Having worked as a technician in a scientific lab, Kay Price was familiar with what research was like. She compared Diet 7-Up and Tab. She had an adequate design, an excellent N = 50, and the potential for interesting results in comparing the taste preferences of 25 men and 25 women. Her paper seems very scientific; she even subtitles her "Operational Definitions." Here are her first three entries:

> Flat test—a test to determine the amount of time it takes for Tab and Diet 7-Up to go flat.
>
> Flat time—the amount of time for Tab and Diet 7-Up to go flat.
>
> Flat—loss of appealing taste, no longer possessing refreshing qualities.

After reading these definitions, could a reader replicate Price's "flat time"? What have her definitions told the reader to do to obtain the same results? Nothing. She has given the description of the term, but not the operations to be performed.

Compare Price's operational definition for "flat time" to Matt Brady's definition of shot pattern:

> The shot pattern can be studied by firing the shotgun into an open sheet of paper. What is most desirable is to have a shot pattern which is concentrated. A greater concentration of shot hitting the target means that more individual pellets will hit the target. And the more pellets that hit the target (in this case a duck or a goose), the greater the likely-hood of a successful kill . . . The shotgun shell's pellet concentration (Shot Pattern Concentration) was determined by counting the greatest number of shot holes found in a circle with a diameter of 20 inches and then dividing the number of holes within the circle by the number of pellets originally in the shotgun shell.

Including No Operational Definition for a "Better" Product

Although most students made operational definitions of at least some specific characteristics or tests, many students did not operationally define the "better product." Although Kay Price addressed the issue of operational definitions by making the list quoted above, she did not put "better diet drink" on the list. Neither she nor Susan Bell had an operational definition of "better." Bell explains to her readers, "The purpose of this research is to describe the experiments performed on paper towels and to present the conclusions that have been reached as to which is the better paper towel." Her paper stays in the descriptive mode; her conclusions describe which is the better paper towel for each of her four tests, not overall. In terms of the five tasks of good/ better/best reasoning (p. 12), she does not complete Task 3—to bring the information about the options (in this case the four tests) into a disciplined relationship with her definition of "good" so that a *single* judgment can be made.

Teacher's Methods, Student Performance, and Implications

As we listened to the 1983 tapes, we heard several students repeat to themselves the phrase, "must operationally define the better product." The tone in their voices, as well as their final papers, revealed that this was a skill that they knew they were expected to demonstrate, but they really didn't know what it was.

Anderson recognized the phrase from her one-hour lecture in which she used Crisco and Wesson Oil as model products. She recalled asking questions like "How would you define 'crispy'?" or "What is the 'better' cooking oil?" She remembered reminding the students in both the 45-minute peer conference on their drafts of the Methods and Materials section and in their last 45-minute peer session to "Be sure that all your operational definitions are perfectly clear."

We realized that many of these upper-level biology students, like the students in Sherman's and Breihan's classes, could not easily move from merely reading or hearing a description of a complex intellectual operation to using it on their own. Since Anderson had assumed that upper-level biology majors knew how to construct operational definitions, she assumed that group work would help students focus on improving their definitions. As Anderson listened to the tapes, she realized, "no wonder peer groups hadn't helped—the blind were leading the blind."

Anderson decided to teach students concretely how to define terms operationally. She used several oral "If we were doing an experiment on . . ." exercises with the 1985 class; they got much better at defining a specific characteristic such as "shot pattern" (see Brady's operational definition, pp. 210–11). But when the students still had trouble defining the better product, we realized that two kinds of operational definitions were critical to success. We called these *specific operational definitions* (e.g., "shot pattern") and *comprehensive operational definitions* ("better" product).

Based on this insight, Anderson developed for her 1986 class a writing activity to help students learn how to construct both kinds of operational definitions. Figure 6.5 is a copy of her Operational Definitions Worksheet. The handwritten comments are the student's and the comments in brackets are ours. Anderson used a simple question as basis for this exercise: "Under which conditions—very wet, moist, or dry—does mold grow best?"

In addition to the worksheet, Anderson asked each student to "write out your comprehensive operational definition of better product" before the second peer conference session. This time, the students knew enough to help each other.

Students in the 1986 class received a higher mean score from the raters on defining operationally, and a larger percentage of students had scores of 3.0 or above (Figure 6.6).

The difference in the average achievement for operational definitions, as measured by the primary trait score for Anderson's 1983 students (2.68) and her 1986 students (3.50), has a $\underline{P}$ value of .01, indicating that the null hypothesis is 1 in 100.

CONTROLLING VARIABLES

The Nature of the Difficulties

In Anderson's experience, controlling variables is a skill that college biology students often use in their laboratory courses. Many lab manuals ask questions such as "Which variables have been controlled in this experiment?" or "What additional factors must be controlled in this experiment?" Teacher-constructed tests and standardized tests commonly use multiple-choice questions to assess this skill. Anderson was confident that her junior and senior science majors, all of whom had taken at least ten semester hours of college science, knew how to control variables in experiments designed by others. In her assignment, however, the students had to control variables within their own designs.

Operational Definitions Worksheet

I. Explain in your own words what an operational definition is. Include an example in your discussion.

a definition which explains a specific process or how a certain task is to be performed.
* *An explanation for a procedure to use something*
        – data matches outcome
        – the procedure can be repeated

[In the three or four minutes allotted for them to answer, many of the students, like this respondent, did not come up with an example. However, these few minutes made them aware that they couldn't think of an example.]

II. In the described mold experiment, state which terms must be operationally defined and define one of them.

Wet ⎞
moist ⎬ Bread → 2 ml H_2O ... 5 ml H_2O
dry ⎠ ⟶ 0 ml H_2O

Lighting – 12 hr light
             12 hr dark

[added later] grow best – most excessive growth during a 14 day period.
(success consistant)

Enviornment – moisture will be contained aerobic in a limited envirinment

Mold growth – excessive = 7 cm +
            moderate = 2-7 cm
            minimum = 0-2 cm

(Do 4 pilot
To get a feel
for time and)

[All students listed very wet," "moist," and "dry." Many recognized that "mold" had to be identified. These were *specific* operational definitions. Only a few students realized that they had to define "grows best"—the *comprehensive* operational definition which would integrate the values of the specific tests. When students had filled out the sheet, Anderson explained the meanings of specific and comprehensive operational definitions. This student then added "grow best" to her list.]

continued

Figure 6.5. Operational Definitions Worksheet.

Figure 6.5 (cont.)

III. Was the term that you defined a specific operational definition or a comprehensive operational definition? As you explain the difference, define the type of term you did not use in II.

[handwritten notes] c-o def. of topic / Research had a *Best beverage* - which product resulted with the most positive responses to experiment on for a taste test, minimum preparation time, + maximum shelf life,

[This student's mind went right to the original research topic that she had chosen and for some reason she wrote that down—an indication of the success of this in-class exercise in helping students to apply the principles directly to their own research projects.]

IV. Examine the terms in the article that you abstracted and identify an example of a specific operational definition and of a comprehensive definition. Explain if these were stated or had to be inferred by the reader.

[At this point groups of students examined a journal article handed out the day before. They worked on this task orally with peers for about 7 minutes until the end of class. Most groups quickly moved to talking about their own research—another indication of their ability to transfer this in-class lesson to their own research projects.]

As we reviewed the 1983 papers, we found that when students developed an adequate experimental design, they controlled variables adequately. When they had poorly designed experiments, they had difficulties in controlling variables as well. Finding this expected high correlation between designing experiments and controlling variables, we really did not try to document how the low-success students went wrong. Quite frankly, to have helped Mike Siliato or Jeremy Lucas control the variables in their designs would have been like "arranging deck chairs on the Titanic." On the other hand, successful students' logs made very clear what they found helpful:

												$\bar{x}$	P Value
1983	1	1.5	1.5	2	3	3	3	3	3.5	4	4	2.68	.01
1986	2.5	3	3	3.5	3.5	3.5	3.5	4	4	4	4	3.50	

Figure 6.6. Comparison of 1983 and 1986 students' primary trait scores for "Defining Operationally." Shaded areas show students receiving scores of 3.0 ("adequate") or better. $\bar{x}$ = mean score. $\underline{P}$ = the null hypothesis is 1 in 100.

1. *Peer conferences were an effective way to help students control variables.* Although this was documented in the 1983 logs, we found two particularly cogent examples in the 1985 logs. On 2/27/85 Ivan Ford records,

> I was eating breakfast and decided to do a comparison test on two types of cornflakes. The idea of a taste test popped immediately into my mind and when my flakes got soggy I decided to do an absorption rate test first thinking of soaking and weighing the flakes at one minute intervals. We broke into groups in class (me, Kathy, Eric, and Mark) and I told them my plans. I thought of having some physical tests to determine crunchiness of dry flakes, a 20 person taste test a nutritional comparison, and some way of telling how many times you can drop the box without getting all those scummy crumbs. They all liked the ideas.

Lisa Land, a student who designed a good experiment to test microwave popcorns, recorded in her log,

> April 4—sat around in class and discussed the paper. Once you see the other ideas it becomes easier—your ideas are on the right TRACK. As I describe what I'm doing + how I'll control the experiment, it's not so bad.

2. *Manipulating the products and/or conducting a pilot helped students do a better job of controlling variables.* For example, Jim Wilkerson did not identify the age of the pen as a variable to control until he wrote with the pens himself. Two days after she wrote her log entry above, Lisa Land wrote in her log,

> April 6—I did a simple chart for my *variables*. Popped the popcorn like the pilot—put into unmarked bags—I took them over to my mother-in-law's first—had the family do my taste tests. They hem-hawed, but they did it. . . . took the rest of the popcorn to my mother's & did the same thing. I put a special mark next to the smoker—? *new variable*. [Italics ours]

Teacher's Methods, Student Performance, and Implications

In 1983, Anderson instructed students in the scientific method in a one-hour lecture, using Crisco and Wesson Oil as examples, and reminding students that it was important to control variables. She broke them into various groups for three 45-minute sessions to work on a variety of topics, including controlling variables.

In 1986, Anderson reviewed the term *control variables* in a 15-minute overview of the scientific method. All students conducted at least one pilot experiment and turned in a rough draft of a pilot report. Students focused on controlling variables in peer groups when they worked on the Methods and Materials section of their papers. The 1983 class average for controlling variables was 2.73; it increased to 3.18 in 1986 (Figure 6.7).

Anderson was most interested in the scores for controlling variables earned by students who had received 3.5 and better for designing good experiments, because those were students who had variables *worth* controlling. Those averages increased from 3.33 in 1983 to 3.64 in 1986. We concluded that controlling variables was closely linked to experimental design. Further, Anderson's assumption that students did know how to control variables was probably correct. These averages, 3.33 and 3.64, are higher than the average scores for any other scientific skill category.

PRESENTING DATA IN GRAPHIC FORM

The Nature of the Difficulties

Anderson encouraged both the 1983 and the 1986 students to use graphics to communicate scientific information, but to be on the safe side, she also required three graphics. In 1983 Anderson spent one 75-minute period lecturing on the basic functions of pie graphs, bar graphs, line graphs, diagrams, flow charts, tables, and photographs of organisms and/or their representations, i.e. X-rays, EKG's, photomicrographs, and so forth. In a second period, she went over the five different types of graphics the students constructed from some fish data she had given them as a homework sheet, and she helped students

												$\bar{x}$	$\underline{P}$ Value
1983	1.5	2	2	2	2.5	2.5	3	3	3.5	4	4	2.73	.10
1986	2	2	2.5	3	3	3	3.5	3.5	4	4	4.5	3.18	

Figure 6.7. Comparison of 1983 and 1986 students' primary trait scores for "Controlling Variables." Shaded areas show students receiving scores of 3.0 ("adequate") or better. $\bar{x}$ = mean score. $\underline{P}$ = the probability under the null hypothesis that improvement is due to chance is 10 in 100.

compose self-contained headings (consistent with APA style guidelines) for their fish graphics.

Looking at the 1983 graphics, we concluded that the two-day "mini-unit" was not a smashing success. Although some graphics were good (see Jim Wilkerson's table on p. 188) and some were poor (see Mike Siliato's table on p. 204), most of them were just mediocre. The students' rough drafts document that they did not experiment with data in different graphic forms. Their tapes and logs also indicate that they picked the graphic first such as, "I'll put a pie graph in my paper" or "I will put some stuff in a table," rather than taking the information and deciding which graphic would most effectively illustrate their findings. Less successful students seemed to reason that any three graphics would do in much the same manner that less successful writers seem to view writing as coming up with a specified number of words. For example, Jeremy Logan records that he "prepared graphics"; we found out that meant he soaked off the Joy label and put it in his paper as "Figure 3."

Teacher's Methods, Student Performance, and Implications

In 1986 Anderson gave the same lecture on graphics. She handed out the same fish data as a homework assignment. But to make explicit the connection between the way they illustrated fish data and the graphics students should use in their household products experiment, she spent the last 20 minutes of each class having students discuss in groups what kinds of household product data would be appropriate to each type of graphic. Anderson emphasized that scientific writers focus on *selecting*, not constructing, the most appropriate graphic in the rough draft stage. The 1986 students used more graphics and they used a greater variety of graphics, as Table 6.6 indicates.

Clearly, providing students with in-class, teacher-directed time to transfer learning principles was quantitatively productive. The primary trait scores for collecting and interpreting data indicates that the 1986 students constructed more effective graphics as well (see Table A.1, Appendix A, p. 247).

INTERPRETING DATA

The Nature of the Difficulties

The other essential skill in using evidence to support a position was interpreting data. Although students collected and communicated data

Table 6.6   Graphics Strategies (1983 and 1986 Classes)

	Totals	
Strategy	1983	1986
Students having 3 required graphics	9	11
Students having more than 3 graphics	4	7
Students having diagrams	2	7
Students having line graphs	1	4
Students having rating scales	3	6
Number of Graphics included in all papers	38	55

N = 11 students (1983); N = 11 students (1986)

in the Results section of the scientific journal format, they had to make sense of that data in the Discussion. In this section, the students had to "put it all together," as Wilkerson did in his Discussion of the better erasable pen.

Teacher's Methods, Student Performance, and Implications

In both 1983 and 1986, Anderson told both groups that the Discussion, Conclusions, and Implications section should "summarize the research, accept or reject the hypothesis, and explain the significance of the research in terms of price and quality." Figure 6.8 compares 1983 and 1986 students' primary trait scores for interpreting data.

Since Anderson's teaching methods for interpreting data were virtually identical, we wondered *how* and *why* 1986 students had been more successful than the 1983 students. First, we focused on quantitative differences between what each class included within the Discussion section. But as we examined the data, we found that differences between the two groups in summarizing, accepting, or rejecting the hypothesis, and discussing price adequately, were small and did not involve the same students. The striking difference was that the 1986 students designed experiments that contained more evidence to support a position (see Table 6.7). Further, they refined both their data collection

												$\bar{x}$	P Value
1983	1	1.5	2.5	3	3	3	3	3	3.5	4	4.5	2.90	.03
1986	2.5	3	3	3.5	3.5	3.5	4	4	4	4	4.5	3.59	

Figure 6.8. Comparison of 1983 and 1986 students' primary trait scores for "Interpreting Data." Shaded areas show students receiving scores of 3.0 ("adequate") or better. $\bar{x}$ = mean score. P = the probability under the null hypothesis that improvement is due to chance is 3 in 100.

Table 6.7   Use of Evidence (1983 and 1986 Classes)

Strategy	1983	1986
Students using special subgroups for interpreting data (see Tables 6.3 and 6.4)	4	7
Students achieving an average of 3.0 or above on the primary trait checklist for other skills	4	8*
Students interpreting data more than adequately (3.5 or above on the primary trait checklist)	3	8*

N = 11 students (1983); N = 11 students (1986)   *Same population

and their conclusions by designating subgroups for whom one product might be better (see Tables 6.3 and 6.4).

We highlight with an asterisk two groups of 8 students because they were *identical* groups. We conclude, therefore, that the differences in the 1983 and 1986 students' achievement in interpreting data can be attributed to the fact that the 1986 students designed better experiments, made better operational definitions, controlled more variables, and collected better data.

We have discussed difficulties that concerned Anderson's expectations for use of the scientific method. Now we discuss the difficulties that arose as students tried to meet Anderson's expectations for the scientific report format.

DIFFICULTIES WITH ORGANIZING THE PAPER

Because the research paper had a prescribed format, students faced two types of organizational problems. They had to organize their information in order to fit it into the appropriate format sections— Title, Introduction, Methods and Materials, Results, and Discussion— and they also had to organize the appropriate information logically within a section.

FORMAT ORGANIZATION

The Nature of the Difficulties

Although practicing scientists have traditionally regarded a standardized, research-report format as an asset, it was the students' nemesis. An interview between 1983 students Hilary Nearing and Susan Bell reveals how frustrating students found this organizational task. For the interview with each other, Nearing and Bell are using a peer review sheet that Anderson has provided, the first question of which is, "I had trouble writing the _____. What part of the paper did you find hardest?" Nearing, who plans to compare a high-phosphate and a low-phosphate detergent to find out which is better, replies:

> *Nearing*: Well, see, I had percent of phosphates in one cup of detergent was 6.3 in one and .3 in the other. Now I don't know whether to put that in my results because it *is*—
>
> *Bell*: Well . . .
>
> *Nearing*: Because my thing is—
>
> *Bell*: Well, see, usually it's, well . . .
>
> *Nearing*: Or would it go in the Conclusion [Discussion section]. See, that, that's particularly what I had trouble with.
>
> *Bell*: I don't know. Results of data, maybe you could put? Under your ta— under your Data and Results? And then put that as your first table with the main characteristics of your, of each detergent, you know, if it's broken up into that?
>
> *Nearing*: Oh. Well, I'm going to have a bar graph representing that, just to show people.
>
> *Bell*: In your Conclusion? And where's that going to go?
>
> *Nearing*: In my, in my—
>
> *Bell*: In your Results?
>
> *Nearing*: My Results—
>
> *Bell*: 'Cause then that would be OK, I mean, that would be telling that information then. I mean if you were going to have a graph for it in your Results and then, then you really don't have to expl—
>
> *Nearing*: [unintelligible syllable] OK go ahead.
>
> *Bell*: Then you really don't have to explain it.
>
> *Nearing*: Price is kind of relative, because it's going to be varied with the amount of phosphate.
>
> *Bell*: Is that what your main factor is?
>
> *Nearing*: Yeah, that's like a variable. Well, I'm going to do phosphate-free and then Cheer which has lots of phosphate.
>
> *Bell*: Oh, OK, oh.
>
> *Nearing*: So I put the amount of phosphate in my Results. It's pretty important for them to know it before they read the Discussion. How about looking at it that way?

Bell: Well, if you're going to have a graph. Are you planning on putting price in the Results? Is that what you're—

Nearing: Yeah.

Bell: How are you going to list that? Are you going to write it out?

Nearing: Yeah, write it out.

Bell: Then I would write the other factors in there, too. In the Results, not the Conclusion. If you're going to put price in the Results,

Nearing: No, I put the price in the Conclusion.

Bell: Oh. Let's see.

This "Who's on first?" routine went on in a peer conference, at the end of which Nearing asked Anderson if she should include the price in the Results. The answer, of course, was no, and Anderson reminded her that, as a nonexperimental factor, it should be stated in the Methods and Materials section first, then discussed at the end.

Students who did not ask for guidance often constructed inappropriate guidelines for themselves. Sharon Tissinger, on her tape, reads a price and says, "It has numbers in it; it goes in Results." Quantification is a characteristic of all scientific writing, not just the Results portion of the format. By the same token, Nearing's percent of phosphate per cup of detergent does not belong in the Results just because it is expressed as a number. It belongs in the Introduction in order to clarify that Nearing has chosen to compare the cleaning abilities of a high-phosphate and a low-phosphate detergent.

In essence, 1983 students placed materials in the wrong sections. They omitted sections. They invented sections. They even put some things into two sections because they couldn't decide which section they belonged in.

When we read the students' logs, we discovered a major reason why they had difficulties: they believed that the order of the format dictated the order of composing. Jeremy Lucas's log reveals this notion:

March 3rd.	Bought 32 oz. each (Joy and Palmolive)
March 4th.	Used about 15 minutes to think of how to start the paper.
March 5th.	Spent 1 hour in the library to write the first page of the paper. (Introduction)
March 10th.	Compared stain removal by these two products. Also compared physical differences.

March 14th.	Wrote 1 and 1/2 pages on the materials and methods. I spent 1 hour on this.
March 17th.	Tested spotlessness on two cups. Still thinking of data for the graphs.
March 18th.	At 2 p.m. I wrote the remaining part of the methods and materials.
	[Lucas has 12 more log entries running through April 9th, 1983. He never mentions the Introduction again]

Believing, as Lucas did, that the order of the format dictated the order of composing, students tried to write their original research papers in sections from the beginning, rather than writing rough drafts of all related information and revising the drafts to meet format demands at a later date. Many 1983 students were never able to resolve the conflict between the order of the format and the order of the composing process—a difficulty that also plagued Sherman's students (p. 80). When Lucas began writing the Introduction, he had not conducted a pilot and had not experimented with the two dish detergents in any way. He seems to have begun with writing the Introduction because, like nine of his ten classmates in 1983, he thought that was where everybody started. Jane Chance, a 1985 student who made a "C" on the original research paper but a "B" in the course, thought so too. When she was asked by a peer which part of the paper was the hardest part to write, she said:

> The Introduction, no question. I didn't have too much problem writing the Methods and Materials and the Results other than phraseology, I suppose. The Introduction I had the most problem with—how to lead into it . . . I went at it the wrong way. I tried to sit down and hammer it out, the Introduction, before I did anything else. I finally had to switch and just write the Methods and Materials and then fill in the Introduction from there.

After struggling with the Introduction, Lucas moved on to the next section of the format—the Methods and Materials section. On March 10, he tested the spot removal qualities of the dish soap. The only writing he did was to record data. He wrote nothing about his procedures, what he found out, or what it meant, because he was too busy writing the first section of Methods and Materials. He finally wrote about his spot test four days after his experimentation. It is not surprising that he left out important information and organized his data poorly. Mike Siliato separated by a number of weeks the experimentation and writing in his "scrub now, write later" plan; he too was unsuccessful.

In addition to the major problem—letting the order of the format dictate the order of composing—some students also thought there should be "transitions" from section to section. In Anderson's view, one function of the scientific format divisions, such as Introduction, Methods and Materials, etc., is to eliminate the need for transitions.

Teacher's Methods, Student Performance, and Implications

In 1983, Anderson lectured on the parts of the scientific journal article and their functions. At that time the students had already read five research articles arranged in that format. She asked the students to "bring in three pages of your Methods and Materials section." This was the basis of a 40-minute peer conference session in which students were free to address other concerns about the paper as well.

Anderson's conclusion? "What a mistake!" By asking the students for three pages from the Methods and Materials section, she forced them to do exactly the activity they needed help with *before* they got to class. She also perpetuated, if not created, for the students the myth that scientists compose their reports in format sections. One student even scratched out text that would have been good for her Conclusions section because she decided it didn't fit in Methods and Materials, and she never brought it back.

In 1986, to counter these problems, Anderson, in a 15-minute lecture on format, clarified that successful scientists write before, during, and after research, and then rearrange their written text to meet format demands. She stressed that the order of the sections in a scientific research paper does not determine the order of composition, and encouraged students to link experimenting and writing together as closely as possible. She listed each unit of the scientific article and explained its function, then gave the students a short research article that she had cut into chunks. In groups of three or four, the students put the "format puzzle" together, the cut-and-paste activity replacing her longer 1983 lecture. All of this helped students to focus on the issue of format in reading a scientific article, and gave them hands-on experience in manipulating material within that format.

Also in 1986, Anderson gave the students a reprint of one of her own published articles to serve as a format model. It is clear from notes, tapes, and rough drafts that the students referred to it for organizing the entire report.

In the next assignment, the students were asked to "bring in three pages of your research." Notice the big change: Anderson did not ask for a specific section of the paper, she asked only for pages of text, thus reinforcing the notion that format did not dictate the order of composition. In class, peer groups discussed where the text they had written would fit within the format. Toward the end of this session, Anderson explained to the students *why* transitions were not necessary between sections because the format itself resolved that writing problem.

But one problem arose with the students' in-class discussion of their pages of text. Although it was Anderson's intent that the three-page assignment would be a "hands on" time for students to put information into all five format sections, as it turned out, students' three pages usually contained information that belonged only in Methods and Materials. Thus the groups worked almost exclusively on Methods and Materials because those were the only pages they had. The primary trait scores for "format organization" measured the way students placed information in all sections. For that reason, we were not surprised that "Scientific Format" was the writing category that showed the smallest margin of increase (Figure 6.9).

SECTION ORGANIZATION

The Nature of the Difficulties

Anderson's students not only struggled to determine which section their information should go into, they also had difficulty in organizing information within the sections. It was a common problem; for example, 45 percent of students in 1983 had a primary trait score below 3.0 for the Methods and Materials section—a score partly dependent upon organizing that section.

Logs and tapes made clear that students thought chronological order was always important. Hilary Nearing and Susan Bell agreed that the Methods and Materials section was easier than the other sections, able to be written, as they said in their peer-response session, "zoom, zoom, zoom." However, they often included extraneous material arranged in

												$\bar{x}$	$\underline{P}$ Value
1983	2	2	2	2	2.5	2.5	4	4	4	4.5	4.5	3.09	.31
1986	2	2	2	2.5	3	3	4	4.5	4.5	4.5	4.5	3.32	

Figure 6.9. Comparison of 1983 and 1986 students' primary trait scores for "Scientific Format." Shaded areas show students receiving scores of 3.0 ("adequate") or better. $\bar{x}$ = mean score. $\underline{P}$ = the probability under the null hypothesis that improvement is due to chance is 31 in 100.

merely chronological order. Bell wrote in her Methods and Materials section about conducting the "first, second, third, and fourth tests." Since these were not a sequence of time-related tests, she should have referred to them as "maximum absorbency test," "hand dryability test," and so forth. Further, the order of the tests in Materials and Methods should have corresponded to the order in the Results section.

In a short, informal assignment asking students to reevaluate this paper and explain what they would do differently next time, Duncan Solski, a 1986 student, replied,

> The overall feeling of the paper was written in chronological order, with words like *then, next,* and *after* to show sequence of events. I think leaving these words out would make the paper sound more like gathered research information and less like a story.

Teacher's Methods, Student Performance, and Implications

In addition to the activities designed to help students with format organization as a whole, Anderson in 1986 instituted an activity to help students move away from chronological organization, particularly in their Methods and Materials sections. In the last peer conferencing session, when students were working on revisions, Anderson asked them to exchange papers and "Circle all the words on one page of the Methods and Materials that imply chronology." After this, they were to reread this section and determine whether the chronology was significant or simply the result of an inappropriate narrative approach. The primary trait scores on the Methods and Materials section went from 3.00 in 1983 to 3.55 in 1986 (Figure 6.10).

ANDERSON'S AND WALVOORD'S CONCLUSIONS

This chapter has explored the nature of students' difficulties in the same six areas of difficulty we constructed for all four disciplines.

												$\bar{x}$	$\underline{P}$ Value
1983	1.5	1.5	2	2	2.5	3	3.5	3.5	4	4.5	5	3.00	.14
1986	1.5	2.5	3	3	3	3.5	4	4.5	4.5	4.5	5	3.55	

Figure 6.10. Comparison of 1983 and 1986 students' primary trait scores for "Methods and Materials." Shaded areas show students receiving scores of 3.0 ("adequate") or better. $\bar{x}$ = mean score. $\underline{P}$ = the probability under the null hypothesis that improvement is due to chance is 14 in 100.

Though students in Anderson's class had to address the good/better/best questions within the scientific framework, and though some of their difficulties arose from the scientific requirement to quantify data, nonetheless, we found that their difficulties fell into the same general categories as those of students in the other classes.

We found similarities, too, in students' strategies. As in the other three disciplines, difficulties arose with roles. Anderson wanted the professional-in-training role of scientist. Many students adopted this role, but we also saw traces of lay roles (the advice-giving parent, the storyteller) and text-processor roles (students relying in inappropriate ways on the product labels). Students experienced difficulties not only in adopting the role of scientist, but also in performing it appropriately—that is, using the scientific method and writing their reports in the appropriate format.

Anderson's teaching methods in 1983 were already using peer and teacher response. Our investigation of the 1983 class showed Anderson where students were still having difficulties, and how her methods were either working in contradiction to the processes she wanted them to use, failing to offer appropriate guidance when it was needed, or placing too much reliance on the advice of peers before they were able to help one another. To direct her changes, Anderson was guided by the information we had gathered and by her own strong conviction that students trying to engage in complex reasoning and methodology need concrete experiences under the guidance of their teacher. In our terms, she taught procedural knowledge procedurally.

After we examined the data from 1983 and Anderson implemented changes, the 1986 section of students performed better, according to the judgment of outside raters, in those areas that Anderson had addressed. Given the small sample (11 students in each class) and our lack of full information about other factors, such as SAT scores (lacking for the many Towson State students who were transfers), we certainly do not have a scientific basis for proving that the improvement resulted from the changed teaching methods. Nonetheless, students improved in every category (Appendix A). In eight of the eleven primary trait categories, the probability that any difference was due to chance was less than 15 percent. In eight of the eleven categories, the probability was less than 15 percent. We think that the changes in teaching methods are likely candidates for helping to explain the improvement. Moreover, our findings about the nature of students' difficulties may provide useful clues about students in other settings trying to learn scientific processes and scientific writing.

But this chapter is not just a report of an "experiment" on our part.

It is the story of a living classroom, a story of teacher and students working together in order that learning could take place for all of them, a story of a teacher's growth and change. Anderson's classroom will never be the same again. So the only way to "replicate" our "experiment" is for other teachers to do what we did: systematically and collaboratively observe students, and then, guided by the best theories and intuitions at their command, try to shape teaching methods that address the difficulties that observation has revealed.

Note

1. Brand names used by the students have been retained for authenticity. However this is student work. In no way do we imply judgments about the relative merits of any product named in this chapter.

7 Conclusion

Barbara E. Walvoord
Loyola College in Maryland

Lucille Parkinson McCarthy
University of Maryland Baltimore County

> Once he grants students the intelligence and will they need to
> master what is being taught, the teacher begins to look at his
> students' difficulties in a more fruitful way: he begins to search
> in what students write and say for clues to their reasoning and
> their purposes, and in what *he* does for gaps and misjudgments.
> He begins teaching anew.
>
> —Mina Shaughnessy, *Errors and Expectations*

Though Walvoord and McCarthy are the authors of this chapter, all
team members have had input, and the chapter is based on the entire
team's study. Thus "we" in this chapter refers to the team as a whole.

We summarized some of our findings in Chapter 1 as a way of
helping readers prepare for the classroom chapters. In this chapter,
we complete that summary and we discuss implications of our study
both for teaching and for further research.

RESEARCH QUESTION 1:
WHAT WERE TEACHERS' EXPECTATIONS?

EXPECTATIONS FOR THE PROFESSIONAL-IN-TRAINING ROLE

Throughout the book, we have used "role" as a conceptual lever to
help us understand the four classrooms (p. 8). In Chapter 1 we
discussed the common expectation that students would assume, in
their thinking/writing processes, the role of "professional-in-training."
We saw that the professional-in-training role differed in each class:

Business: the decision maker: In the upper-level business course, the

228

professional-in-training was a decision maker who had the responsibility to consider the complexity of a situation, but who assumed that, though the decision had to be explained and supported, the decision was his or hers to make, and would be implemented.

History: the arguer/debater: In the freshman CORE history class, the role was that of professional in society, but not necessarily a historian. This professional was knowledgeable about history and able to use historical evidence to argue in the public forum about human problems, such as the price of political stability. She or he was also able to clarify her or his own values in the give-and-take of debate.

Psychology: the social scientist/counselor/friend: In the human sexuality class, students were preparing for a variety of professions, many of them in social services. The expected role was an amalgam of several interrelated roles. The student was to use social science knowledge to counsel a friend who was receiving the letter. As social scientist/counselor/friend, the student had a responsibility to guide and inform, to remain nonjudgmental, and to facilitate the decisions of the friend/client.

Biology: the research scientist: In the upper-level biology course, the role was that of an entry-level scientist in a research and development laboratory, whose responsibility was to use the scientific method to make judgments about products.

Further research might explore other classrooms to discover other role variations. Are there classrooms where some version of the professional-in-training role is *not* wanted? What roles are expected in those classes? What other versions of the professional-in-training exist in classrooms? Are aspects of the roles common to particular disciplines?

To teachers, we suggest that role expectations may be tacit rather than explicit, as they were for our team before the study. We found it helpful for ourselves and our students to define the type of professional-in-training roles we expected, and then to ask whether our teaching methods were appropriately communicating and encouraging those roles.

EXPECTATIONS FOR GOOD/BETTER/BEST REASONING

In Chapter 1 (pp. 7–8) we summarize our finding that teachers were asking good/better/best questions and that answering those questions in all four classes required students to perform five tasks. Here we add that the classes differed in how those tasks were explained in the teachers' models for good/better/best reasoning. Particularly, the classes differed along these dimensions:

1. The strictness of the requirement for quantification
2. The language and configuration of the teacher's model for good/ better/best reasoning
3. Who decided whether something was "good" or "best"
4. What type of definition was required

1. *Strictness of the requirement for quantification*: The strictest requirement for quantification was found, of course, in the biology class, where all results had to be expressed in quantitative terms. The business course textbook showed a quantitative method—factor rating (p. 75)— for completing the tasks of good/better/best reasoning, but the teacher deliberately made room for nonquantifiable factors. The history and psychology classes were least rigid about quantifying, but in those classes, too, there was some expectation for indicating which factors were most important.

2. *The language and configuration of the teacher's model for good/ better/best reasoning*: Each teacher used different language and different models to talk about the reasoning process. The business, psychology, and biology teachers saw definition in good/better/best reasoning as a beginning point; the history teacher saw definition as a connector (see Figure 6.1, p. 181).

The differences in the teachers' models for reasoning strongly influenced how reasoning was taught and learned in each classroom. Our study affirms Anne Herrington's (1988) finding, in a naturalistic study of a college literature class: "The lines of reasoning used in the students' papers mirrored the class" (146).

Those who use the Toulmin model (p. 127) for teaching or research need to be aware that the *sequence* of the elements in the model and the *language* used to describe those elements may be quite different in various classrooms.

3. *Who decided whether something was "good," "better," or "best"?* In business, history, and biology, the student made the decision and explained/defended it (Catonsville is the best stadium site; General Perez should adopt the English style of government; brand X is better than brand Y). In the psychology class, much of the responsibility for making specific decisions about what should be done (i.e., what birth

control methods to use) was left to the letter recipient. The student letter-writer, in the role of social scientist/counselor/friend, facilitated the decision by offering information, analysis, and descriptions of the decision-making process. However, only if the client/friend who received the letter was a danger to self or others would the writer actually make a decision about what should be done.

4. *What type of definition of "good," "better," or "best" was required?* The biology teacher wanted an operational definition; the other teachers wanted what Sherman called a "useful" definition (pp. 88–89). None of the teachers wanted a dictionary definition. All teachers expected a definition that was constructed by the students to serve a particular purpose or support a particular argument.

Research is needed on the forms that the five tasks may take in other settings. What language and models for good/better/best reasoning exist in other classrooms? Are the models discipline-specific— that is, would all business teachers tend to have the same model? What are other common kinds of reasoning beside good/better/best reasoning in college classes? What models and language do teachers use to present the reasoning process?

For teachers, we suggest making the model of reasoning explicit. That step helped us better understand our own expectations and communicate them to students.

RESEARCH QUESTION 2:
WHAT WERE THE DIFFICULTIES?

Chapter 1 defined "difficulty" and discussed our use of the term (pp. 5–6). The classroom chapters explored the six areas of difficulty we constructed for all four classrooms:

1. Gathering sufficient specific information
2. Constructing the audience and the self
3. Stating a position
4. Using appropriate discipline-based methods to arrive at and support the position
5. Managing complexity
6. Organizing the paper

These were certainly not the only areas or the only ways of

constructing the areas in which difficulties arose in all four classrooms. Further research might investigate the difficulties that occurred in settings different from ours. The difficulties we have constructed, however, may guide teachers' efforts to help their students.

RESEARCH QUESTION 3:
HOW DID TEACHERS' METHODS AND STUDENTS' STRATEGIES APPEAR TO AFFECT THE DIFFICULTIES?

In each chapter, we discussed teachers' methods and students' strategies that seemed to affect the difficulties. We treated students' strategies and teachers' methods as a pair, because of our conviction that difficulties are caused neither by students alone nor by teachers alone, but by complex interactions. In this concluding chapter, however, to get the advantage of a somewhat different angle on students' strategies and teachers' methods, we slice against that grain, treating, first, students' strategies as a group, then teaching methods.

STUDENTS' STRATEGIES

We have discussed a large number of student strategies that seemed to affect the difficulties. Here we summarize some of the most frequent and salient.

Students' Roles

Throughout the book we have discussed the three main roles we found students adopting: the professional-in-training role the teacher wanted, and two roles teachers did not want: text-processor and layperson. Our data suggest that, at least to some extent, students may be able to choose their roles deliberately and that teachers can influence this choice.

Further research might try to specify the roles that students adopt in other settings. What factors influence students' adoption of roles? How much variation in roles does a single student exhibit among all his/her classes? Does the text-processor role represent a stage in some students' development? How are roles related to other elements such as the students' and teachers' past experiences, the classroom dynamics, gender, culture, or the students' anxiety, motivation, or other characteristics? Does teaching students to define roles and role expectations help them?

Many of the student strategies we discuss in the rest of this section are related to roles; for example, the textbook-processor role implies certain strategies for using models and approaching the textbook.

Students' Use of Models from Other Settings

Our students *did* transfer knowledge from one classroom to another. In each classroom, we saw students guide their thinking and writing by models they had learned elsewhere, such as the "term paper," "reflection paper," "thesis and subs," or the model of the streetcorner debate. Sometimes these models were either inappropriate, or the student applied them in ways that were not helpful, but at times, too, the models did serve students well. Teachers, we noted, might elicit certain models such as the "reflection paper" by the length of the paper, its source of information, or the phrasing on the assignment sheet.

The "thesis/subs" model was prevalent in the Loyola College classes, where the model was directly taught in Breihan's history course, and where it was used by students in the business class as a carryover from composition. We noted that high-success students used it more than low-success students in Sherman's class. But we also noted that students often had difficulty applying the model, and that the thesis/subs model might encourage some students to use a limited "find reasons"strategy, in which they merely searched for reasons or advantages to support their recommendations.

More research is needed into what models students have when they arrive at college. What models do they most commonly use? How do students interpret teachers' messages about models? How do students select appropriate models? What intellectual or contextual factors contribute to making a model so rigidly fixed as to hinder the student's ability or willingness to change it, ignore it, or learn new models? Research on, for example, what "term paper" means to students will surely profit from the research on "schemata" for stories and other forms (e.g., Stein and Trabasso 1982).

It would also be interesting to study further any situation like Loyola where a single model is strongly taught in a freshman composition course, and trace how various students use that model over the years of their schooling, and, perhaps, afterwards as well. Such a study might help elucidate how students use their freshman composition training. McCarthy's 1987 study of a single Loyola student has made a start in that direction.

Students' Approaches to the Textbook and Other Source Texts

We noted that some students approached all textbook material as declarative knowledge, while teachers viewed some textbook material as procedural knowledge (p. 59). Investigators might explore students' notions of texts and how those notions change. What factors can change a student's view of texts? Is a single student capable of viewing texts differently in different classes? How do culture, socioeconomic class, age, or other factors influence students' approaches to texts?

Students' Strategies for Using Assignment Sheets

Students relied heavily on written assignment sheets, treating them as the most important guides to the task and often interpreting them narrowly and literally as recipes and as rulebooks (pp. 57–58). The teacher's language on the assignment sheet seemed a contributing factor in a number of students' difficulties. Further research might investigate the assignment sheet's role in a wider variety of classroom settings. Previous research on "charter documents" (McCarthy, in press) will probably be relevant.

Students' Reading Comprehension

Reading comprehension appeared more and more complex as we saw how the meaning of that term depended upon purpose and setting. For example, Sherman's students had to interpret procedural information as procedural, not declarative (p. 59), and Breihan's students had to understand how information could be used as evidence—had to see texts as voices in a debate. Research might explore further these multiple meanings of "reading comprehension" and investigate how students learn appropriate strategies for comprehension in different settings.

Students' Approaches to Definition

Definition, we found, was a crucial element for good/better/best reasoning in all four classes. Defining "good," "better," or "best" was one of the five tasks of good/better/best reasoning (p. 12). Teachers expected students to *construct* definitions that would serve certain functions in investigation or in argument. Students, however, often viewed definitions as fixed entities that could be correct or incorrect and that could be *found* in a source text and used unchanged. Further investigations might continue to explore the role of definition in various academic disciplines. How do students learn definition in childhood? What does definition mean to them? What is the role of definition in the different cultures, schools, and other settings from which students come? How do students move from a concept of definition as a fixed, found, "correct" statement to definition as a constructed tool for argument or research? What underpinnings are needed to make such a move possible?

Students' Categories for "Seeing"

In assignments where students collected information from observation (including experimentation) rather than from texts, they sometimes did not appear to realize their need for specialized, discipline-based categories with which to "see" (p. 62). Further research might explore students' notions about observation as a method of inquiry. How do students attach value to observation? How does their view of observation as a mode of inquiry compare to their view of reading as a mode of inquiry? Do some students readily adopt appropriate categories in a variety of disciplines? If so, how do they learn to do that?

Students' Ways of Distinguishing the Sequences of Decision Making, Composing, and the Paper

We found that students often acted as though all three of these sequences must be the same. Further research might explore student notions and uses of sequence in other settings.

Students' Ways of Combining Reason with Feelings and Solution-Searching with Rationale-Building

Combining reason with feelings and solution-searching with rationale-building were necessary to good/better/best assignments in all four classes (Tasks 4 and 5). Trying to integrate these elements created complex difficulties in all the classes. Students in the layperson role tended to rely too heavily on feelings and on rationale-building. Students in the professional-in-training role sometimes were confused about how to combine feelings within the reasoning process their teacher expected. Researchers might explore how Tasks 4 and 5 are worked out in other settings. There may be stages in students' development of the ability to integrate feelings and evidence. (Perry's 1970 scheme is one attempt to show such stages). How do discipline-based differences affect students' ways of combining feelings and evidence? How do teachers in various settings assign value to feelings? to rationale-building? What models do students choose to help them in integrating feelings with evidence, and rationale-building with solution-searching? How do age, culture, gender, and former schooling affect the integration?

Students' Strategies for Pre-Draft Writing

We defined "pre-draft writing" as any writing that preceded the drafting of at least two-thirds of what the student considered to be the paper. We identified some of the many functions of pre-draft writing and indicated that high-success students seemed to do more pre-draft writing and different kinds of pre-draft writing than low-success students (pp. 91–92). These findings need to be tested in other settings.

We suggested that students needed forms of pre-draft writing that would help them with good/better/best reasoning Task 3: bringing different kinds of information together in a disciplined way so that a single judgment could be made. Investigators might explore further how the discipline or the classroom setting influence students' ways of relating different kinds of information. How do various kinds of instruction influence students' use of pre-draft writing? Would composition-class instruction in certain types of pre-draft writing that allow such connections among different types of information be useful or usable by students in later courses?

Students varied greatly in their outlining for different papers in the same course, causing us to question whether previous studies of the low incidence of outlining across many types of writing may mask the high incidence of outlining for certain types of papers. Further research might investigate students' notions, and practice, of outlining.

These student strategies are some of the most salient and frequently occurring in our study of the four classrooms. We suggest that teachers might gain important insights by investigating these strategies among their own students.

TEACHERS' METHODS

The Power of Teaching

This book is an argument for the power of teaching to shape thinking and writing. That argument is made by our constructions about how teaching methods went awry as well as about how they succeeded. The argument is also made through our descriptions of how the different models for good/better/best reasoning shaped the nature of thinking and writing in each classroom. Also, the chapter on Anderson's biology class shows how students' thinking and writing changed in a later class, after she had changed her teaching methods. One conclusion the four teachers carried away from our study was the sense that students' ability and motivation—the two aspects the teachers had most commonly blamed for students' shortcomings—played less significant roles than the teachers had thought. We saw students trying hard to meet teachers' expectations—harder than we had often given them credit for. Students' failures to meet their teachers' expectations were often directly traceable to mixed signals by the teacher, or to instruction that was needed but not provided. After seeing in our data how his assignment sheet had led to students' misunderstandings and difficulties, one of our teachers remarked wryly, "In other words, I got what I deserved."

The Effects of Teacher Research in the Classroom

So how can teachers deserve, and get, better learning, thinking, and writing among their students? Our first answer to that question is— by *observing* students systematically. All four members of the team whose classes we studied had attended writing-across-the-curriculum workshops and were at various stages in trying out the teaching methods that had been discussed. It was our *observation of our classrooms*, however, that enabled us to see whether, and how, our methods were working, and that gave us clues about how to help our students more effectively. Marshall's (1984a) and Langer and Applebee's (1987) studies of high school teachers have emphasized that teaching methods learned in writing-across-the-curriculum seminars may lose their force because they are contradicted by other things the teacher is doing, because they are sabotaged by students' goals and ways of working, or because they are incorporated by teachers into old patterns of interacting with students and into old ways of using writing for evaluation.

Our study confirms that this may happen. But it also suggests a remedy: teacher research. A key phrase was repeated by each of our teachers in some form or another as they analyzed data from our study: "Oh, if I'd only known the students were doing that, I would have. . . ." And then would come ideas for change. Thus we would recommend that workshops on teaching not only suggest teaching methods that other teachers have found helpful, but also give participants the tools and the encouragement to conduct systematic inquiry into their own classrooms to discover how those teaching methods are working in their own settings.

Principles for Effective Teaching

Our investigation gave us nine guiding principles for reshaping our teaching in response to what we learned about our students' thinking and writing.

1. *Make the teaching methods fit the writing and thinking processes of high-success students.* Our investigations of difficulties in our classrooms often showed us where our teaching methods ran counter to the writing and thinking strategies that high-success students were using in spite of us. For example, Anderson's early request for a draft of "your Introduction and Methods and Material sections" led students into difficulty because it implied, wrongly, that the order of the final paper should dictate the order of composing. Robison's early web nicely emphasized some aspects of what she wanted, but ignored what was an early consideration for her high-success students—delineating their letter recipients.

2. *Present procedural knowledge procedurally.* In all four classes, we found that verbal descriptions of a process, whether presented in class or in a textbook, were difficult for students to translate into action. Further, students often treated procedural knowledge about how to do something as declarative knowledge to be summarized, not used to guide a process. We concluded that procedural knowledge often needs to be taught procedurally—by concrete experiences under the guidance of the teacher who leads students physically and directly through the procedure. This was the key, for example, to the exercises

about mold that Anderson added to help her biology students apply what she had earlier only *said* about how to formulate operational definitions. It was the key to Breihan's history class debates, which physically placed students on opposite sides of the classroom in an actual debate, conveying unmistakably to them that they were to take a position and construct arguments to defend it. Sequenced writing assignments, when well planned, were a powerful instrument to guide students as they learned to use the methods of the discipline.

3. *Define clear goals for informal, ungraded writing.* Our investigation convinced us of the usefulness of informal, ungraded writing, but showed us how important it is to plan that writing to achieve specific goals. We saw Breihan use informal writings completed outside of class, which he collected and marked, and Anderson use informal writings completed outside and inside class, which she rarely collected. What made both kinds of informal writing effective was that the teacher shaped and revised those writing assignments, based on information about students' thinking and writing processes and on clear learning goals.

4. *Guide peer response.* In both classes that used teacher-structured peer response—psychology and biology—we concluded that such response could be helpful or unhelpful, depending upon whether the peers actually knew enough to help one another. Particularly, peers seemed unable, without considerable guidance and instruction, to help each other with major issues in good/better/best reasoning. In Anderson's biology class, specific instruction aimed at the whole class appeared to enable peers to help each other more effectively because they knew better what they were doing and what to look for. In both classes, peer groups did better when they had specific things to look for and specific guidelines. Our data caused us to question the oft-used model of peer response as the "first-line" response, followed by teacher response. Further studies are needed on the role of peer response and the roles of students within peer response in a variety of college classrooms. Anne Herrington's 1989 paper usefully explores outcomes of peer response beyond merely whether it improves students' papers.

5. *Make teacher draft response consistent with the writing process and the reward system.* One technique frequently recommended in writing-across-the-curriculum seminars is teacher response to students' drafts. In two of our classrooms—history and business—teacher draft response was a powerful impetus for students' revision and improvement of drafts. Students revised directly from the comments, made revisions

for virtually every suggestion, and most of the time improved the papers. In the psychology classroom, however, few students revised at all in response to teacher comments on a draft. The difference seemed due in part to the fact that in the psychology class the teacher's response came later in the composing process; i.e., after students had received peer response, revised those drafts, and typed a draft for teacher response. Also, in the psychology classroom, less credit toward the final grade was awarded for revision, and the suggestions for revision were made at a late point in the spring semester. Beach (1979) records significant gains in the quality of high school students' revised papers as a result of teacher response to drafts. Our study indicates that such gains may depend heavily upon context and may not hold for all classrooms.

6. *Craft the assignment sheet with care.* Because of the way students approach the assignment sheet as a recipe and rulebook, it is important to craft the assignment sheet with great care. Robison's CRAFT acronym (p. 151) is a guide to the kinds of information the sheet usually needs to include. Teachers need also to attend to the sequence of the decision-making and composing processes, and to the organizational patterns for the finished paper, that students may infer from the sheet. This is particularly important, given students' tendency not to separate those sequences and to interpret recursive processes linearly.

7. *Give explicit instructions and guidance, especially when designating a peer audience and/or a familiar setting and topic for student writing.* In business, psychology, and biology, the teachers designated a "peer" audience and/or a familiar setting for certain assignments. These designations were part of those teachers' strong emphasis upon helping students to relate course learning to their own experiences and to move away from the text-processing role—students merely summarizing or synthesizing written texts for a teacher they envisioned as merely checking their textbook knowledge. We noted the success of such peer audience designations in capturing students' interest and involvement—for example in Sherman's Stadium and McDonald's-Popeye's assignments. We do not agree with Bartholomae (1985) that assigning a peer audience is "an act of hostility" on the part of the teacher because it fails to train students in the "expert" stance they must assume for college writing. Bartholomae (and some students) assume that the students would write as nonprofessionals—for example, as a baseball fan to other baseball fans or as friend to friend.

Our teachers, on the other hand, expected students to view themselves and their peer classmates as professionals-in-training (business and biology) or as client-like seekers of help (psychology). In both cases, the peer audience was chosen by the teacher to give direct practice to students in the professional roles they would someday assume. In the psychology class, many students showed great ingenuity in constructing themselves as "experts" in their letters. The appropriate response by teachers, we believe, is not to eliminate the peer audience or the familiar setting for assignments, but rather to help students assume appropriate roles in that context and to construct their audiences appropriately.

8. *Offer early guidance.* Early guidance by the teacher, as students first defined the task, gathered information, made notes, planned the paper, and produced the first draft, seemed crucially important to students' success in all our classes. Draft response alone might appear too late for students to amend certain kinds of problems whose origins lay in early stages, particularly since students rarely returned to their original sources as a result of teacher response to drafts. Further investigations might uncover circumstances in which students do return to original sources, or might investigate aspects that help students make better use of late guidance, such as teacher draft response. However, it seems productive also to turn our attention to developing better ways of guiding students in early stages of their planning, information gathering, role taking, and envisioning of the paper they will write or the reasoning tasks they will perform.

9. *Use language in the modes you want students to use.* In each classroom, we found students mimicking the language of the teacher and the classroom. In the psychology class, for example, students who established successful tone in the letters seemed to model directly from their teacher's classroom talk and the language she gave them on the assignment sheet. In the history class, the dialogic talk of the classroom, particularly embodied in the seven in-class debates, seemed to help students achieve the dialogic thinking and writing that was so highly valued in that classroom. Further research could explore more fully the relationship between classroom talk and the forms that students' planning, thinking, and writing can take. Particularly, it would be important to note whether forms of higher-order thinking can be taught to students through forms of classroom talk, as Breihan's students seemed to learn the dialogue of argument and counterargument through the debates and classroom discussions.

WHAT CLASSROOM RESEARCH MEANT TO US

In addition to the findings that we have constructed and presented here for others to interpret and use, our seven-year collaboration produced knowledge that we ourselves have used. Each of us believes that what we learned about these four classrooms enabled us to become more effective teachers. In mid-career, when we might have become bored or cynical about teaching the same classes year after year, the project has made our undergraduate classrooms places of learning and growth for us, and has sustained our interest in our students—how they learn and how they can be guided.

Our study suggests research for classroom teachers as well as for composition researchers. Our team members began to reap the rewards of our research as soon as we had looked at the first student packets, as soon as we had constructed the primary trait scale, as soon as we had coded and then analyzed how our students used pre-draft writing. Our interdisciplinary collaboration, with its mix of perspectives, helped us see our classrooms in new ways and effect changes there. We believe that important rewards can come to any teacher who undertakes systematic investigation of his or her classroom, even within a limited scope, alone or with a collaborator. This project has taught us about our discipline-based ways of knowing—how, as Geertz puts it, "we organize our significative worlds." It has also helped us understand how our students struggle as they try out our languages and work to meet our expectations. Becoming learners in our own classrooms has enabled us, in Shaughnessy's words, "to teach anew."

Appendix A

Primary Trait Analysis for Anderson's Biology Class

This appendix contains two items: the primary trait scoring sheet developed by Anderson and used by outside raters, and scores for the 1983 and 1986 classes (Table A.1). See pp. 35–36 for explanation of the primary trait analysis procedure.

Primary Trait Scoring Sheet for Anderson's Class

Please evaluate the original research paper and assign an appropriate number of points for each section. In each category, higher numbers represent greater mastery. Please do not award partial scores.

Title

5 – Is appropriate in tone and structure to science journal; contains necessary descriptors, brand names, and allows reader to anticipate design.

4 – Is appropriate in tone and structure to science journal; most descriptors present; identifies function of experimentation, suggests design, but lacks brand names.

3 – Identifies function, brand name, but does not allow reader to anticipate design.

2 – Identifies function or brand name, but not both; lacks design information or is misleading.

1 – Is patterned after another discipline or missing.

Introduction

5 – Clearly identifies the purpose of the research; identifies interested audience(s); adopts an appropriate tone.

4 – Clearly identifies the purpose of the research; identifies interested audience(s).

3 – Clearly identifies the purpose of the research.

2 – Purpose present in Introduction, but must be identified by reader.

1 – Fails to identify the purpose of the research.

243

Scientific Format Demands

5 – All material placed in the correct sections; organized logically within each section; runs parallel among different sections.

4 – All material placed in correct sections; organized logically within sections, but may lack parallelism among sections.

3 – Material placed in the right sections, but not well organized within the sections; disregards parallelism.

2 – Some materials are placed in the wrong sections or are not adequately organized wherever they are placed.

1 – Material placed in wrong sections or not sectioned; poorly organized wherever placed.

Methods and Materials Section

5 – Contains effectively, quantifiably, concisely organized information that allows the experiment to be replicated; is written so that all information inherent to the document can be related back to this section; identifies sources of all data to be collected; identifies sequential information in an appropriate chronology; does not contain unnecessary, wordy descriptions of procedures.

4 – As above, but contains unnecessary information, and/or wordy descriptions within the section.

3 – Presents an experiment that is definitely replicable; all information in document may be related to this section; however, fails to identify some sources of data and/or presents sequential information in a disorganized, difficult pattern.

2 – Presents an experiment that is marginally replicable; parts of the basic design must be inferred by the reader; procedures not quantitatively described; some information in Results or Conclusions cannot be anticipated by reading the Methods and Materials section.

1 – Describes the experiment so poorly or in such a nonscientific way that it cannot be replicated.

Nonexperimental Information

5 – Student researches and includes price and other nonexperimental information that would be expected to be significant to the audience in determining the better product, or specifically states nonexperimental factors excluded by design; interjects these at appropriate positions in text and/or develops a weighted rating scale; integrates nonexperimental information in the Conclusions.

4 – Student acts as above, but is somewhat less effective in developing the significance of the nonexperimental information.

3 – Student introduces price and other nonexperimental information, but does not integrate them into Conclusions.

2 – Student researches and includes price effectively; does not include or specifically exclude other nonexperimental information.

1 – Student considers price and/or other nonexperimental variables as research variables; fails to identify the significance of these factors to the research.

Designing an Experiment

5 – Student selects experimental factors that are appropriate to the research purpose and audience; measures adequate aspects of these selected factors; establishes discrete subgroups for which data significance may vary; student demonstrates an ability to eliminate bias from the design and bias-ridden statements from the research; student selects appropriate sample size, equivalent groups, and statistics; student designs a superior experiment.

4 – As above, but student designs an adequate experiment.

3 – Student selects experimental factors that are appropriate to the research purpose and audience; measures adequate aspects of these selected factors; establishes discrete subgroups for which data significance may vary; research is weakened by bias *or* by sample size of less than 10.

2 – As above, but research is weakened by bias *and* inappropriate sample size.

1 – Student designs a poor experiment.

Defining Operationally

5 – Student constructs a stated comprehensive operational definition and well-developed specific operational definitions.

4 – Student constructs an implied comprehensive operational definition and well-developed specific operational definitions.

3 – Student constructs an implied comprehensive operational definition (possibly less clear) and some specific operational definitions.

2 – Student constructs specific operational definitions, but fails to construct a comprehensive definition.

1 – Student lacks understanding of operational definition.

Controlling Variables

5 – Student demonstrates, by written statement, the ability to control variables by experimental control and by randomization; student

makes reference to, or implies, factors to be disregarded by reference to pilot or experience; superior overall control of variables.

4 – As above, but student demonstrates an adequate control of variables.

3 – Student demonstrates the ability to control important variables experimentally; Methods and Materials section does not indicate knowledge of randomization and/or selected disregard of variables.

2 – Student demonstrates the ability to control some, but not all, of the important variables experimentally.

1 – Student demonstrates a lack of understanding about controlling variables.

Collecting Data and Communicating Results

5 – Student selects quantifiable experimental factors and/or defines and establishes quantitative units of comparison; measures the quantifiable factors and/or units in appropriate quantities or intervals; student selects appropriate statistical information to be utilized in the results; when effective, student displays results in graphs with correctly labeled axes; data are presented to the reader in text as well as graphic forms; tables or graphs have self-contained headings.

4 – As 5 above, but the student did not prepare self-contained headings for tables or graphs.

3 – As 4 above, but data reported in graphs or tables contain materials that are irrelevant and/or not statistically appropriate.

2 – Student selects quantifiable experimental factors and/or defines and establishes quantitative units of comparison; fails to select appropriate quantities or intervals and/or fails to display information graphically when appropriate.

1 – Student does not select, collect, and/or communicate quantifiable results.

Interpreting Data: Drawing Conclusions/Implications

5 – Student summarizes the purpose and the findings of the research; student draws inferences that are consistent with the data and scientific reasoning and relates these to interested audiences; student explains expected results and offers explanations and/or suggestions for further research for unexpected results; student presents data honestly, distinguishes between fact and implication,

and avoids overgeneralizing; student organizes nonexperimental information to support conclusion; student accepts or rejects the hypothesis.

4 – As 5 above, but student does not accept or reject the hypothesis.

3 – As 4 above, but the student overgeneralizes and/or fails to organize nonexperimental information to support conclusions.

2 – Student summarizes the purpose and findings of the research; student explains expected results, but ignores unexpected results.

1 – Student may or may not summarize the results, but fails to interpret their significance to interested audiences.

Table A.1   Primary Trait Scores for Anderson's 1983 and 1986 Classes

	1983	1986	$\underline{P}$ Values*
Title	2.95	3.22	.24
Introduction	3.18	3.64	.14
Scientific Format	3.09	3.32	.31
Methods and Materials	3.00	3.55	.14
Non-Experimental Info	3.18	3.50	.24
Designing the Experiment	2.68	3.32	.07
Defining Operationally	2.68	3.50	.01
Controlling Variables	2.73	3.18	.10
Collecting Data	2.86	3.36	.14
Interpreting Data	2.90	3.59	.03
Overall	2.93	3.42	.09

*$\underline{P}$ values: The probability values calculated were the $\underline{P}$ values of a T distribution with 20 degrees of freedom. The values were determined by interpolation between standard tabulated values for the T distributions (see Fisher and Yates 1973; Table F.3 in Dayton and Stunkard 1971).

Appendix B

Characteristics of Students: Entire Class and Focus Group

This appendix presents the characteristics of the students in each class as a whole and in the focus group. (See p. 40 for our use of focus groups.) In Anderson's biology class, the entire class (13 students enrolled, 11 submitting data) was used as a focus group. (For characteristics of that class, see p. 18.)

Table B.1 Sherman's Business Class: Characteristics of Entire Class and Focus Group

	Entire Class	Focus Group
Mean Verbal SAT	460	444
Class		
Junior	73%	71%
Senior	27%	29%
Mean Course Grade (4 = A)	2.9	3.0
Minority	7%	14%
Female	52%	79%
English as a Second Language	2%	7%
Older than 24 Years	7%	14%

N = Entire class (44 students); focus group (14 students).

Table B.2 Breihan's History Class: Characteristics of Entire Class and Focus Group

	Entire Class	Focus Group
Mean Verbal SAT	542	533
Class		
Freshman	81%	79%
Sophomore	19%	21%
Mean Course Grade (4 = A)	3.1	3.2
Female	56%	53%
Minority	4%	0
English as a Second Language	0	0
Older than 24 Years	0	0

N = Entire class (27 students); focus group (19 students).

248

Table B.3   Robison's Psychology Class: Characteristics of Entire Class
and Focus Group

	Entire Class	Focus Group
Mean Verbal SAT	448	430
Class		
Freshman	3%	0
Sophomore	10%	17%
Junior	33%	25%
Senior	50%	58%
Nondegree	3%	0
Mean Course Grade (4 = A)	3.2	3.3
Female	100%	100%
Minority	23%	25%
ESL	17%	17%
Older than 24 Years	10%	8%

N = Entire class (30 students), focus group (12 students).

Works Cited

Alley, Michael. 1987. *The craft of scientific writing.* Englewood Cliffs, N.J.: Prentice-Hall.

Applebee, Arthur N., with contributions by Judith Langer, Russel Durst, Kay Butler-Nalan, James Marshall, and George Newell. 1984. *Contexts for learning to write: Studies of secondary school instruction.* Norwood, N.J.: Ablex.

Applebee, Arthur N., Russel K. Durst, and George E. Newell. 1984. The demands of school writing. In Arthur N. Applebee (Ed.), *Contexts for learning to write: Studies of secondary school instruction* (55–77). Norwood, N.J.: Ablex.

Applebee, Arthur N., Judith A. Langer, Ina V. S. Mullis, and Lynn B. Jenkins. 1990. *The writing report card, 1984–1988: Findings from the nation's report card.* Princeton, N.J.: Educational Testing Service and National Assessment of Educational Progress. Report No. ISBN-8-88685-096-7; NAEP No. 19-W-01.

Aristotle. 1954. *Rhetoric; Poetics.* Trans. W. Rhys Roberts (*Rhetoric*) and Ingram Bywater (*Poetics*). New York: Modern Library.

Banton, Michael. 1985. Role. In Adam Kuper and Jessica Kuper (Eds.), *The social science encyclopedia* (714–16). London: Routledge & Kegan Paul.

Bartholomae, David. 1985. Inventing the university. In Mike Rose (Ed.), *When a writer can't write: Studies in writer's block and other composing-process problems* (134–65). New York: Guilford.

Basseches, Michael. 1980. Dialectical schemata: A framework for the empirical study of the development of dialectical thinking. *Human Development* 23: 400–21.

Bazerman, Charles. 1983. Scientific writing as a social act: Research, theory, and practice. In Paul V. Anderson, R. John Brockmann, and Carolyn R. Miller (Eds.), *New essays in technical and scientific communication* (156–84). Farmingdale, N.Y.: Baywood.

Beach, Richard. 1979. The effects of between-draft teacher evaluation versus student self-evaluation on high school students' revising of rough drafts. *Research in the Teaching of English* 13: 111–19.

Becher, Tony. 1987a. The disciplinary shaping of the profession. In Burton R. Clark (Ed.), *The academic profession: National, disciplinary and institutional settings* (271–303). Berkeley, Calif.: University of California Press.

———. 1987b. Disciplinary discourse. *Studies in Higher Education* 12: 261–74.

Behrens, Laurence. 1978. Writing, reading, and the rest of the faculty: A survey. *English Journal* 67(6): 54–60.

Belenky, Mary Field, Blythe M. Clinchy, Nancy R. Goldberger, and Jill M. Tarule. 1986. *Women's ways of knowing: The development of self, voice, and mind.* New York: Basic Books.

Berkenkotter, Carol. 1983. Decisions and revisions: The planning strategies of a publishing writer. *College Composition and Communication* 34: 156–69.

Berkenkotter, Carol, Thomas N. Huckin, and John Ackerman. 1988. Conventions, conversations, and the writer: Case study of a student in a rhetoric Ph.D. program. *Research in the Teaching of English* 22: 9–44.

Berlin, James. 1988. Rhetoric and ideology in the writing class. *College English* 50: 477–94.

Biddle, Arthur, and Daniel Bean, with Toby Fulwiler. 1987. *Writer's guide: Life science.* Lexington, Mass.: D. C. Heath.

Bizzell, Patricia L. 1978. The ethos of academic discourse. *College Composition and Communication* 29: 351–55.

Bloom, Benjamin S. (Ed.). 1956–1964. *Taxonomy of educational objectives: The classification of educational goals.* 2 vols. New York: David McKay.

Bransford, John, R. Sherwood, N. Vye, and J. Rieser. 1986. Teaching thinking and problem solving: Research foundations. *American Psychologist* 41: 1078–89.

Breihan, John R. 1986. Prewriting in college history courses. *Perspectives* 24(3): 20–21. American Historical Association.

Bridgeman, Brent, and Sybil B. Carlson. 1984. Survey of academic writing tasks. *Written Communication* 1: 247–80.

Britton, James, Tony Burgess, Nancy Martin, Alex McLeod, and Harold Rosen. 1975. *The development of writing abilities* (11–18). London: Macmillan Education for the Schools Council.

Brodkey, Linda. 1987. *Academic writing as social practice.* Philadelphia, Pa.: Temple University Press.

Bruffee, Kenneth. 1987. Kenneth Bruffee responds. *College English* 49: 711–16.

Chodorow, Nancy. 1978. *The reproduction of mothering: Psychoanalysis and the sociology of gender.* Berkeley, Calif.: University of California Press.

Clifford, James. 1983. On ethnographic authority. *Representations* 1(2): 118–46.

Collins, Allan, and Dedre Gentner. 1980. A framework for a cognitive theory of writing. In Lee W. Gregg and Erwin R. Steinberg (Eds.), *Cognitive processes in writing* (51–72). Hillsdale, N.J.: Lawrence Erlbaum.

Colomb, Gregory G., and Joseph M. Williams. 1985. Perceiving structure in professional prose: A multiply determined experience. In Lee Odell and Dixie Goswami (Eds.), *Writing in non-academic settings* (87–128). New York: The Guilford Press.

Connor, Ulla. 1990. Linguistic/rhetorical measures for international persuasive student writing. *Research in the Teaching of English* 24: 67–87.

Connor, Ulla, and Janice Lauer. 1985. Understanding persuasive essay writing: Linguistic/rhetorical approach. *Text* 5: 309–26.

Cooper, Charles R. 1983. Procedures for describing written texts. In Peter

Mosenthal, Lynne Tamor, and Sean A. Walmsley (Eds.), *Research on writing: Principles and methods* (287–313). New York: Longman.

Cooper, Charles R., with Roger Cherry, Barbara Copley, Stefan Fleischer, Rita Pollard, and Michael Sartisky. 1984. Studying the writing abilities of a university freshman class: Strategies from a case study. In Richard Beach and Lillian S. Bridwell (Eds.), *New directions in composition research* (19–52). New York: The Guilford Press.

Cooper, Marilyn, and Michael Holzman. 1983. Talking about protocols. *College Composition and Communication* 34, 284–93.

————. 1985. Reply. *College Composition and Communication* 36: 97–100.

Corey, G. 1984. Role expectations. In Raymond J. Corsini (Ed.), *Encyclopedia of psychology*. Vol. 3 (249–50). New York: Wiley.

Day, Robert A. 1979. *How to write and publish a scientific paper*. Philadelphia, Pa.: ISI Press.

Dayton, C. Mitchell, and Clayton L. Stunkard. 1971. *Statistics for problem solving*. New York: McGraw-Hill.

Denzin, Norman K. 1978. *Sociological methods: A sourcebook*. 2d ed. New York: McGraw-Hill.

Doheny-Farina, Stephen. 1986. Writing in an emerging organization: An ethnographic study. *Written Communication* 3: 158–85.

Ede, Lisa, and Andrea Lunsford. 1984. Audience addressed/audience invoked: The role of audience in composition theory and pedagogy. *College Composition and Communication* 35: 155–71.

Elbow, Peter. 1986. *Embracing contraries: Explorations in learning and teaching*. New York: Oxford University Press.

Ericsson, K. Anders, and Herbert A. Simon. 1980. Verbal reports as data. *Psychological Review* 87: 215–51.

————. 1984. *Protocol analysis: Verbal reports as data*. Cambridge, Mass.: MIT Press.

Faigley, Lester. 1986. Competing theories of process: A critique and a proposal. *College English* 48: 527–42.

Faigley, Lester, and Kristine Hansen. 1985. Learning to write in the social sciences. *College Composition and Communication* 36: 140–49.

Faigley, Lester, and Stephen Witte. 1981. Analyzing revision. *College Composition and Communication* 32: 400–14.

————. 1984. Measuring the effects of revisions on text structure. In Richard Beach and Lillian S. Bridwell (Eds.), *New directions in composition research* (95–108). New York: The Guilford Press.

Fish, Stanley Eugene. 1980. *Is there a text in this class? The authority of interpretive communities*. Cambridge, Mass.:Harvard University Press.

Fisher, Donald A., and Frank Yates. 1963. *Statistical tables for biological, agricultural, and medical research*. New York: Hafner.

Flower, Linda S. 1990. The role of task representation in reading to write. In Linda S. Flower, Victoria Stein, John Ackerman, Margaret J. Kantz, and Kathleen McCormick, *Reading to write* (35–75). New York: Oxford University Press.

Flower, Linda S., and John R. Hayes. 1980. The cognition of discovery: Defining a rhetorical problem. *College Composition and Communication* 31: 21–32.

————. 1981a. Plans that guide the composing process. In Carl H. Frederiksen and Joseph F. Dominic (Eds.), *Writing: The nature, development, and teaching of written communication*. Vol. 2: *Writing: Process, development and communication* (39–58). Hillsdale, N.J.: Lawrence Erlbaum.

————. 1981b. A cognitive process theory of writing. *College Composition and Communication* 32: 365–87.

————. 1985. Response to Marilyn Cooper and Michael Holzman. "Talking about protocols." *College Composition and Communication* 36: 94–97.

Frederiksen, Carl H., and Joseph F. Dominic. 1981. Introduction: Perspectives on the activity of writing. In Carl H. Frederiksen and Joseph F. Dominic (Eds.), *Writing: The nature, development, and teaching of written communication*. Vol. 2: *Writing: Process, development and communication* (1–20). Hillsdale, N.J.: Lawrence Erlbaum.

Garvey, Catherine. 1977. The contingent query: A dependent act in conversation. In Michael Lewis and Leonard Rosenblum (Eds.), *Interaction, conversation, and the development of language* (63–93). New York: Wiley.

Gazzam [Anderson], Virginia Johnson, and Barbara Walvoord. 1986. Science and writing: Linking research with classroom models. In *Science Education Information Report*. Columbus, Oh.: National Association for Research in Science Teaching and SMEAC Information Reference Center at Ohio State University.

Geertz, Clifford. 1973. *The interpretation of cultures: Selected essays*. New York: Basic Books.

————. 1976. "From the native's point of view": On the nature of anthropological understanding. In Keith H. Basso and Henry A. Selby (Eds.), *Meaning in Anthropology* (221–37). Albuquerque, N.M.: University of New Mexico Press.

————. 1983. The way we think now: Toward an ethnography of modern thought. In Clifford Geertz, *Local Knowledge* (147–63). New York: Basic Books.

Gere, Anne R. 1977. Writing and WRITING. *English Journal* 66(8): 60–64.

Gilligan, Carol. 1982. *In a different voice: Psychological theory and women's development*. Cambridge, Mass.: Harvard University Press.

Gilmore, Perry, and Allan A. Glatthorn. 1982. *Children in and out of schools: Ethnography and education*. Washington, D.C.: Center for Applied Linguistics.

Goswami, Dixie, and Peter R. Stillman. (Eds.). 1987. *Reclaiming the classroom: Teacher research as an agency for change*. Upper Montclair, N.J.: Boynton/Cook.

Greeno, James G. 1980. Some examples of cognitive task analysis with instructional implications. In Richard E. Snow, Pat-Anthony Frederico, and William E. Montague (Eds.), *Aptitude, learning, and instruction*. Vol. 2: *Cognitive process analyses of learning and problem solving* (1–21). Hillsdale, N.J.: Erlbaum.

Guba, Egon G. 1981. Criteria for assessing the trustworthiness of naturalistic inquiries. *Educational Communications and Technology Journal* 29: 75–91.

Gumperz, John Joseph. 1971. *Language in social groups; Essays by John J. Gumperz.* Stanford, Calif.: Stanford University Press.

Harste, Jerome C., Virginia A. Woodward, and Carolyn L. Burke. 1984. Examining our assumptions: A transactional view of literacy and learning. *Research in the Teaching of English* 18: 84–108.

Hayes, John R., and Linda S. Flower. 1983. Uncovering cognitive processes in writing: An introduction to protocol analysis. In Peter Mosenthal, Lynne Tamor, and Sean A. Walmsley (Eds.), *Research on writing: Principles and methods* (207–20). New York: Longman.

Hays, Janice N., Kathleen M. Brandt, and Kathryn H. Chantry. 1988. The impact of friendly and hostile audiences on the argumentative writing of high school and college students. *Research in the Teaching of English* 22: 391–416.

Heath, Shirley Brice. 1982. Ethnography in education: Defining the essentials. In Perry Gilmore and Allan Glatthorn (Eds.), *Children in and out of school: Ethnography and education* (33–55). Washington, D.C.: Center for Applied Linguistics.

———. 1983. *Ways with words: Language, life, and work in communities and classrooms.* New York: Cambridge University Press.

Herrington, Anne Jeannette. 1983. Writing in academic settings: A study of the rhetorical contexts for writing in two college chemical engineering courses. *Dissertation Abstracts International, 45,* 104A. (University Microfilms, 1985, No. 84–09, 508)

———. 1985. Writing in academic settings: A study of the contexts for writing in two college chemical engineering courses. *Research in the Teaching of English* 19: 331–61.

———. 1988. Teaching, writing, and learning: A naturalistic study of writing in an undergraduate literature course. In David Jolliffe (Ed.), *Writing in academic disciplines.* Vol.2: *Advances in writing research* (133–66). Norwood, N.J.: Ablex.

———. 1989. Revision with peer and instructor review in an anthropology class: What does it mean to say knowledge is "negotiated"? Paper presented at annual meeting of Conference on College Composition and Communication, Seattle, March 17.

Hillocks, George, Jr. 1986. *Research on written composition: New directions for teaching.* Urbana, Ill.: ERIC Clearinghouse on Reading and Communication Skills and the National Conference on Research in English.

Hymes, Dell. 1972a. Introduction. In Courtney B. Cazden, Vera P. John, and Dell Hymes (Eds.), *Functions of language in the classroom* (xi–lvii). New York: Teachers College Press.

———. 1972b. Models of the interaction of language and social life. In John Gumperz and Dell Hymes (Eds.), *Directions in sociolinguistics* (35–71). New York: Holt, Rinehart & Winston.

———. 1974. *Foundations in sociolinguistics: An ethnographic approach.* Philadelphia, Pa.: University of Pennsylvania Press.

Kahane, Howard. 1980. The nature and classification of fallacies. In J. Anthony Blaire and Ralph H. Johnson (Eds.), *Informal logic: The first international symposium* (31–39). Point Reyes, Calif.: Edgepress.

Kantor, Kenneth J. 1984. Classroom contexts and the development of writing intuitions: An ethnographic case study. In Richard Beach and Lillian S. Bridwell (Eds.), *New Directions in Composition Research* (72–94). New York: The Guilford Press.

Kennedy, Mary Lynch. 1985. The composing process of college students writing from sources. *Written Communication* 2: 434–56.

Klemp, George O., Jr. 1982a. Assessing student potential: An immodest proposal. In Clark Taylor (Ed.), *Diverse student preparation: Benefits and issues. New Directions for Experimental Learning* 17 [Special issue]: 37–48. San Francisco, Calif.: Jossey-Bass.

———. 1982b. Job competence assessment: Defining the attributes of the top performer. In Ruth Salinger (Ed.), *The Pig in the Python and Other Tales* (55–67). Collection of research papers presented before the 1981 ASTD National Conference. Washington, D.C.: American Society for Training and Development.

Kurfiss, Joanne Gainen. 1988. *Critical thinking.* ASHE-ERIC Higher Education Report No. 2. Washington, D.C.: Association for the Study of Higher Education.

Langer, Judith A. 1984. Where problems start: The effects of available information on responses to school writing tasks. In Arthur N. Applebee (Ed.), *Contexts for learning to write: Studies of secondary school instruction* (135–148). Norwood, N.J.: Ablex.

———. 1985. Musings . . . A sociocognitive view of language learning. *Research in the Teaching of English* 19: 325–27.

Langer, Judith A., and Arthur N. Applebee 1987. *How writing shapes thinking: A study of teaching and learning.* NCTE Research Report No. 22. Urbana, Ill.: National Council of Teachers of English.

Lanham, Richard A. 1979. *Revising prose.* New York: Charles Scribner's Sons.

Larkin, Jill H., Joan I. Heller, and James G. Greeno. 1980. Instructional implications of research on problem solving. In Wilbert J. McKeachie (Ed.), *Learning, cognition, and college teaching. New Directions for Teaching and Learning* 2: (51–65). San Francisco, Calif.: Jossey- Bass.

Larson, Richard L. 1982. The "research paper" in the writing course: A nonform of writing. *College English* 44: 811–16.

Latour, Bruno, and Steve Woolgar. 1979. *Laboratory life: The social construction of scientific facts.* Beverly Hills, Calif.: Sage.

LeCompte, Margaret D., and Judith Preissle Goetz. 1982. Problems of reliability and validity in ethnographic research. *Review of Educational Research* 52: 31–60.

Lincoln, Yvonna S., and Egon G. Guba. 1985. *Naturalistic inquiry.* Beverly Hills, Calif.: Sage.

Lloyd-Jones, Richard. 1977. Primary trait scoring. In Charles Cooper and Lee Odell (Eds.), *Evaluating writing: Describing, measuring, judging* (33–66). Urbana, Ill.: National Council of Teachers of English.

Mallonee, Barbara C., and John R. Breihan. 1985. Responding to students' drafts: Interdisciplinary consensus. *College Composition and Communication* 36: 213–31.

Marshall, James D. 1984a. Process and product: Case studies of writing in two content areas. In Arthur N. Applebee (Ed.), *Contexts for learning to write: Studies of secondary school instruction* (149–68). Norwood, N.J.: Ablex.

———. 1984b. Schooling and the composing process. In Arthur N. Applebee (Ed.), *Contexts for learning to write: Studies of secondary school instruction* (103–119). Norwood, N.J.: Ablex.

Mathison, Sandra March. 1988. Why triangulate? *Educational Researcher* 17(2): 13–17.

McCarthy, Lucille Parkinson. 1987. A stranger in strange lands: A college student writing across the curriculum. *Research in the Teaching of English* 21: 233–65.

———. (In press). A psychiatrist using DSM-III: The influence of a charter document in psychiatry. In Charles Bazerman and James Paradis (Eds.), *Textual dynamics of the professions*. Madison, Wisc.: University of Wisconsin Press.

McCarthy, Lucille Parkinson, and Barbara E. Walvoord. 1988. Models for collaborative research in writing across the curriculum. In Susan McLeod (Ed.), *Strengthening programs for writing across the curriculum* (77–89). San Francisco, Calif.: Jossey-Bass.

McMillan, Victoria E. 1988. *Writing papers in the biological sciences*. New York: St. Martin's.

McPeck, John E. 1981. *Critical thinking and education*. New York: St. Martin's. Oxford: Martin Robertson.

Meese, George P. 1987. Focused learning in chemistry research: Suzanne's journal. In Toby Fulwiler (Ed.), *The journal book* (337–47). Portsmouth, N.H.: Heinemann, Boynton/Cook.

Meyer, Bonnie J. F. 1975. *The organization of prose and its effects on memory*. New York: American Elsevier.

———. 1985. Prose analysis: Purposes, procedures, and problems. In Bruce K. Britton and John B. Black (Eds.), *Understanding expository text: A theoretical and practical handbook for analyzing explanatory texts* (11–64). Hillsdale, N.J.: Lawrence Erlbaum.

Miles, Matthew B., and A. Michael Huberman. 1984. Drawing valid meaning from qualitative data: Toward a shared craft. *Educational Researcher* 13(5): 20–30.

Nelson, Jennie, and John R. Hayes. 1988. *How the writing context shapes college students' strategies for writing from sources*. Technical Report No. 16. Berkeley, Calif.: University of California and Carnegie Mellon University, Center for the Study of Writing at University of California, Berkeley, and Carnegie Mellon University.

Nisbett, Richard E., and Timothy DeCamp Wilson. 1977. Telling more than we can know: Verbal reports on mental processes. *Psychological Review* 84: 231–59.

North, Stephen M. 1986. Writing in a philosophy class: Three case studies. *Research in the Teaching of English* 20: 225–62.

Nystrand, Martin. 1990. Sharing words: The effects of readers on developing writers. *Written Communication* 7: 3–24.

Odell, Lee. 1986. Foreword. In Art Young and Toby Fulwiler (Eds.), *Writing across the disciplines: Research into practice* (ix–xi). Upper Montclair, N.J.: Boynton/Cook.

Odell, Lee, Dixie Goswami, and Anne Herrington. 1983. The discourse-based interview: A procedure for exploring the tacit knowledge of writers in nonacademic settings. In Peter Mosenthal, Lynne Tamor, and Sean A. Walmsley (Eds.), *Research on writing: Principles and methods* (221–36). New York: Longman.

Ong, Walter J., S.J. 1975. The writer's audience is always a fiction. *Publications of the Modern Language Association of America*, 90: 9–21.

Park, Douglas B. 1982. The meanings of "audience." *College English* 44: 247–57.

Pechenik, Jan A. 1987. *A short guide to writing about biology.* Boston: Little, Brown.

Perfetto, Greg A., John D. Bransford, and Jeffery J. Franks. 1983. Constraints on access in a problem solving context. *Memory and Cognition* 11: 24–31.

Perkins, D[avid] N. 1985. Postprimary education has little impact on informal reasoning. *Journal of Educational Psychology* 77: 562–71.

Perl, Sondra Anne. 1978. Five writers writing: Case studies of the composing processes of unskilled college writers. *Dissertation Abstracts International*, 39, 4788A. (University Microfilms No. 78–24, 104)

———. 1979. The composing processes of unskilled college writers. *Research in the Teaching of English* 13: 317–36.

Perry, William G. Jr., 1970. *Forms of intellectual and ethical development in the college years.* New York: Hart, Renehart and Winston.

Philips, Susan U. 1982. The language socialization of lawyers: Acquiring the "cant." In George Spindler (Ed.), *Doing the ethnography of schooling* (176–209). New York: Holt, Rinehart and Winston.

Pratt, Mary L. 1977. *Toward a speech act theory of literary discourse.* Bloomington, Ind.: Indiana University Press.

Robison, Susan Miller. August 1983. *Crafting the psychology assignment: Techniques to improve student writing.* Paper presented at the American Psychological Association Annual Convention, Anaheim, California.

Rohman, D. Gordon. 1965. Pre-writing: The stage of discovery in the writing process. *College Composition and Communication* 16: 106–12.

Rorty, Richard. 1982. *Consequences of pragmatism: Essays, 1972–1980.* Minneapolis, Minn.: University of Minnesota Press.

Rose, Mike. 1983. Remedial writing courses: A critique and a proposal. *College English* 45: 109–28.

Rosenblatt, Louise. 1978. *The reader, the text, the poem: The transactional theory of the literary work.* Carbondale, Ill.: Southern Illinois University Press.

Scardamalia, Marlene. 1981. How children cope with the cognitive demands of writing. In Carl H. Frederiksen and Joseph F. Dominic (Eds.), *Writing: The nature, development, and teaching of written communication.* Vol. 2:

Writing: Process, Development, and Communication. Hillsdale, N.J.: Lawrence Erlbaum.

Schwegler, Robert, and Linda Shamoon. 1982. The aims and process of the research paper. *College English* 44: 817–24.

Selfe, Cynthia Leigh. 1981. The composing processes of four high and four low writing apprehensives: A modified case study. *Dissertation Abstracts International,* 42(07), 3168A. (University Microfilms No. 1848)

Shaughnessy, Mina P. 1977. *Errors and expectations: A guide for the teacher of basic writing.* New York: Oxford University Press.

Shih, May. 1986. Content-based approaches to teaching academic writing. *TESOL Quarterly* 20: 617–48.

Simon, Herbert A. 1979. Problem solving and education. In David T. Tuma and Frederick Reif (Eds.), *Problem solving and education: Issues in teaching and research* (81–96). Hillsdale, N.J.: Erlbaum.

Singer, Daniel, and Barbara Walvoord. 1984. Process-oriented writing instruction in a case method class. In John A. Pearce II and Richard B. Robinson, Jr. (Eds.), *Proceedings of the Academy of Management* (121–25). Boston, Mass.: Academy of Management. (ERIC Document Reproduction Service No. ED 249 500)

Sperling, Melanie, and Sarah Warshauer Freedman. 1987. A good girl writes like a good girl: Written response to student writing. *Written Communication* 4: 343–69.

Spindler, George. 1982. Introduction and editorial commentary. In George Spindler (Ed.), *Doing the ethnography of schooling: Educational anthropology in action* (1–18 et passim). New York: Holt, Rinehart and Winston.

Spradley, James P. 1979. *The ethnographic interview.* New York: Holt, Rinehart and Winston.

————. 1980. *Participant observation.* New York: Holt, Rinehart & Winston.

Stein, Nancy L., and Tom Trabasso. 1982. What's in a story: An approach to comprehension and instruction. In Robert Glaser (Ed.), *Advances in Instructional Psychology,* Vol. 2 (213–267). Hillsdale, N.J.: Erlbaum.

Sternglass, Marilyn S., and Sharon Lynn Pugh. 1986. Retrospective accounts of language and learning processes. *Written Communication* 3: 297–323.

Sullivan, Francis J. 1987. *Placing texts, placing writers: Sources of readers' judgments in university placement-testing.* NCTE Promising Researcher report. Unpublished manuscript, Temple University, Philadelphia, Pa.

Swarts, Heidi, Linda S. Flower, and John R. Hayes. 1984. Designing protocol studies of the writing process: An introduction. In Richard Beach and Lillian S. Bridwell (Eds.), *New directions in composition research* (53–71). New York: The Guilford Press.

Tomlinson, Barbara. 1984. Talking about the composing process: The limitations of retrospective accounts. *Written Communication* 1: 429–45.

Toulmin, Stephen, Richard Rieke, and Allan Janik. 1984. *An introduction to reasoning.* 2d ed. New York: Macmillan.

Voss, James F., Sherman W. Tyler, and Laurie A. Yengo. 1983. Individual differences in the solving of social science problems. In Ronna F. Dillon and Ronald R. Schmeck (Eds.), *Individual differences in cognitive processes,* Vol. 1 (205–32). New York: Academic Press.

Voss, James F., Terry R. Greene, Timothy A. Post, and Barbara C. Penner. 1983. Problem-solving skill in the social sciences. In Gordon H. Bower (Ed.), *The Psychology of Learning and Motivation,* Vol. 17 (165–213). New York: Academic Press.

Walvoord, Barbara. 1985. *Writing: Strategies for all disciplines.* Englewood Cliffs, N.J.: Prentice-Hall.

Walvoord, Barbara E., and H. Fil Dowling, Jr., with John R. Breihan, Virginia Johnson Gazzam, Carl E. Henderson, Gertrude B. Hopkins, Barbara Mallonee, and Sally McNelis. 1990. The Baltimore area consortium. In Toby Fulwiler and Art Young (Eds.), *Programs that work: Models and methods for writing across the curriculum,* (273–286). Portsmouth, N.H.: Heinemann, Boynton/Cook.

Whiteman, Marcia F. (Ed.). 1981. *Variation in writing: Functional and linguistic-cultural differences.* Vol. 1 of Carl H. Frederiksen and Joseph F. Dominic (Eds.), *Writing: The nature, development, and teaching of written communication.* Hillsdale, N.J.: Lawrence Erlbaum.

Index

The Research Team

Left to right: John R. Breihan, Virginia Johnson Anderson, Barbara E. Walvoord, A. Kimbrough Sherman, Susan Miller Robison, and Lucille Parkinson McCarthy.

Virginia Johnson Anderson is an associate professor of biology at Towson State University and an active member of the Baltimore Area Consortium for Writing Across the Curriculum. Anderson has published in leading science education journals, served as the keynote speaker at numerous professional meetings including NEA-Alaska, directed five state and national research grants, conducted workshops in over forty colleges and schools, taught preschool science in a summer camp program for eight years, and received an award for innovations in college science teaching from the National Science Teachers Association. She feels that conducting workshops in writing activities to enhance scientific thinking and reporting has been her most rewarding professional achievement.

John R. Breihan is associate professor of history at Loyola College, where he has taught since 1977. Educated at Princeton and Cambridge, his major field of research and publication is late 18th-century British history. He has also served as codirector of Loyola's writing-across-the-curriculum program, Empirical Rhetoric. In addition to publishing articles on this subject, he has made presentations about writing instruction to the Conference on College Composition and Communications and other writing conferences, and has conducted faculty workshops at several colleges on issues involved in cross-curricular writing.

Lucille Parkinson McCarthy is assistant professor of English at the University of Maryland Baltimore County. She has published articles on students' and professionals' writing in academic and medical settings and has recently coauthored a book on the emotional problems of handicapped children. Her current research interests focus on writing in philosophy and psychiatry.

Susan Miller Robison is a psychologist in private practice in Ellicott City, Maryland and a professor of psychology at the College of Notre Dame of Maryland. Robison is the author of *Discovering and Sharing Your Gifts*, a leadership manual published by the National Council of Catholic Women. She consults nationally on stress management, leadership, writing across the curriculum, and executive stress (especially for women executives). In her off-work hours, Susan competes in amateur ballroom dance competitions with her husband Philip.

A. Kimbrough Sherman is an associate professor of decision science and dean of graduate programs in management at Loyola College in Maryland. He has taught a variety of business courses at large and small private and public universities. His research interests are in quality, production technology, and expert systems.

Barbara E. Walvoord is professor of writing/media at Loyola College in Maryland. She has initiated and directed writing-across-the-curriculum programs both at Loyola College and at Central College in Pella, Iowa. She was cofounder and for several years codirector of the Maryland Writing Project, an affiliate of the National Writing Project. She was also cofounder and director of the Baltimore Area Consortium for Writing Across the Curriculum (BACWAC), which includes virtually every public and private school, kindergarten through university, in the greater Baltimore area. In addition to articles and conference presentations about writing, she has published two textbooks and a book for teachers—*Helping Students Write Well: A Guide for Teachers in All Disciplines* (2nd ed. New York: Modern Language Assn., 1986). For the past twenty years she has conducted workshops and consulted on campuses across the country.